AF684732

Chinese Family Business and the Equal Inheritance System

This book disputes the traditional argument that the equal inheritance system hinders the growth of Chinese family business, approaching this not only in terms of economic capital, but also in terms of human capital such as education and leadership, and social networks.

Zheng argues that most of the family business patriarchs only focus on the passing of economic capital, but give little attention to human capital and social capital when they come to the stage of transferring control to the next level. It further elaborates that the equal inheritance system itself isn't the destructive force that weakens family business competitiveness, but can assist economic development by generating dynamism and capital.

Based on extensive primary research, the work discusses how equal division encourages sibling comparison, analysing how such comparisons initially generate stress and anxiety, but ultimately galvanize competition, benefiting the business. The author also assesses how family division can offer initial economic human and social capitals that can motivate siblings to start their own businesses and be free from the subjugation sometimes associated with a family firm. Through the evaluation of these issues the book argues that the equal inheritance system can be regarded as the origin of the self-employment mentality, which not only fosters the growth of Chinese family business, but plays a crucial role in promoting economic development.

Providing a valuable contribution to the field, this work will be of great interest to all scholars of Chinese and Asian business.

Victor Zheng is currently Research Assistant Professor of the Centre of Asian Studies, HKU. His research interests includes: Chinese family business and inheritance; Hong Kong commercial history and society; social indicators; and social development.

Routledge contemporary China series

1 **Nationalism, Democracy and National Integration in China**
Leong Liew and Wang Shaoguang

2 **Hong Kong's Tortuous Democratization**
A comparative analysis
Ming Sing

3 **China's Business Reforms**
Institutional challenges in a globalised economy
Edited by Russell Smyth and Cherrie Zhu

4 **Challenges for China's Development**
An enterprise perspective
Edited by David H. Brown and Alasdair MacBean

5 **New Crime in China**
Public order and human rights
Ron Keith and Zhiqiu Lin

6 **Non-Governmental Organizations in Contemporary China**
Paving the way to civil society?
Qiusha Ma

7 **Globalization and the Chinese City**
Fulong Wu

8 **The Politics of China's Accession to the World Trade Organization**
The dragon goes global
Hui Feng

9 **Narrating China**
Jia Pingwa and his fictional world
Yiyan Wang

10 **Sex, Science and Morality in China**
Joanne McMillan

11 **Politics in China since 1949**
Legitimizing authoritarian rule
Robert Weatherley

12 **International Human Resource Management in Chinese Multinationals**
Jie Shen and Vincent Edwards

13 **Unemployment in China**
Economy, human resources and labour markets
Edited by Grace Lee and Malcolm Warner

14 **China and Africa**
Engagement and compromise
Ian Taylor

15 **Gender and Education in China**
Gender discourses and women's schooling in the early twentieth century
Paul J. Bailey

16 **SARS**
Reception and interpretation in three Chinese cities
Edited by Deborah Davis and Helen Siu

17 **Human Security and the Chinese State**
Historical transformations and the modern quest for sovereignty
Robert E. Bedeski

18 **Gender and Work in Urban China**
Women workers of the unlucky generation
Liu Jieyu

19 **China's State Enterprise Reform**
From Marx to the market
John Hassard, Jackie Sheehan, Meixiang Zhou, Jane Terpstra-Tong and Jonathan Morris

20 **Cultural Heritage Management in China**
Preserving the cities of the Pearl River Delta
Edited by Hilary du Cros and Yok-shiu F. Lee

21 **Paying for Progress**
Public finance, human welfare and inequality in China
Edited by Vivienne Shue and Christine Wong

22 **China's Foreign Trade Policy**
The new constituencies
Edited by Ka Zeng

23 **Hong Kong, China**
Learning to belong to a nation
Gordon Mathews, Tai-lok Lui and Eric Kit-wai Ma

24 **China Turns to Multilateralism**
Foreign policy and regional security
Edited by Guoguang Wu and Helen Lansdowne

25 **Tourism and Tibetan Culture in Transition**
A place called Shangrila
Åshild Kolås

26 **China's Emerging Cities**
The making of new urbanism
Edited by Fulong Wu

27 **China–US Relations Transformed**
Perceptions and strategic interactions
Edited by Suisheng Zhao

28 **The Chinese Party-State in the 21st Century**
Adaptation and the reinvention of legitimacy
Edited by André Laliberté and Marc Lanteigne

29 **Political Change in Macao**
Sonny Shiu-Hing Lo

30 **China's Energy Geopolitics**
The Shanghai cooperation organization and Central Asia
Thrassy N. Marketos

31 **Regime Legitimacy in Contemporary China**
Institutional change and stability
Edited by Thomas Heberer and Gunter Schubert

32 **U.S.–China Relations**
China policy on Capitol Hill
Tao Xie

33 **Chinese Kinship**
Contemporary anthropological perspectives
Edited by Susanne Brandtstädter and Gonçalo D. Santos

34 **Politics and Government in Hong Kong**
Crisis under Chinese sovereignty
Edited by Ming Sing

35 **Rethinking Chinese Popular Culture**
Cannibalizations of the canon
Edited by Carlos Rojas and Eileen Cheng-yin Chow

36 **Institutional Balancing in the Asia Pacific**
Economic interdependence and China's rise
Kai He

37 **Rent Seeking in China**
Edited by Tak-Wing Ngo and Yongping Wu

38 **China, Xinjiang and Central Asia**
History, transition and crossborder interaction into the 21st century
Edited by Colin Mackerras and Michael Clarke

39 **Intellectual Property Rights in China**
Politics of piracy, trade and protection
Gordon Cheung

40 **Developing China**
Land, politics and social conditions
George C.S. Lin

41 **State and Society Responses to Social Welfare Needs in China**
Serving the people
Edited by Jonathan Schwartz and Shawn Shieh

42 **Gay and Lesbian Subculture in Urban China**
Loretta Wing Wah Ho

43 **The Politics of Heritage Tourism in China**
A view from Lijiang
Xiaobo Su and Peggy Teo

44 **Suicide and Justice**
A Chinese perspective
Wu Fei

45 **Management Training and Development in China**
Educating managers in a globalized economy
Edited by Malcolm Warner and Keith Goodall

46 **Patron–Client Politics and Elections in Hong Kong**
Bruce Kam-kwan Kwong

47 **Chinese Family Business and the Equal Inheritance System**
Unravelling the myth
Victor Zheng

Chinese Family Business and the Equal Inheritance System

Unravelling the myth

Victor Zheng

Routledge
Taylor & Francis Group
LONDON AND NEW YORK

First published 2010
by Routledge
2 Park Square, Milton Park, Abingdon, Oxon OX14 4RN

Simultaneously published in the USA and Canada
by Routledge
270 Madison Ave, New York, NY 10016

Routledge is an imprint of the Taylor & Francis Group, an informa business

© 2010 Victor Zheng

Typeset in Times by Wearset Ltd, Boldon, Tyne and Wear
Printed and bound in Great Britain by TJI Digital, Padstow, Cornwall

All rights reserved. No part of this book may be reprinted or reproduced or utilized in any form or by any electronic, mechanical, or other means, now known or hereafter invented, including photocopying and recording, or in any information storage or retrieval system, without permission in writing from the publishers.

British Library Cataloguing in Publication Data
A catalogue record for this book is available from the British Library

Library of Congress Cataloging in Publication Data
A catalog record for this book has been requested

ISBN10: 0-415-55638-4 (hbk)
ISBN10: 0-203-86141-8 (ebk)

ISBN13: 978-0-415-55638-5 (hbk)
ISBN13: 978-0-203-86141-7 (ebk)

To my beloved wife and daughters

Contents

Figures and tables

Figures

Tables

Acknowledgements

This book is a revised version of my PhD dissertation, which would not have been completed without the help and support of many people and institutions. First and foremost, I am particularly indebted to my supervisor, Professor Wong Siu-lun, who not only gave me academic advice and guidance, but also unfailing support and encouragement. I would like to thank Professor Chan Kwok-bun of Hong Kong Baptist University, Professor Thomas Wong of the University of Hong Kong and Professor Joseph Lee Tse-hey of Pace University for their valuable comments and help at different stages. Without their encouragement and assistance, the publication of this book would not be possible.

My deepest gratitude goes to the Chinese family business research team of the Centre of Asian Studies (HKU), whose members include Professor Wong Siu-lun (as head), Dr Sun Wenbin, Dr Ho Tsaiman and Dr Louella Cheng. I admit that many of my ideas and theories on Chinese family business have been sharpened in this series of meeting and discussions.

I am also indebted to the Chaozhou respondents in this study who were kind to accept my request for interviews and shared with me all aspects of their lives, not only their business affairs. Moreover, I am most thankful to have had great help from a leading office furniture company in Hong Kong, whose general manager kindly allowed me to undertake participant observation in his company. However, I regret that I cannot thank them by name as I promised anonymity. I am obliged to thank my uncle, Mr Cheng Kin-ping, who introduced me to Mr Lam Fung-lam, secretary of the Chaozhou Chamber of Commerce (CCC). With their valuable assistance and support, I could successfully interview 35 CCC members.

I have received help from a number of others at various stages of my research. They are Mr Simon Tam, Professor Kao Cheng-shu, Ms Teresa Tsai, Ms Stephanie Rogers, Ms Jennifer Eagleton and Professor Pamela Stewart. During the later stage of research, my research assistant, Miss Jocko Yuen, also provided great help. To all of them, my sincere and grateful thanks are given.

I am also indebted to a number of anonymous but professional librarians in the Hong Kong Collection of the Hong Kong University Main Library for their kind assistance when needed. I must also thank the Hong Kong Research Grant Council (Reference No. HKU7459/08) for funding follow-up research, which I used to fine-tune my arguments.

Last, but not least, my wholehearted thanks must go to my beloved wife, Kit-ping, who not only acted as first reader and chief sounding board and whose ideas and suggestions greatly improved this book, but also provided unfailing care, love, patience and understanding during the tiresome re-writing process. My little three daughters, Xin-qiao, Xin-ling and Xin-yan, enriched my dull academic life with their very special 'symphony' of laughter and tears. In short, I would like to reiterate that without all of the above, the publication of this book would not be possible.

Victor Zheng
Centre of Asian Studies
University of Hong Kong

Abbreviations

CCC	Chaozhou Chamber of Commerce
CPPCC	Chinese People's Political Consultative Conference
HSBC	Hong Kong and Shanghai Banking Corporation
IC	integrated circuit
IRD	Inland Revenue Department
JP	Justice of Peace
KBE	Knight Grand Cross Order of the British Empire
LCST	Lee Chung Shing Tong
MBE	Member of the British Empire
MPDN	*Ming Pao Daily News*
NPC	National People's Congress
OBE	Order of British Empire
PCP	Po-Chai-Pill
PLK	Po Leung Kuk
PRC	People's Republic of China
SHKP	Sun Hung Kai Properties
TWGH	Tung Wah Group of Hospitals
YCH	Yan Chai Hospital

Introduction

Unravelling the myth

I

Nina Wang Kung Yu-sum, Asia's richest woman, died in 2007. She was the chairwoman of privately held property giant Chinachem.[1] Her personal assistant said of her: 'She had been working in the office over the past few weeks. She also made the decisions on investments in allotments of new shares, and the recent purchase of land in the New Territories was done under her instructions' (*South China Morning Post* 5 April 2007).

Nina Wang preferred to be known as Chinachem's chairlady. She had undergone a marathon legal battle with her father-in-law, Wang Din-shin (aged 96) to control the estate of her late husband, Teddy Wang. It included the Chinachem property empire. At the conclusion of legal proceedings she was cleared of forging Teddy Wang's will.

According to *Forbes* magazine's 2007 rich list, Nina Wang was the 204th richest person in the world, with a net worth of HK$32.7 billion. There was much speculation about the distribution of her fortune. Soon after her death, a similar lawsuit commenced over her own estate and over the validity of her own will.

II

Bitter sibling rivalry unfolded inside the boardroom of Sun Hung Kai Properties (SHKP) in 2008. The brothers, Walter Kwok Ping-sheung, Thomas Kwok Ping-kwong and Raymond Kwok Ping-luen, struggled for control of the HK$325 billion empire their late father, Kwok Tak-seng, had built.

It was a highly public dispute, replete with charges of mismanagement, questions about the undue influence of a woman friend, charges that the eldest brother, Walter, suffered from a psychological disorder, media leaks and court injunctions. It ended with Walter Kwok's ousting as chairman on 27 May 2008.

> [T]he power struggle at SHKP also raises a long list of questions about the quality of its corporate governance. Throughout the dispute there were

> allegations and counter-allegations of questionable management practices, though most directors sided with the two younger brothers. But the installation of their 79-year-old mother, Kwong Siu-hing, as the new chairman also raised eyebrows.
>
> (*South China Morning Post* 9 June 2008)

SHKP's boardroom battle is unrivalled in Hong Kong's recent corporate history in terms of drama, intrigue and acrimony. The family feud cast a shadow over the company and raised concerns about the opaque succession plans at other family-controlled companies in Hong Kong – some of which are still run by their octogenarian founders.

III

An investigation into a pair of secret trusts set up in 1979 for six of the eight Eric Ho Tung children led to a sequence of lawsuits between the Ho Tungs. In 2006 the high court ruled that Eric Ho Tung had no right to disinherit Sean and another son, Anthony, from two trusts worth HK$100 million. The trusts were to be paid out when Eric Ho Tung died.

In 2009 Sean Ho Tung lost his bid for a slice of the estate left behind by Sir Robert Ho Tung. Like other grandchildren of Sir Robert who were born after his death, Sean was not entitled to be a beneficiary of Sir Robert's will.

> Mr. [Sean] Ho Tung, son of billionaire philanthropist Eric Ho Tung, was born nine years after his great-grandfather died. Some of his siblings were also born after Sir Robert's death. That meant they should not receive any money from the estate.
>
> (*South China Morning Post* 21 March 2009)

When talking about the development and inheritance of a Chinese family business, words such as paternalism, cronyism and nepotism rapidly come to mind. Unprofessional management, poor succession planning, constant family feuds and extreme sibling rivalry are also seen as characteristics of Chinese family businesses. Some may even see these things as inherent in Chinese culture.

With many doubts, but a strong curiosity about the developmental pattern of Chinese family business, this book tries to unravel the mythology around Chinese family business through the frequently criticized but seldom discussed equal inheritance system. In order to test the conventional negative impression that Chinese family business is inefficient, ill-managed, short-lived, unstable and filled with internal rivalry, fieldwork was conducted in the period 1997–2000. A total of 35 Chaozhou merchants from 26 families were interviewed. In addition, 20 wealthy long-established Hong Kong families were also selected for closer study and comparison.

As expected, many of the studied family businesses have suffered from some of the above-mentioned problems. However, many of them overcame them to become extremely successful business concerns generation after generation through rational separation of family disputes and business management.

After in-depth analysis, some salient findings were revealed. First, it is found that the equal inheritance system does not necessarily lead to internal family conflict and rivalry. Quite the opposite, equal arrangements among heirs can alleviate sibling disputes and disagreements. In other words, the equal inheritance system per se has a certain constructive function that can reduce business instability and family conflict instead of provoking internal rivalry.

Second, it is also found that the equal inheritance mechanism does not definitely lead to the levelling of capital and suffocation of business development. In fact, for the wealthy families studied, it is found that although they divided their family estate from generation to generation, the dominating shares in their family-controlled companies were seldom affected. In fact, after making their family-controlled businesses listed companies, not only did their family wealth increase drastically as the businesses expanded, the sense of keeping the business under family control is also further enhanced. Thus, it is quite clear that although family estates divide from generation to generation, family control over certain companies does not generally follow this path as most family members see that concentration of shares can give each member or *fang* (branch) better protection, or to be more specific, can better serve each member's interests.

After cross-examining families with a successful transmission of leadership and those with a less successful succession, it was further found that in those less successful successions, family attention was only focused on the passing on of economic capital. Little attention is given to the transmission of human capital and social capital. For those successful succession families, apart from a clear transfer of ownership of family estates and company shares from one generation to the next, their patriarchs also paid attention to education and the re-establishment of new leadership, business networks and personal connections.

Looking from a positive perspective, we can see that the equal inheritance system can in fact assist economic development by generating competition and capital. Equal division is a criterion for sibling comparison. Comparison generates stress and anxiety, with each member trying to outdo the others, while galvanizing competition. On the other hand, family division can offer initial capital that can motivate siblings who want to be free from subjugation to start their own businesses. In other words, the equal inheritance system, in fact, can be regarded as the origin of the self-employment mentality, which not only doesn't hinder the growth of Chinese family business, but plays a crucial role in promoting economic development.

To conclude, a strong self-employment mentality drives Chinese family business to develop its own special pattern or structure, while *jiazu jituan* (literally, family-based consortium) is the most distinctive type of structure that I propose as a description to differ it from the Japanese zaibu (or kietartu) or the Korean chaebol. For this type of family business, different family members diversify into different businesses or professions. These businesses or professions may or may not relate to each other. However, they maintain a certain level of interconnection under the banner of the family (*jiazu*). They can compete and/or support each other during a time of expansion, reorganization, difficulties or crises. In short, if patriarchs can handle the inheritance issue properly, their family businesses not only can be highly competitive and resilient, but also can be maintained from generation to generation.

Notes

1 Chinachem is a cash-rich conglomerate that owns more than 200 buildings in Hong Kong. It is the only major local developer not yet listed on the city's stock exchange.

1 Equal inheritance and family business continuity

Family businesses contribute to most of the gross national product and provide most places of employment. In the United States, up to 90 per cent of all enterprises are family-owned In Spain, 75 to 90 per cent of the total jobs are provided by small family-owned businesses (Gallo 1988). Family businesses also proliferate in Canada, Europe, Latin America and Asia (Ward 1987a, 1987b; Swinth and Vinton 1993). Litz (1995) even estimates that family-owned businesses comprise over 95 per cent of all business establishments worldwide.

The dominant role of family businesses in the Hong Kong economy is also obvious. Evers (2000: B3) reports,

> [T]raditional Chinese family businesses, like the empires of Li Ka-shing, Robert Kwok [Kuok] or Mochtar Riady [also known as Lee Man-tjin], now make up over 70 per cent of the Hang Seng capitalization and a huge chunk of stock markets across Asia.

In other words, family businesses could be considered the lynchpin of the modern economy.

The problem of continuity

Although the family business is recognized for its vital role in the economy, its short life span is frequently criticized and negatively stereotyped. Americans talk about 'rags to riches to rags' or 'shirt-sleeves to shirt-sleeves in three generations'. The French say 'it is easier to make money than to keep it'. The Chinese say 'great wealth doesn't last beyond three generations' (*daifu buguo sandai*) or 'a gentlemen's grace becomes extinct in three generations' (*junzi zhize, sandai erzhan*). Whatever the saying is, one thing is common – most people consider family business unstable and short-lived. Ward (1987b: 1) succinctly describes the developmental path of family business: '[T]he first generation builds the business, the second generation "milks" or "harvests" it, and the third generation must either auction what is left to the highest bidder or start all over again.'

In order to support this generalization, Ward (ibid.) conducted structural research on the issue in the United States in 1986. Unsurprisingly, in his survey of 200 family manufacturing firms, he found that their firms' life was short. Only three out of ten survived into the second generation. To be specific, only 16 per cent of all family businesses would be transferred to the third generation. Most small firms went out of existence after ten years. In other words, the transience of family firms is obvious.

In fact, Ward is not the only one to come to this conclusion. Other scholars also draw similar conclusions from their research (Beckhard and Dyer 1983; Davis and Stern 1980; Lansberg 1988). What are the main obstacles that hinder the development of family business? In their nationwide survey, Winter and Fitzgerald (1993: 106) summarize their findings: '[O]ne-fifth of the respondents indicated economic reasons for quitting, the remainder indicated family, health and retirement, or employment reasons.' Beckhard *et al.* (1987: xv) go a step further and write:

> Family businesses tend to have relatively short life spans. Problems such as succession, the interplay of family issues and business decisions, the professional development of family members, the transition of non-family management, the retention of competent non-family employees, and the balance of personal and corporate finances are all factors that make the survival of the family firms perilous.

Danco (1987: xiv) places the responsibility directly on family members and points out succinctly as follows,

> Family businesses fail because they [family members] allow themselves to be destroyed slowly but surely, by the action – or more accurately, the inaction – of their owners/managers. The businesses fail because, more often than not, these people never make the decision needed to ensure the vitality of their companies in an ever-changing, even more complex world.

Although very few family businesses pass from generation to generation, some of them still can overcome the structural issues and last for centuries. For instance, in Japan, Daimaru was set up in 1717, Mitsukoshi in 1673, Matsuzakaya in 1896. These are still well-known names today (Chen 1988). In European countries, family businesses that last beyond three generations are also common. For example, in Italy, the Agnelli family set up their car business in 1899, while in England, the Sainsbury family founded their distribution business in 1897. Other notable examples, such as the Kristiansen family (1932) in Denmark, the Dassault family (1928) in France, the Swarovski family (1885) in Austria, the March family (1926) in Spain, the Brenninkmeyer family (1841) in Holland, the Goulandris family (1900) in Greece and the Schmidheiny family (1912) in Switzerland are also frequently quoted (Lam 1993).

If there are successful cases in other cultures, what about Chinese family businesses? When talking about Chinese family business, many people will immediately think that very few of them last over three generations (Qi 1984,

1985). Some scholars even comment critically that 'longevity has never been a characteristic even of traditional Chinese family firms' (Wong *et al.* 1992: 370). If this is really the case, what are the main factors that contribute to the completely different development path of Chinese family business? If it is not the case, can we find counter examples? What are the core reasons that enable some of them to survive over three generations?

Before commencing the discussion, let me define the term 'family business'. Leach (1991: 3–4) writes,

> A family business is one which, quite simply, is influenced by a family or by a family relationship.... The family, as a body, may effectively control business operations because it owns more than 50 per cent of the voting shares, or because family members fill a significant number of the top management positions.

Another scholar, Miyamoto (1984: 206), suggests that family firms are 'firms in which the majority of capital is held by a single family'. Ward (1987b: 6) further includes one more core element into the definition. He suggests that it is '[a] business that will be passed on for the family's next generation to manage and control.' Tong (1991: 180) simply regards that '[a] business may be considered as a family enterprise if a family exercises effective control over it.' In order to have a thorough discussion, in this research a broader concept is used, i.e. if a single family can exercise a majority control over the business it can be regarded as a family business.

Perceptions of family business

When talking about family businesses, many people may have a general impression that they are full of problems or strife. Some of them even think that they will fold during or after transmission. They attribute this to family conflict, inherent weaknesses of the inheritance mechanism, management ideology and the overlapping relations among them. If all these are true, I will ask some theoretical questions: First, as a fundamental social unit, why are there dividing and conflicting forces inside the family? Second, as a business organization, how can family members keep effective control of their businesses? Third, in what way can family control be maintained from one generation to the next? I will examine these arguments one by one in the following paragraphs.

The first hurdle faced by family businesses is internal conflict between family members. Harvey and Evans (1994: 331) state that 'family businesses are fertile fields for conflict'. Some other scholars even specify these conflicts as parent–son conflict, sibling conflict, and in-law conflict (Levinson 1971; Donnelley 1964; Calder 1961; Gibbon and Hadekel 1990). What are the reasons for such conflicts? Levinson (1971) points his accusing finger at the founder. He claims that the founder, intentionally or unintentionally, wants to retain his power. Even when he reaches retirement age, he does not want to surrender his power.

In Levinson's words, the founder has 'married with the career or the business. The business is an instrument of him. So, he has great difficulties giving up.' Other scholars comment that the family business represents all the value of the founder. He subconsciously wants to keep his domination while he is still alive (Lansberg 1988; Alcorn 1982).

Tong (1991: 181) argues that even though the founder has declared his intention to retire, his influence still remains strong in the business: 'The role of the founder does not end with his retirement, [but] continues to influence the decision-making process.' Rosenfeld (1998: 178) also comments, 'Men are still entrepreneurial, even at eighty-five. They scheme more.' Indeed, this 'I do not want to surrender power' mentality is considered as the major source of father–son(s) conflict.

If the successor does not want to play a subservient role for too long and tries to seize power from the founder, the level of distrust will accelerate. Direct confrontation between the son and the founder will eventually bubble up to the surface. It will ultimately endanger the succession process and hamper business performance. As a result, many successors, even when they are over 60, still prefer to play a subordinate role during their father's reign.

Distrust of the successor's ability can be detrimental (Lansberg 1988; Leach 1991). Chan and Chiang's (1994: 62) story vividly addresses the main worry of one of their first-generation respondents: 'He realizes that continuity is a major problem and worries about the lack of patience, integrity and resoluteness of the next generation.' In the eyes of the founder, his son is always impatient, inexperienced and less independent. Fearing the successor cannot effectively and properly manage the family business, the founder is less eager to release his control. Thus, the successor has less opportunity to build his leadership. The recursive causality is that inexperience will further be exposed during a time of crisis. The awkwardness of the successor reinforces the father's perception. Then, the successor will get less chance to practice leadership and his image of incompetence will be reconfirmed. Finally, the family business will suffer.

Overruling a successor's decision also has a negative impact on family businesses (Lansberg 1988; Handler 1990). As human beings, making mistakes is inevitable, especially when the successor first takes up the role of leader. A father who frequently overrules a successor's decisions, fearing that a particular decision is immature or will affect company profitability will seriously weaken the heir's leadership. The successor will find it difficult to rein in subordinates. Employees will be ambivalent and they will wonder who has the final say and who they should listen to. By definition, the successor is the new leader of the company. But in reality, the retired father is the paramount figure. Unclear leadership and swaying business policy both hurt the family and the business. Overruling a successor's decision upsets the successor and invites further discontent.

Different perceptions and values between father and son is another area that invites conflict (Levinson 1971; Handler 1990). The upbringing between the two generations is different. Generally, the father comes from a poor family. Poverty and lack of options forces him to leave school earlier, work earlier and mature earlier. The son, on the contrary, comes from a well-off family. He does not need to worry about how he is going to live. Usually he studies abroad and obtains a good academic qualification. Due to the complete contrast in background, their mentality and beliefs are different. A large number of scholars argue that the styles and value systems of the younger generation are different from that of the founder-owner. They explain that since the new generations have gained higher education, they think differently from the founder. Such divergent views on life, career, marriage and family will inevitably create tension between the two generations. The new generation may not treasure the small family business. Instead, they prefer to become a professional, to get involved in politics or to migrate to Western countries (Menkhoff 1990; Cunningham and Ho 1994).

Even if the father does something inappropriate, no one can oust him against his will. The sons cannot topple the father's paramount position both in the family and in the company. If they do so, they have to bear huge moral sanctions, as well as risking of being 'dethroned' by the father. It is taboo in the company (culture) to disobey the rule of the founder (Alcorn 1982). In other words, the family is a breeding ground of conflict. If such conflict cannot be properly diverted or solved, separation and dissension will be the inevitable result (Omohundro 1974).

Favouritism is one of the reasons for sibling conflict, and very often parents are unaware of its impact (Alcorn 1982). Parents often have different expectations and degrees of satisfaction for each of their children. To win the heart of their parents, there will be competition among children. Favouritism deepens children's jealousy of each other and weakens their mutual cooperation (Levinson 1971). When tension accumulates to a certain level, conflict will finally come to the surface and become destructive.

Like favouritism, second guessing the successor or making comparisons between sons also generates conflict and jealousy (Kets de Vries 1988). Some fathers may praise one son in front of others in the hope that others can learn lessons from them. Such 'teaching methods', however, will create negative feelings among siblings and widen their misunderstanding.

Family conflict may also be intensified when children marry. The joining of in-laws makes family relationships more complicated (Cohen 1976). Bickering between in-laws, brothers and sisters are frequent occurrences. Couples will address grievances and frustrations to each other. They will complain about the favouritism of parents or the unequal share of domestic chores, or may criticize other family members' misconduct. Such incessant gossip reinforces the couples' bad feelings of being hard done by and will worsen their relationship with the rest of the family. If conflict between the in-laws remains unchecked, misunderstandings will finally lead to a devastating outcome.

However, some scholars may see the question from another angle. They argue that the inherent cultural system is the reason for family business dissension. For instance, Freedman (1979) points out that partition occurs in Chinese families when the family head passes away. Formerly, the power was strongly controlled in the hands of the father. The death of the father implies the transfer of power to the eldest son (or brother). However, severe competition among sons makes it difficult for the eldest son to draw all members together. The equal-share principle further adds fuel to the fire and drives members apart. The overt competition among in-laws also worsens each other's relationship. In other words, the death of the family head is the crucial factor that affects family division (Freedman 1957, 1971).

In fact, some scholars also blame the coparcenary principle as the key factor that shortens the life of the family and its business, as it implies male heirs have equal right to family property. Sons from the same ancestor have 'jural equality' to family property (Chen 1985a, 1985b; Wang 1977; Chau 1991; Liu 1959; Wolf 1981; Diamond 1969; Johnston 1910). By simple calculation, when the founder dies, his estate will be divided amongst his heirs. If he has four sons, each son will get one-quarter of it. If he has eight sons, each son will only get one-eighth. In the next generation or next round of division, the ratio will become even smaller. In other words, family property and its business share will get smaller and smaller after each partition.

In his book, *Ladder of Success in Imperial China*, Ho (1976) presents us with a persistent and striking downward trend of social mobility for the majority of mandarin officials in the Qing dynasty (1644–1912). He attributes this tendency to the coparcenary inheritance system and concludes that the Chinese family is constantly subjected to the process of economic levelling. In his eyes, the relationship between the progressive dilution of property and the inability of high-status families to perpetuate themselves is clear. Based on Ho's findings, Chau (1991) compares the Chinese coparcenary system with the Japanese primogeniture system, a system of inheritance in which a single heir, usually the eldest male of the oldest branch in the family, gets the estate. He summarizes that the coparcenary inheritance system is 'dysfunctional, [has] downward mobility and lack of corporate longevity', while the primogeniture system is 'functional, assisting capital formation and corporate longevity'.

DeGlopper (1972) also suggests that Chinese family businesses do not follow the pattern of European and Japanese models in terms of generational succession. He uses the term 'amoeboid fission' to indicate the Chinese succession pattern and puts forward that the 'amoeboid fission' is a result of the equal inheritance system. Yeung (2000b: 59) also blames the inheritance system as prohibitive to business growth by promoting incessant fragmentation. He writes: 'Many Chinese family firms experience a downsizing effect when the family firm is broken down into separate business units, each headed by a son or a nephew.' In a nutshell, all these scholars assert that the inheritance system itself is a centrifugal force that not only suffocates capital accumulation, but also weakens the competitiveness of the business.

Another approach suggests that family businesses rely too much on the contribution of family members. It is frequently quoted that family members are generally assigned to important management posts, but the assignment is not due to qualifications or performance, rather to personal relationship. Outside professionals rarely reach the top echelon of a family firm. Nepotism (employment based on kinship) and paternalism (power and control held in the hands of father) are common features. Employees are assessed by the level of trust and loyalty instead of efficiency and job performance (Redding 1990, 1991; Mackie 1992; Fukuyama 1995). The over-concentration of business networks and personal ties in the father's hands are also very dangerous in case of the father's serious illness or sudden death. No other family member can really fill his shoes. Over-reliance on family and kin members is also believed to narrow the scope of business vision and ideas.

Second, a negative image remains about inheriting the family enterprise. If successors can successfully take up and expand the business, people will attribute such success to their progenitor's merit rather than the successors' contributions. If they fail, they will be condemned as 'prodigal' or the 'culprit' who ruined the family enterprise. People will put strong pressure on those inheriting an undertaking. Leach (1991: 140) comments that

> To enter the already established family firm, however, [was regarded] as a 'no win' option – if they succeed, people will say 'well, why not, he started after all the hard work had been done', while if they fail, they have squandered a talented opportunity and destroyed a family legacy.

In other words, it is generally believed that it will be difficult to attract the best talent to take on a family undertaking.

Drastic reformation and expansion during the leadership changeover period makes family firms vulnerable. Usually, people have the common perception that the successor reaches the apex of the management ladder because they are born with a silver spoon in their mouth, and there is doubt about their capability. Furthermore, people will compare the successors with their predecessors and blame the successors as being less competent or less hardworking (Qi 1981, 1984). Some successors do not accept this comparison and want to prove their ability to the world. As a result, after taking up the helm, they may carry out radical reform in the hope of emerging from their predecessor's shadow. If these reformations are conducted without proper planning, or the changes are too drastic, then the business may face serious trouble. In-depth study has found that if restructuring takes place without the cooperation of the whole company, these reformations will most likely end in failure (Barnes and Kriger 1986).

Everything has its lifecycle: birth, growth, maturity and death. Both family and firms follow their own lifecycle. It becomes quite complicated when the lifecycle of both family and business go hand-in-hand (Lansberg 1988; Davis and Stern 1980; Rosenblatt 1991). According to Kwong (1984), each family will usually go through a cycle of formation, extension, completed extension, contraction, completed contraction and finally dissolution. He further suggests that when a couple marries, a nuclear family forms (formation). When the couple has children, the family size expands, while the structure swells and extends (extension and completed extension). When their children grow up, marry and form their own nuclear families, the former family contracts. Finally, when the old couple dies, this family dissolves (contraction and completed contraction).

In fact, the family lifecycle usually runs parallel to the business lifecycle. When young, the founder tries hard to build up his own enterprise. His unremitting toil makes him successful and his business grows. Competition, technology and consumption pattern affects the founder's business. If the founder does not upgrade his skills and know-how to meet changing consumer demand, his business will lose its competitiveness.

Even though the founder wants to pass the business onto his children, his children may not be willing to take over the reins. Generally, his children may prefer to set up their own nuclear families and create their own businesses or simply work in large corporations. They treasure their independence and freedom. This centrifugal force should not be underestimated. Following the business lifecycle, family business also reaches its waning stage. If his children take over the business, they have to conduct reformation in order to rejuvenate the business. Such reformation is perceived as more difficult than starting a new enterprise. If the founder dies before his successors take up the business, transmission will become more complicated. In Navin's (1991) study, he discovers that most firm owners died before their children could take control of the business. Such unfavourable factors weaken the sons' intention to take on a family enterprise.

To avoid discontinuity of the business when the founder dies, a proper transfer of management and control is necessary. If there is no transmission preparation, as Tong (1991: 197) writes, 'The moment he [the founder] relaxes his control, without proper transfer of power, the family business inevitably divides.' In fact, the lack of a succession plan is frequently criticized as detrimental to family continuity (Lansberg 1988; Leach 1991; Beckhard and Dyer 1983). During the start-up period, the founder usually pays too much attention to creating the business, but neglects the issue of succession. In the later stage, after reaching the time for expansion, the founder gets too deeply involved in their business and finds it very difficult to give up power. They may overlook the importance of a well-formulated succession plan.

Some founders may have the misconception that passing on leadership is just like changing hands on the steering wheel. Once the successors have a 'licence', they can drive at any time. Thus, they underestimate the complexity of leadership training. In fact, the change of leadership is not a simple event. It involves things like workers' loyalty, authority, personal ties, business networks, and crises management. All of these require a continuous and lengthy period of training. Leach (1991: 13, 128) therefore comments: 'The father himself is often ambivalent about succession because he is worried about the ability of his children and how he is to approach favoring one at the expense of the others.'

The interconnectedness of Chinese, family and business

From the above arguments, an integrated approach can be formulated. Generally speaking, 'Chinese family business' is operated by three major interrelated components. Literally, they are 'Chinese', 'family' and 'business'. 'Chinese' implies the Chinese cultural environment or Confucian moral code. 'Family' means the system is subjected to family domination or ownership. 'Business' assumes that the operation follows economic and business principles.

Although each system operates according to its own rules, it also interacts with the others. Interaction generates feedback. Positive feedback in each system can facilitate family business development and growth. Negative feedback, on the contrary, creates inefficiency and conflict. The survival of the business will therefore be threatened (Figure 1.1). To sum up, the inherent weaknesses of these three main systems can be summarized as follows:

1 Culture system: the equal inheritance system levels the family business capital and therefore creates a tendency to downsize. It weakens the business competitive edge. A negative image attributed to inheritance problems prohibits successors from taking up the family business. Neglecting to develop a succession plan further threatens business transmission and continuity.
2 Family system: inherent internal conflicts generate tension amongst family members who hurt each other and ultimately plague business operations. Paternalism and nepotism does not welcome professional non-family members' contribution, but turns to cronyism, and therefore reduces organization flexibility and efficiency and inevitably weakens business performance.

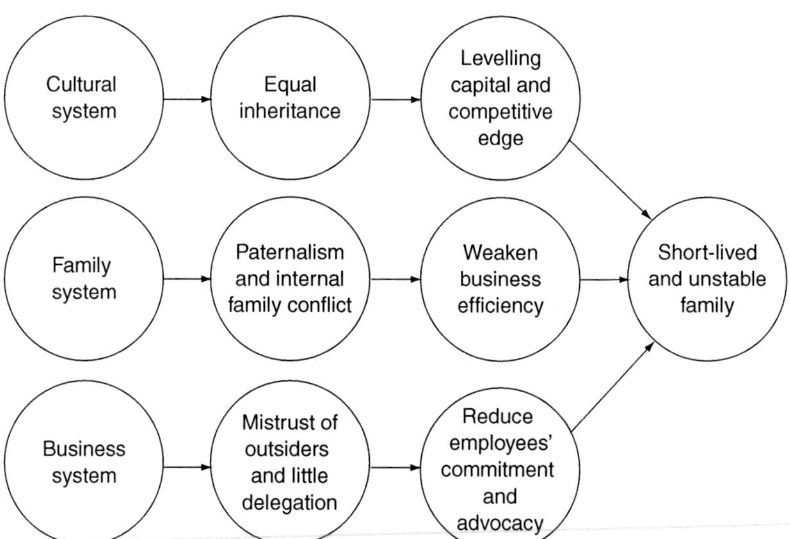

Figure 1.1 Chinese family business: an interconnected system.

3 Business system: wrong timing of expansion and unplanned reformations are serious mistakes that are often committed by new leaders. The decline of the business cycle makes poor family management even worse. Over-concentration of power and a low level of delegation discourage employees' cooperation, commitment and advocacy, and also complicate the process of succession.

In short, conventional theories argue that the equal inheritance system levels off capital accumulation while internal family conflict weakens siblings' cooperation. Over-concentration of power and lack of commitment further affects business efficiency. The weakness of each system means that negative interaction plagues the family business and further depletes its chance for survival. All these imply that Chinese family business is inefficient, dissentious, short-lived and unstable.

The above arguments seem logical and flawless on the surface. However, if one takes a deeper look, one can find that the real picture does not resemble this. First, most of these arguments lack empirical support and some are normative and subjective. They do not quantify the effect of each factor but only summarize some unsuccessful family businesses and reach some grossly inaccurate conclusions (Yeung 2000a). In fact, this kind of analysis does not investigate why some family businesses fail while others succeed.

Second, all these arguments seem to over emphasize the weaknesses of the family and cultural systems in addition to inefficient management, but neglect the impact of natural family and business cycles. In fact, the expansion or decline of family or business may reflect different stages of the cycles. It may not directly relate to the family system and cultural system at all. The change in ideology, technology, consumption patterns, market competition and product innovation can directly affect the lifecycle of an industry or a family. For instance, Ward (1987b) suggests that suppliers and customers who alter the 'rules of the game', or competitors that quickly copy successful strategies, also shape the business environment. In other words, to close down a business is merely a commercial decision. Thus, one should not magnify the effect of family or cultural factors.

Third, the conventional argument places too much emphasis on the negative and destructive effect of family conflict. It does not mean all family conflicts are malicious, hostile or dissenting. In fact, some conflicts can be benign, positive and constructive (Freedman 1991; Jehn 1997; Cosier and Harvey 1998). A certain level of conflict can stimulate family members' functional competitiveness, innovation and incentives. Family members should 'learn to address conflict, welcome it, use it as an opportunity to grow. Remember that two (or more) heads are better than one if they can disagree' (Kaye and McCarthy 1996: 71–2). A reasonable approach in family business is therefore not to accumulate and invite destructive conflict, but to encourage constructive and positive competition.

Fourth, personal connections and business networks can be functional to business operations. The invisible linkages with suppliers, customers or contacts in the social and political arenas can reduce transaction costs on the one hand, and enlarge profit margin on the other. In addition, an intertwined and well-connected network can serve a protective function for the family businesses (Landa 1983; Wong 1996). It can erect social barriers against outsiders, preventing them from diluting the family's profit margin.

Fifth, a one-sided accusation of the equal inheritance principle does not favour dialectic and scientific discussion. An oversimplified comparison between the primogeniture and coparcenary system, and a narrow conclusion that equal inheritance amongst heirs discourages family unity and business continuity is unfair. Division of a family estate does not equate to disintegration of the business. Many family businesses can still be kept intact even after portions of company shares are assigned to various family members.

In fact, equal inheritance among children is more compatible with modern society, which emphasizes fairness and justice. In America, the elimination of primogeniture was declared in 1785 in Virginia, with other states soon following (Gundersen 1998). In Chinese tradition, although only male heirs have equal rights in accessing ancestral property, and female family members are still excluded from the line of inheritance, such an arrangement is fairer than primogeniture, a system that dictates only the eldest son has the right to access his father's property (Sung 1982; Yue 1989).

In fact, not many Chinese family firms have operated successfully and have survived beyond three generations. In Taiwan, for example, five wealthy families, the Lin Jia-yin family (1820), the Gu Xian-rong family (1887), the Lin Ping-hou family (1847), the Yan Dou-meng family (1803) and Chen Fu-qian family (1860s) have survived for over 100 years. Today, these five families still play influential roles in Taiwan (Sima 2000).

In Hong Kong, there are also many similar cases. Famous examples such as the Li Shek-pang family, the Ho Tung family, the Chau Wing-tai family, the Fung Pak-liu family, the Lee Leung-yick family, the Hui Oi-chow family, the Fung Ping-shan family and the Wing On the Kwok's family are frequently quoted, not only in the popular media, but also in business and academic circles. Logically, we may ask: Why can these families avoid all the above-mentioned inherent weaknesses of dissension and keep their businesses viable over generations?

Theoretical framework and research objectives

As we all know, the life of a human being is limited, while the life of an organization can vary depending on how carefully it is looked after. Like all kinds of organizations, if a family business wants to outlive a person, a successful transmission from one generation to the next is vital. However, when talking about inheritance, not only the passing on of ownership should be addressed – the transfer of leadership and business networks also needs closer examination.

In reality, when we talk about inheritance and transmission of family business, we usually follow Karl Marx's view that economic capital determines the mode of production, relation of production and socio-political structure, and therefore only focus on the transfer of physical or economic capital such as cash, bank deposits, machinery and property. We may overlook intangible human and social capital, and seldom give attention to the passing on of personality, leadership, personal ties and business connections, and give little awareness to its effect on social behaviour and organization structure.

As we all know, although intangible social capital is abstract and difficult to assess or calculate, it really 'facilitates certain actions of individuals who are within the structure' (Coleman 1990: 302). Its influence on various arenas such as day-to-day transactions, clientele management, interaction with customers and organization reformation is in-depth, far-reaching and very fundamental (Bourdieu 1986; Granovetter 1985; Fukuyama 1995). In other words, during preparation for 'passing the baton', if we don't give due attention to the transfer of human capital and social capital (especially network capital) on top of economic capital, the possibility of maintaining family business vitality and continuity from one generation to the next would definitely be in doubt.

Before commencing systematic discussion of the transmission of the three types of capital, some basic concepts and theoretical framework must first be outlined. To begin with, we may ask, 'What is inheritance?' According to Goody (1976, 1987): 'Inheritance, in a strict sense, is transmission of relatively exclusive rights at death.' However, economists view inheritance both more broadly and more narrowly than the strict definition. Menschik and Jianakplos (1998: 45) argue:

> In a broader sense, economists' interest in inheritance is a concern with the intergenerational transfer of wealth.... Economists also recognize wealth to consist of more than tangible or financial assets. Human capital, the knowledge and education embodied in individuals, is [also] part of an individual's wealth.

In other words, apart from the transfer of economic capital, economists suggest inclusion of human capital. Brittain (1977: 124) points out that although economists have enriched the concept, there is still an 'explanatory gap' involved in the transfer process. He suggests that such a gap is due to the inadequate measurement of human capital: '[Other factors] involved are the inheritance of ability, ambition, and other measured characteristics like speech and dress that may affect earning power both directly, and indirectly through their effect on education.' Although the scope of definition is expanded, some vital parts are still missing. First, it does not include leadership as one of the key elements of human capital. Second, it does not cover a person or family's social capital that also determines social behaviour and affects social relations.

In everyday life, being a leader and leadership are key concepts that are frequently heard but seldom analysed regarding their real meaning. Interpretation is mainly based on individual perception and understanding of the terms. In family business, leadership also plays an important role that should not be overlooked or underestimated. According to *Webster's Third New International Dictionary*

(1986), leadership is defined as '(1) the office or position of a leader; (2) the quality of a leader, [i.e.] capacity to lead, or the act of leading; and (3) a group of persons who lead.' Weber tries to take this a step further and suggests a special type of leadership – charismatic leadership – to differentiate it from ordinary leadership. In his concept, charismatic leadership should consist of some indefinable essence:

> Certain quality of an individual personality by virtue of which he is set apart from ordinary men and treated as endowed with supernatural, superhuman, or at least especially exceptional powers or qualities. These are not accessible to ordinary persons, but are regarded as of divine origin or as exemplary, and on the basis of them the individual concerned is treated as a leader.
>
> (Weber 1947: 329)

In addition, Weber also points out that such a special personality trait is 'the gift of grace'. It can not be learned or taught, but can be awakened or tested. In order to make the concept clearer, he further elaborates:

> There is no such thing as 'appointment or dismissal', no career, and no promotion. There is only a 'call' at the instance of the leader on the basis of the charismatic qualification of those he summons, one of the form routinization of charisma ... by the designation on the part of the original charismatic leader of his own successor and his recognition on the part of the followers. Legitimacy is acquired through the act of designation.
>
> (ibid.: 331–5)

Echoing Weber's definition, Richardson and Thayer (1993: 5) concisely explain, '[Charismatic leadership is] a special quality of leadership that captures the popular imagination and inspires unswerving allegiance and devotion ... a person who has some divinely inspired gift, grace, or talent.' Such gifted essence generates charisma that attracts followers.

By convention, charismatic leadership only applied to great leaders who had mass appeal and who had brought revolutionary change to society (Bendix 1971). However, some scholars argue that Weber himself does not confine the application of this theory to 'great leaders'. In fact, this concept can also apply to daily life (Shils 1965). For example, a popular singer's performance on the stage that drives the audience wild is also one kind of charismatic appeal. A family leader, who can persuade his family members and employees to devote themselves wholeheartedly to the business and can mobilize resources for investment is another kind of charismatic leader. In other words, leadership is a broad concept. It applies to the social and political, as well as to the family circle. In business circles, however, it is usually translated as another term, entrepreneurship.

In the past, when explaining economic growth, most scholars attempted to shed light on the concept of entrepreneurship. But we may ask: What is entrepreneurship? Schumpeter, a close friend of Weber, sees entrepreneurship as a spirit of economic innovation and motivation. He further suggests that it is the prime mover for economic growth. According to Schumpeter (1934: 93–4), entrepreneurship refers to the following spirit:

> First of all, there is the dream and the will to found a private kingdom, usually, though not necessary, also a dynasty.... Then, there is the will to conquer: the impulse to fight, to prove oneself superior to others, to succeed for the sake, not of the fruits of success, but of success itself.... Finally, there is the joy of creating, of getting things done, or simply of exercising one's energy and ingenuity.

In order to solidify the concept, Schumpeter (ibid.: 66) further suggests five conditions to measure entrepreneurship.

1 The introduction of a new good.
2 The introduction of a new method of production.
3 The opening of a new market.
4 The conquest of a new source of supply of raw material or half-manufactured goods.
5 The carrying out of the new organization of any industry.

As a way to simplify Schumpeter's theory, Kao (1995: 12) comprehensively defines entrepreneurship as 'the process of doing something new and/or something different for the purposes of creating wealth for the individual and adding value to society'. There has been extensive discussion on the topic of entrepreneurs and entrepreneurship in business, economics and sociology. Many of the arguments usually diverge from one another and may blur attempts at constructive analysis (Kirzner 1973, 1979; Leibenstein 1978). Yu (1997) simply categorizes them into two main groups: Schumpeterian entrepreneurship and Kirznerian entrepreneurship. Schumpeterians emphasize innovative economic activities, while Kirznerians stress arbitrage economic activities.

Clearly, Schumpeterian entrepreneurs innovate new products or new ideas from scratch and become the prime movers of economic activities, while Kirznerian entrepreneurs discover the existence and/or the value of available knowledge, and imitate the innovation to arbitrage profit opportunities. Although their nature and style are different, they are both facilitators and coordinators of economic activities. In this study, in order to simplify discussion, we adapt Schumpeter's idea of entrepreneurship.

Similarly, although the terms of social capital and social network are frequently heard, little solid research has been done on it. Bourdieu (1986) argues that members of the capitalist class are able to reproduce their position in society by accumulating not just economic capital, but also social and cultural capital. In other words, the privileged class will usually try to use their social network for safeguarding their interests. Allen (1987: 23) puts it more succinctly: 'Nothing succeeds like money, manners and connections.'

What is a social network? Scott (1988: 109) writes, 'Individuals are, as it was, tied to one another by invisible bonds which are knitted together into a criss-cross mesh of connections, much as a fishing net or length of cloth is made from intertwined fabrics.' Clearly, a social network means that a network is constructed to serve a social purpose or function, while personal ties can simply refer to one's personal connections with other people.

Each Chinese family enterprise is generally viewed as a 'bamboo web', characterized by 'tight-knit contacts, strong leadership from a far-sighted patriarch and unswerving loyalty and obedience from staff' (Evers 2000: B3). In order to have a better understanding of this kind of structure, Numazaki (1986) chose to conduct intensive fieldwork in Taiwan. After that he found that business groups there were primarily based on personal connections among businessmen and families. He even discovered that most of the enterprise groups were not independent actors. Rather, they were 'embedded in a web of partnerships'. Then, I would like to ask the following question: Why do Chinese family enterprises stress so heavily the informal personal ties and social connections instead of formal systems or a black-and-white contract?

Williamson (1975) tries to explain it from a different perspective. He argues that the emergence of a social network and personal ties is due to the failure of the market, or to be more specific, to market imperfections, such as transaction costs, business uncertainty and idiosyncratic exchange. Thus, institutions like townsmen associations (*tongxianhui*), clansmen associations (*zongqinhui*) and particularistic personal ties are thought to help organize economic relationships more efficiently.

Fukuyama (1995) goes a step further and points out that Chinese society belongs to a 'low trust' type which only puts trust in family members. Non-family members are generally regarded as outsiders and little trust is given. In other words, building personal ties and social connections strengthens the relationship between family members or establishes mutual trust with particular non-family members for a special purpose. Clearly, from Fukuyama's standpoint, modern capitalism cannot take root in 'low trust' societies.

Some other scholars take social network analysis as their research method or design. They use it for interpreting actors' manoeuvres within cultural constraints and normative boundaries to see how the informal system interacts with the formal system or how they supplement each other in affecting social behaviour (Whitten and Whitten 1972). For whatever reasons and from whatever perspective, it seems clear that the use of personal ties and social connections is due to the inadequacy of formal systems or the inefficiencies of the free market.

Since human capital and network capital are equally important and have far-reaching effects on doing business. Neglecting these elements will clearly blur the perception of family business development and transmission. In order to achieve a balanced perspective, social and cultural aspects must be added for analysis in this book. In other words, from a sociological point of view, inheritance not only should include the transmission of private property rights, but also the transmission of education and leadership, as well as the inculcation of personal connections and social networks.

To borrow Brittain's (1977: 102) words, inheritance should also focus on 'the acquisition of a possession condition or trait from the past generation'. Therefore, when talking about inheritance, we should not narrowly focus on economic capital and the passing on of ownership of physical property. Human and social capital, including the inculcation of personal ties, leadership style and business connections, should be equally dealt with.

Another key concept is succession. Generally, succession represents

> (1) the action of a person or thing following, or succeeding to the place of, another; (2) the coming of one person or thing after another; also (3) the passing from one act or state to another ... that to which a person succeeds as heirs; an inheritance.
>
> (*Compact Oxford University Dictionary* 1993: 1950)

Succession can be testate or intestate. Intestate succession occurs when a person dies without a will, while testate succession refers to the disposition of property at death in accordance with the terms of a will (Sussman *et al.* 1970: 16). The entitlement to succession of property on death is governed either by the will or by the rules of intestacy, or by a combination of both (Sherrin 1994).

Generally speaking, a will is a statement of intention and expectation that does not take effect until after death. To be specific, a will is '[a] written instrument, legally executed by which a man makes disposition of his estate, to take effect after death' (*The American College Dictionary* 1956). There are four kinds of will substitutes: gifts, trusts, life insurance and joint ownership of property with right of survivorship. Succession of family property via a will has become formalized and systematized in the modern Western world.

> A legally devised plan to transfer and conserve patrimonial capital in one generation becomes in the next generation an organizational framework for extended family relations – actually a formal model or surrogate of the family, with law rather than the founding entrepreneurial patriarch as its source of authority.
>
> (Marcus 1980: 859)

Another question that needs to be clarified is the meaning of ownership. Similarly, according to the *Compact Oxford English Dictionary* (1993: 1250), ownership is defined as:

> The fact or state of being an owner; legal right of possession; property, proprietorship, dominion.... Ownership or property may be described accurately enough in the following manner: the right to use or deal with some given subject in a manner, or to an extent, which, though it is not unlimited, is indefinite.

In his book, *Ownership and Control of the One Hundred Largest Corporations in Malaysia, Kuala Lumpur*, Lim (1981: 4) simply states, 'Ownership is usually defined as the legal rights over the use, disposal and fruits of the means of production in society.' Kao (1995: 130) sees ownership from another perspective, and suggests that it is 'making decisions and entitlement to the harvest'.

The entitlement to the harvest means economic benefit: It is the right of decision making that has the most far reaching effect on the individual. In other words, the transfer of ownership not only means the passing of legal rights of possession, property or proprietorship from one party to another, but should also include the rights of making decision and holding responsibility for risk and profit.

To sum up, the main objectives of this book are: to examine the transfer of economic capital, human capital and social capital; to explain why some of the Chinese family businesses can overcome the succession problems and can manage their businesses from generation to generation; to explore the origin of the self-employment mentality with special reference to the equal inheritance system; and more importantly, to cross-examine how the equal inheritance system affects economic development in Chinese societies such as Hong Kong.

In the following chapters I will first outline the research methodology and the overall developmental process of the studied family businesses. Then, light will be shed on the preparation and transfer of economic capital, human capital and network capital in three separate chapters. Special characteristics and the inheritability of these three types of capital will also be discussed. After that, I will summarize all the major research findings in the final chapter by cross-examining how Chinese family businesses restructure their organizations in order to adapt to the ever-changing and highly competitive environment. Finally, I will argue that if businesses can take economic capital, human capital and social capital equally into account during succession, and more importantly, can overcome difficulties and crises at each stage, the probability of maintaining their business vitality and continuity from one generation to the next will be high.

In order to make the research objective clear and the presentation more consistent, all Chinese terms, place names, person names, company names, idioms and proverbs in this book are transliterated by using the Mandarin *pinyin* system, except for those Chinese terms, place names, company names and person names commonly used in the Hong Kong popular media or are Romanized according to the *Gazetteer*. Most individual Chinese terms, names, place names and company names can be found in the glossary.

2 Methodology and sketches of the studied families

Before giving detailed presentation of the study, a brief account of the fieldwork and methodology is necessary. In this chapter, I will first explain the rationale in using Chaozhou (also known as Teochiu, Chiuchow or Chiuchau) merchants and long-established families in Hong Kong as two major reference groups. Then, I will outline the procedure used in formulating the research idea, the process of gathering data and the application of scientific methodology. After that, I will briefly describe some of the respondents in order to provide some background about these targeted groups.

In the second part of this chapter, attention will be given to the long-established families by sketching out the developmental path they generally followed. Some special mechanisms adopted by this group of families to overcome crises at different times will also be addressed briefly. To begin with, let us discuss the rationale in formulating the research idea.

Formation of the research idea

The prime aim of this research is to study inheritance and succession in Chinese family businesses. As discussed in the previous chapter, conventional theories strongly criticize Chinese culture, management style and its family system, and come to the conclusion that family business in the Chinese guise is inefficient, conflicting and short-lived. The aim of this study is to test these assertions and examine whether these conventional theories are correct or not.

Looking from this perspective, we can identify that the equal inheritance system is the starting point of the discussion. However, it would be too vague and too ambitious if we put all inheritance issues into one research basket. In order to make this study feasible and down-to-earth, we should first delineate the research boundary. In this research, long-established families and the Chaozhou merchants in Hong Kong are selected as the two main reference groups to supplement each other. The long-established families are those with a long history in Hong Kong. Their businesses have been transmitted over several generations and their success clearly deviates from the traditional wisdom that Chinese family businesses cannot go beyond three generations. Their experience can offer many useful insights, such as how they overcome problems in transmission and sustain their businesses; their strategies in maintaining the vitality of their businesses; and whether this mechanism can be learnt by other families.

Why did I choose Chaozhou merchants in Hong Kong as the other reference group? It is a long story. In 1995, when I first studied the rice industry in Hong Kong, I found that Chaozhou rice merchants had engaged in this business for several generations. Later, I learnt that these people had settled down in Hong Kong as early as the 1840s, and also played influential roles in many other industries. Thus, I believe that through studying this group, the myths surrounding family business transmission and transformation could be more or less unravelled. Therefore, I chose the Chaozhou community as the reference group for closer study. Can Chaozhou merchants learn some lessons from other long-established families? Do they have any different mechanisms in transferring their wealth, leadership and personal ties? Can their businesses also survive over three generations? All these are interesting questions that I will deal with in subsequent chapters.

Chaozhou people are known for being hardworking, family-centred, patriarchal, thrifty, clannish and superstitious (Sparks 1978). Although some Chaozhou people have settled down in Hong Kong for over a century, and are supposed to have been assimilated into the 'host' culture, their identity as people of Chaozhou is still easily recognized. In other words, one can delineate the research boundary and assess their adaptability without difficulty, and ostensibly, I chose them as another reference group to cross-examine the above arguments.

Fieldwork and methodology

The fieldwork is divided into two major parts: intensive interviews and direct participant observation. Intensive personal interviews were mainly conducted from 1997 to 2000. Follow-up telephone calls or second interviews in some cases also took place during the writing of this book. Participant observation was carried out from June 2000 to February 2001 in a leading office furniture company in Wan Chai, Hong Kong.[1]

From the fieldwork point of view, the first basic questions are: How can the transfer of ownership, leadership and personal connection be studied? Where can the information needed be gathered? Answering these questions requires not only defining and examining the in-depth aspect of the transmission mechanism, but also evaluation of the method and philosophy that Chinese businessmen usually follow. Using appropriate method(s) in gathering relevant data is pivotal. Since the transmission of family business is complicated, the data needed must be in-depth, detailed and comprehensive. The use of structured questionnaires for collecting data is far from ideal and was therefore rejected. The main reason is that intensive qualitative material is more important, not relatively superficial responses to simple questions. In this case, intensive personal interviews were the main technique chosen.

Generally speaking, each research method has its own strengths and weaknesses. Intensive personal interviews may also generate bias. First, personal subjectivity is inevitable. Keeping this in mind, I tried my best to minimize this. Throughout the interview I tried to keep my sense of neutrality and objectivity. Second, there may be interviewee reaction. The interviewees may try to avoid those issues/events that may tarnish their image, promote family conflict or affect business profitability, while over-emphasizing or exaggerating those issues/events that enhance their status and reputation. I have also tried to keep this to the minimum by counterchecking through other sources or interviews. Third, the personal interview is criticized as being time consuming. Since in-depth and detailed information are considered crucial, time is not a major consideration here.

The strengths of the personal interview, on the contrary, are numerous. Direct contact with the interviewees can be achieved. With face-to-face dialogue, it is possible to minimize over-reaction by allowing interviewees to clarify statements, and making follow-up questions possible and manageable. Through discussion with interviewees, the interviewer can immediately explore other related areas via follow-up questions. Apart from the advantages for research, personal connections can be built up through personal interviews. Such connections make follow-up interviews and other kinds of interactions, such as social gatherings and business conferences, possible. Therefore, intensive personal interview is the method of choice here.

Besides primary data, secondary data was gathered from different channels, especially for the large families. Relevant data from newspapers, magazines, companies' annual reports, corporate histories, memoirs of family leaders, private correspondents, minutes of board of directors meetings, records from company registries and even advertising and publication leaflets were obtained. Most of these can be found in the Hong Kong Public Records Office, Company Registry, public libraries, and more importantly, the Hong Kong Collection, which is located in the Main Library at the University of Hong Kong. Such materials offer constructive information to supplement the analysis.

Data collection

Collection of data was the most time consuming part of this research. After formulating the research topic and finishing the literature review, the target groups, as well as their basic information, were outlined. Then, intensive personal interviews to collect primary data were conducted. It took nearly two-and-a-half years to gather all the necessary data. For the secondary data, most of the time was spent in sifting data that was related to the study at the Public Records Office, Company Registry, or in libraries. On some occasions, firm visits and marketplace observations were also carried out.

Although one of the targeted reference groups was Chaozhou merchants in Hong Kong, not all of them were suitable for this study. Each selected family firm had to meet a particular criteria. First, firms had to be family-owned or mainly controlled by a single family. In other words, it should tally with the definition of family business or family firm: 'A single family can exercise effective control over the company.' Second, the firms should have been established for at least 20 years. This makes sense as only those businesses could experience a transmission of leadership. Third, the firms should be about to transfer leadership and ownership in the foreseeable future. For instance, in the coming 5–10 years, the leadership should be passed to the next generation. Alternatively, they have already passed their businesses to new management, or those firms who are currently and actually controlled and operated by the second or third generation.

There were also other criteria for selecting the interviewees. Ideally speaking, it is hoped that the founder, successor, family members and some employees could be interviewed. It is speculated that the perspective of each might be different. Such diverse points of view could offer resourceful information on the overall nature of the firm. Moreover, it was hoped that at least two interviewees from a different level in the hierarchy of a single firm or family could be interviewed. However, in reality, it was quite difficult to achieve this goal. However, this was in itself rather telling, since if only one person could be interviewed, it meant the interviewee did not like his/her successors/employees to be interviewed. The interview would then shed light on those areas such as succession arrangements, family conflict and employment relations.

The major criteria in choosing long-established family businesses are simpler. First, these businesses should have been in operation for at least 100 years (approximately three generations). Second, their headquarters should be located in Hong Kong. Third, for practical reasons, data or information that related to these families should be available in the Public Records Office or in various libraries. There may be a problem of representativeness in selecting the cases. However, it is understandable that these cases are not the main study group. They are used only for supplementary purposes. Therefore, I believe this minor weakness does not affect the value and the main theme of this study. It is hoped that the experience from the long-established families can be used to draw a brief comparison with the Chaozhou in Hong Kong.

Having identified the criteria in selecting target firms and delimiting the study group, the method and procedure of gathering information should also be elaborated. First, I contacted my uncle, who was one of the directors of the CCC. With his introduction and recommendation, I visited the CCC in August 1997. The executive, Mr F.L. Lam, welcomed my visit and gave me a list of all directors. That list contained basic information about all the CCC directors, such as their name, post, telephone number, address and major businesses.

Based on the list, I mailed each director a formal letter with the signature of my supervisor, Professor Wong Siu-lun, which outlined the research goals, rationale and content, and invited them for an interview. Many of them replied positively. For those who declined to be interviewed, they recommended other directors instead. As a result, I successfully interviewed 35 informants (Table 2.1). Most of these interviews were held at the interviewees' company. A few of them were held in the clubhouse of the CCC as they held key positions in the association in that period. On average, each interview lasted one-and-a-half

Table 2.1 Summary of Chaozhou family businesses

Interviewees	*Major businesses*
F1, F1's son	General trading, poultry feed, property investment
F2	General trading, semi-conductor, property investment
F3, F3's brother, F3's son	Rice trading, ice-cream making, property investment
F4, F4's son, F4's director	Rice importation, warehousing, wood trading, insurance, banking
F5	Goldsmith shop, imitation jewellery, taxi services
F6	I-C production, property investment
F7, F7's director	Banking, financial investment, real estate
F8	Trading, plastic, clocks and watches, real estate
F9	Gold trading, banking, insurance, real estate investment
F10	Denim manufacturing, property investment
F11	Button production, shipping, household appliances, cement trading
F12	Rice importation, wholesaling and retailing, warehousing
F13	Rice wholesaling, textiles and garments, property investment
F14, F14's son	Fabric cotton, property investment, restaurant
F15	Gold trading, money shop (*qianzhuang*), rice importation
F16	Rice retailing, non-deposit-taking, property investment
F17	Plastic flowers and ornaments, property investment
F18	Dry food trading, property investment
F19, F19's daughter	Rice importation, property investment, warehousing
F20	Textiles and garments, property investment
F21	Decoration products, leather clothes, car parks, property investment
F22	Secretarial and taxation services, property investment
F23	Solicitors and notaries
F24	Fur and feather clothing, property investment
F25	Textiles and garments, camera production
F26, F26's wife	Garments and textiles, travel agency, property investment

Source: Interviews 1997–2000.

hours. Some of them lasted over four hours, including an hour for lunch or dinner. Such lengthy interviews gave me adequate time to make clarifications and ask follow-up questions.

Sketches of the Chaozhou families

In Hong Kong and overseas, Chaozhou merchants are identified as hardworking, ambitious, frugal and economical in doing business. Before the sketches of the studied Chaozhou families in Hong Kong, some background information about this group and its special features is needed. Literally, Chaozhou means 'tidal county', and is situated in the coastal area of northern Guangdong Province. Like most parts of China, Chaozhou is primarily an agricultural region. When the rapid increase in population in the early Qing period coincided with years of famine, draught and social unrest, many people starved, and were eventually forced to leave their home towns to travel to adjacent regions like Fujian, Guangxi, Jiangsu and Zhejiang; or further away to places like Southeast Asia, Australia and America to seek their fortune. Because of this background, Chaozhou became one of the highly recognized *qiaoxiangs*, home towns for the overseas Chinese (Chan 1964; Chan 1974).

In the past, Chaozhou was divided into 11 *xians* (counties). They were Dabu, Huilai, Fengshun, Chaoan, Jieyang, Puning, Raoping, Chaoyang, Shantou, Nanao and Chenghai (Lam 1992). At present, Chaozhou is subdivided into four administrative regions. Jiedong, Jiexi, Puning and Huilai are under Jieyang City's administration. Chaoan and Raoping are under Chaozhou City's control. Chenghai, Nanao and Chaoyang belong to Shantou City, while Dabu and Fengshun are governed by Meizhou City (Guangdong Sheng Dituce 1994). When talking about 'Chaozhou', we mean the traditionally defined area that covered the 11 *xians* (Greater Chaozhou) rather than the present-day Chaozhou City. The Han River, the second largest river in Guangdong, runs through these four cities. The capital city of Chaozhou is Shantou, which is located at the mouth of the Han River.

Chaozhou people came to settle in Hong Kong as early as the 1840s. Hong Kong is a Cantonese-speaking (*Guangdong hua* or *yueyu*) region, while Chaozhou people speak their own dialect (*Chaozhou hua*). When they first arrived, due to the difference in dialect, they could not efficiently communicate with the local people. Most of the new immigrants could not find jobs; nor could they join the colonial government. As a result, many of them could only work as coolies in Western District. Some started their own small- or medium-scale retail businesses, and a few of them even joined triad societies. Living in a foreign place, they gathered together for mutual protection and assistance. During festivals, homesick Chaozhou people usually organized group worship (like the Hungry Ghost Festival), cultural activities (Chaozhou music and opera), and social functions (sharing Chaozhou *kungfu* tea together, a special style of brewing and drinking Chinese tea) to express their attachment to their home towns. Chaozhou people were frequently labelled as chauvinistic (male dominant), quarrelsome, clannish, superstitious, and even with a proclivity for involvement in crime and narcotics (Sparks 1978; Lau 1985; Lai 1990; Wang 1949).

If the Shanghainese are categorized as industrialists who brought capital, machinery and skills to Hong Kong (Wong 1988), then the Chaozhou people could be regarded as the supporting labour force. However, we must accept that both types of people displayed equally strong entrepreneurial spirit. According to certain reliable statistics, the first batch of Chaozhou people came to Hong Kong around the 1840s (Chan 1964; Lai 1990; Sparks 1978). Ko Chor-yuen, Chan Wun-wing and Chan Hoi-tai were Chaozhou pioneers in Hong Kong. They set up trading companies in Western District, specializing in dry food, silk, rice, tea and porcelain (Chan 1994).

Before the turn of the twentieth century, the re-export of goods were the key businesses in Hong Kong. Due to their strong connections in Southeast Asia, especially Thailand, Burma, Malaysia and Singapore, Chaozhou merchants dominated certain businesses such as rice, herbal medicine, porcelain, paper, tea, seed and charcoal. Trade gave rise to other businesses. After the 1910s, they gradually extended their businesses to banking, insurance, transportation and property. Liu Po-shan, Chan But-son, Ngai Shing-kwan, Ma Kam-chuan and Lui Ming-choi emerged during this period.

The fall of Kuomintang rule in the Chinese mainland and the imposition of a USA-led trade embargo against Communist China switched the Hong Kong trading base from re-export to manufacturing. The huge influx of refugees at different periods, a large proportion coming from Chaozhou, provided the momentum for Hong Kong's economic take-off. Different from re-export trading, manufacturing was labour-intensive and factory workers needed to work extremely hard. The Chaozhou people acquired such a work ethic during the hard times back home and therefore gained an upper hand in the manufacturing business. Li Ka-shing came to prominence in the plastic flowers industry, Lam Pak-yan in the garment industry, Choi Cheung-kok and Cheng Yick-chi in the steel and ironwork industry, Chuang Ching-um in the watch and clock industry, and Chan Tai-ho in the toy industry.

Moving into the 1990s, most Chaozhou merchants in Hong Kong have diversified their businesses and market outlets. The return of sovereignty of Hong Kong to China in 1997 and deepening economic reform in the People's Republic of China (PRC) further linked Hong Kong to the Chinese mainland. The Chaozhou community in Hong Kong also extended their network to their home cities and invested heavily there.

The CCC is regarded as one of the oldest townsmen associations in Hong Kong. It was founded by a group of Chaozhou merchants in 1921 and served as a de facto organization for Chaozhou residents in Hong Kong. Different from clansmen and townsmen associations, the CCC emphasizes commercial linkages rather than place of origin or surname. However, it also serves some functions as a townsmen association (Ng-lun and Ho 1996; Cheng 1996), since the CCC serves the de facto function for Chaozhou people in Hong Kong, and many influential Chaozhou merchants are members. With recommendations from the CCC, I conducted my survey successfully and obtained much valuable information.

If we take a brief look at the 35 respondents, who represent 26 families, we can easily find that their fields of business vary greatly, from dry food trading to construction, banking, insurance, legal firms, property investment, public utilities, entertainment, and even to high-technology and internet companies (Table 2.1). No wonder Chaozhou people are recognized as one of the main forces driving the Hong Kong economy! In order to build a comprehensive picture of this group of families, a summary of their fields of business is necessary.

Certain characteristics can be generalized from this data. First, it is found that the founding entrepreneurs were usually refugees from the Chinese mainland who came from poor family backgrounds. At the very beginning, they worked under somebody else's roof, usually relatives or fellow villagers. Later, when they had the opportunity and accumulated a certain amount of savings, they might choose to start their own businesses and, if luck was on their side, become prosperous. When they stepped down in their old age, these founding entrepreneurs expected their offspring to take up the family businesses.

Second, compared to the first generation, the second or later generations had a far better education. Their professional training and new knowledge drove the family businesses to another stage of expansion. A common feature is that when the new generation joined the family businesses, reformation, restructuring and modernization were frequently introduced.

Third, it is also found that even when they had divided their family estate, they could resolve conflicts and disagreements internally by themselves and so keep their businesses intact. Diversification and collaboration was the top of the agenda in many family businesses when they were transferred to the third and later generations.

If we look closely at Table 2.2, we can see that of these 35 respondents, 14 are from the first generation, 15 from the second generation, four from the third generation, and two were employees (executive directors). Among these 14 first-generation migrants, most (11) came to Hong Kong for economic reasons. Two came due to political upheavals (the advent of Communism) and one came due to the imminence of war (the Japanese invasion). The respondents' ages ranged from 35 to 87. Ten of the respondents were over 70 years of age. Although some interviewees have retired and have handed over the management to their successors, they still hold key positions in the company. Evidence also shows that all of them still keep their own offices in the company. Some of them even have personal secretaries.

Respondents' age at the time of arriving Hong Kong is another interesting element. If the age of 21 or above is defined as maturity, then a clear picture can be obtained. Most interviewees were adolescents when they arrived (71.4 per cent). Having spent most of their childhood in Hong Kong, it was conceivable that they would adjust easily to the host environment. As expected, in this sample, I only interviewed two female respondents (Table 2.3). This data indirectly reflects the less favourable social position of females in the Chaozhou community.

Not all of the respondents were born in Chaozhou (18) or Hong Kong (13). Two were born in Shanghai, one in Vietnam and one in Singapore. This pattern reflects the fact that Chaozhou people are scattered all over Southeast Asia and other parts of the globe. Among the 21 respondents who were not born in Hong Kong, most had connections to Hong Kong prior to their arrival. Some respondents claimed they had relatives in Hong Kong (Table 2.4). Reunion with their father or grandfather was the main reason for coming to the city. Such data at least shows that most had kin connections in Hong Kong.

In fact, to leave one's home town and make a living in a totally unfamiliar place was a hard and quite risky decision. When someone decided to emigrate, the person would weigh rationally many factors. Poverty, famine and escape from military conscription were some of the push factors. Hope and the myth that one could earn large amounts of money abroad were some of the pull

Table 2.2 Background of interviewees (by individual)*

Interviewee	*Generation*	*Age*	*Place of birth*	*Age on arrival*	*Years living in HK*
F1	1	82	Chaozhou	19	63
F1's son	2	48	Hong Kong	–	48
F2	2	87	Chaozhou	20	67
F3	2	78	Chaozhou	14	64
F3's brother	2	76	Chaozhou	12	64
F3's son	3	35	Hong Kong	–	35
F4	2	69	Chaozhou	15	54
F4's son	3	37	Hong Kong	–	37
F4's executive director	n/a	61	Singapore	1	60
F5	2	54	Chaozhou	17	37
F6	2	51	Hong Kong	–	51
F7	3	36	Hong Kong	–	36
F7's executive director	n/a	45	Hong Kong	–	45
F8	2	52	Hong Kong	–	52
F9	2	55	Hong Kong	–	55
F10	1	81	Chaozhou	23	58
F11	1	79	Shanghai	27	52
F12	1	75	Chaozhou	23	53
F13	2	72	Shanghai	19	53
F14	1	74	Chaozhou	21	53
F14's son	2	38	Hong Kong	–	38
F15	2	85	Chaozhou	18	67
F16	2	56	Hong Kong	–	56
F17	1	58	Chaozhou	20	38
F18	1	64	Chaozhou	21	43
F19	2	66	Hong Kong	–	66
F19's daughter	3	41	Hong Kong	–	41
F20	1	61	Chaozhou	20	41
F21	2	50	Chaozhou	2	48
F22	1	59	Chaozhou	18	41
F23	1	48	Chaozhou	12	36
F24	1	66	Vietnam	21	45
F25	1	56	Chaozhou	20	36
F26	1	60	Chaozhou	14	46
F26's wife	1	56	Hong Kong	–	56

Source: Interviews 1997–2000.

Note

* The base year in calculating interviewees' ages is 2000.

factors. Having a kin connection was only one of the key elements motivating emigrants to migrate (Chan and Chiang 1994: 127–66). In short, it is a general belief that Chaozhou people have extensive personal or ethnic connections overseas, including Thailand, Singapore, Malaysia and Hong Kong, from as early as the middle of the eighteenth century (Skinner 1957, 1958). For a brief discussion and introduction about the 26 Chaozhou families, please refer to the Appendix at the end of this book.

Table 2.3 Background of interviewees (by category)

Categories	*No. (%)*
Place of birth	
Chaozhou	18 (51.5)
Hong Kong	13 (37.0)
Shanghai	2 (5.7)
Singapore	1 (2.9)
Vietnam	1 (2.9)
Total	35 (100.0)
Generation	
First generation	14 (40.0)
Second generation	15 (42.9)
Third generation	4 (11.4)
Employees	2 (5.7)
Total	35 (100.0)
Age (in 2000)	
30–50	9 (25.7)
51–70	16 (45.7)
Above 70	10 (28.6)
Total	35 (100.0)
Age at time of arrival	
Under 10	1 (4.8)
11–15	5 (23.8)
16–20	9 (42.8)
21–5	5 (23.8)
Over 25	1 (4.8)
Total	21 (100.0)
Sex	
Male	33 (94.3)
Female	2 (5.7)
Total	35 (100.0)

Source: Interviews 1997–2000.

Sketches of the long-established families

After two-and-a-half years of intensive archival study, through repeated visits to the Public Records Office and various libraries, I gathered numerous items of information in relation to the long-established families studied. After in-depth analysis, it is found that although some businesses have died out, some successfully managed their internal family conflicts and successfully solved the equal inheritance or division issue.

From this group of long-established families, I selected 20 for closer study. These are: (1) Wang Lo Kat – the Wang family; (2) Yeo Hiap Seng – the Yeo family; (3) the Vitasoy Group – the Lo Kwai-cheung family; (4) Lee Kam Kee –

Table 2.4 Kin contact in Hong Kong at time of arrival

Interviewee	*Grandfather*	*Father*	*Brother*	*Sister*	*Relatives/ villagers*	*No contact*
F1				✗		
F2		✗	✗			
F3		✗			✗	
F4		✗				
F5	✗					
F10					✗	
F11					✗	
F12					✗	
F13					✗	
F14					✗	
F15		✗				
F17					✗	
F18					✗	
F20		✗				
F21		✗				
F22			✗			
F23		✗				
F24					✗	
F25						✗
F26		✗				

Source: Interviews 1997–2000.

the Lee Kam-tong family; (5) Ma Pak Leung – the Ma family; (6) Lee Chung Shing Tong – the Lee Siu-kay family; (7) Eu Yan Sang – the Eu family; (8) Ying Kee – the Chan Chiu-ying family; (9) Kin Tai Long – the Chan Wun-wing family; (10) Kwong Sang Hong – the Fung Fook-tin family; (11) the Ho Tung family; (12) the Li Shek-pang family; (13) the Lee Leung-yick family; (14) the Fung Pak-liu family; (15) the Chau Wing-tai family; (16) the Ho Oi-chow family; (17) the Fung Ping-shan family; (18) the Cheung Chuk-shan family; (19) the Tang Chi-ngong family; and (20) the Wing On Kwok family.

Based on the nature of their business and family wealth, I roughly divided them into two sub-groups. The first sub-group's families generally engaged in a single business and enjoy a relatively smaller family wealth, while the second sub-group's families invest extensively and enjoy a relatively larger family wealth. In the subsequent paragraphs, I will briefly talk about those families engaging in a single business and those who enjoy a relatively smaller amount of wealth (when compared to the super-rich).

Generally speaking, Wang Lo Kat, Yeo Hiap Seng and the Vitasoy Group are still very famous in the soft drink market; Lee Kam Kee is regarded as a well-known brand name in the sauce and condiment business; Ma Pak Leung, Lee Chung Shing Tong and Eu Yan Sang are treated as market leaders in the Chinese medicine business; Ying Kee is one of the oldest tea-trading firms; and Kin Tai Long still has deep roots in the rice business, while Kwong Sang Hong is famous in the cosmetics business. For these families, their family names represent the product or the business, just like Xerox is synonymous with photocopying, Coca Cola with cola, and McDonalds with hamburgers. In other words, their family names are closely associated to the industries in which they are engaged.

The Wang Lo Kat Tea Shop, founded by Wang Cha-pong, alias 'Lo-kat', in 1850 in Guangzhou (it later become a brand name of a soft drink), is a famous Chinese herbal tea trademark in Chinese communities. Consumers there believed that Wang's herbal tea had a medicinal effect, and was especially good for curing infectious diseases. It was even reported that Wang Lo Kat was once summoned by the Qing Emperor, Tongzhi, to act as one of the Imperial family's doctors. Lo Kat's sons Kwai-shing, Kwai-cheung and Kwai-fa helped him manage the business when they were young. With their assistance, Wang opened branches around Guangzhou and became one of the city's wealthy families.

Hang-li and Hang-yu were key members who represented the third generation of the Wang family. Following in their progenitors' footsteps, they further expanded their branches from Guangzhou to the whole South China region, including such places as Shanghai, Fujian, Suzhou and Hangzhou, and later also set up direct sales outlets in Hong Kong and Macau. A large proportion of their teabags were even exported to Southeast Asian countries. Thus the Wang Lo Kat Tea Shop not only became a brand name within the Chinese mainland, but also in overseas Chinese communities.

During the Japanese invasion, Wang Lo Kat's business faced a serious setback. Many of their shops were either destroyed or forced to close. Hang-yu moved to Hong Kong and settled there. After the end of the Second World War, Yu-hon, son of Hang-yu, took over the leadership of the family business, and reconnected their entire network. With Yu-hon's effort, Wang Lo Kat Tea Shop gradually recovered. Unfortunately, in the 1960s, due to inappropriate over-expansion, the family business was taken over by outsiders. Yu-hon was upset and moved to the USA. However, his wife, Tsai Lai-king, and their children remained in Hong Kong and tried to regain their family business. After years of struggle they finally won back control of Wang Lo Kat Tea Shop in 1971.

Under the fifth generation leaders like Kin-chuen, Kin-han and Kin-yee, the family business rebounded in the late 1980s. They repackaged their traditional herbal tea into a modern soft drink and commenced a worldwide marketing campaign (Wang 1986; M.P. Cheng 1997). Today, although Wang Lo Kat herbal tea only holds a minor share of the soft drink market and there are many family disputes, the brand maintains strong consumer loyalty.

Yeo Hiap Seng is another key brand in the soft drink market. Its founder, Yeo King-lian, was born to a poor family in Fujian Province in 1860. In 1892 he started his business by opening a small sauce and condiment factory in Zhangzhou, Fujian. His products were popular and soon become a famous brand in South China. King-lian's eldest son, Tian-yan, helped his father when he was young, while other sons like Tian-shing, Tian-kow and Tian-wah joined the family enterprise after they had finished their university studies.

During the Japanese invasion, Tian-yan moved the business to Hong Kong and later to Singapore. The Second World War ended in 1945 and Tian-yan decided to stay in Singapore, purchasing a large plot of land in Bukit Timah Road for the sauce brewery factory.

Under Tian-yan's leadership, Yeo's group expanded dramatically. They diversified their business from sauce brewery to canned food, soft drinks and property. In 1950 third-generation members like Chee-yeow, Chee-wai and Chee-hey joined Yeo Hiap Seng. In the late 1960s Yeo Hiap Seng was listed in the Singapore Stock Exchange. They also expanded to Malaysia, Hong Kong and other Southeast Asian countries. Their market outlets covered the USA, Canada and European countries in the 1980s.

Unfortunately, almost during the same period, in the late 1980s, following the entry of the fourth generation, Way-hing, Way-li, Way-cheung and Way-din, internal disputes increased. The conflict became even more serious when outsiders became involved. This conflict became a talking point in the Singaporean and Malaysian Chinese communities. Some of the family members were forced to leave the company against their will. The whole family paid a high price for this internal conflict. However, although Yeo Hiap Seng experienced a serious setback in the 1990s, it gradually recovered. Today, the Yeos still play an influential role in Singapore, Malaysia and Hong Kong (Chan 1992; Chan and Ho 1992; Lan 1999).

Compared to other long-established families, the Vitasoy Group is only a 70 years 'young' company. It was started by a man called Lo Kwai-cheung with a little bean in 1940. Lo Kwai-cheung, eldest son of Lo Chun-hing (a loyal employee of Eu Tong-sen, patriarch of Eu Yan Sang), left his home town, Meixian, to join his father in Penang in the late 1920s when he was a boy. When he first arrived, he studied at a local English secondary school and was sent to the University of Hong Kong in 1934 to study economics. Upon graduation, Lo Kwai-cheung returned to Penang and was recruited as 'business secretary' to Eu Tong-sen on his father's recommendation.

After two or three years' work, Lo Kwai-cheung accumulated some money and business connections. In the late 1930s, he returned to the Chinese mainland and Hong Kong to seek out opportunities and was surprised to see severe war-related malnutrition in both places. Having got the idea that soybeans could be turned into a milk-like drink with high protein content, Lo Kwai-cheung experimented in 1939 and successfully produced 'soya milk'. Then, he set up the Hong Kong Soya-bean Products Company (the former name of the Vitasoy Group) in 1940, with the assistance of his brothers, to try to sell the product to the general public.

At the beginning, since not too many customers were familiar with this totally new product, turnover was not as high as expected. However, after persistent effort and promotion, 'soya milk' became a highly popular drink in the local market as it was delicious, nutritious and affordable. Having earned their 'first bucket of gold', the Lo brothers, under the leadership of Lo Kwai-cheung, took on a series of expansionary measures, such as synchronizing the distribution network, introducing new production lines, and more importantly, obtaining the sole-agents status from the soft drink giants Pepsi Cola Limited and Green Spot Limited in the 1950s.

With a number of well-known brands in its hands, the Vitasoy Group expanded rapidly and quickly became the market leader. Because of its success, Lo Kwai-cheung became one of the most influential businessmen and was invited to serve as an urban councillor and later as a legislative councillor by the colonial government from the 1960s to the 1970s. Also in the 1970s, Lo Yau-lai, son of Lo Kwai-cheung, joined the Vitasoy Group and gradually emerged as the second-generation leader. In 1978, Lo Kwai-cheung stepped down as general manager and passed the helm to Yau-lai. Under the leadership of Yau-lai, the Vitasoy Group experienced another stage of development, not only through introduction of a variety of new products, but also through setting up new assembly lines in the New Territories and the Chinese mainland.

Also around the 1970s, as many of the second-generation members became adults, some were invited to join the Vitasoy Group, while many chose to start their own businesses. For instance, Lo Tang-cheung and Lo Kai-muk started Café de Coral, a leading fast-food chain in Hong Kong. Lo Fong-cheung followed his brother's footsteps and founded the Fairwood Restaurant and Sun Generation Restaurant fast-food chains, becoming one of the key competitors in the fast-food market. Lo Kai-fook, a member of the third generation, started his own fast-food chain, the East-East Noodle and Fook Do-Do Restaurant. The Lo Kwai-cheung family nearly monopolizes the restaurant market in Hong Kong. Although Café de Coral, Fairwood and Sun Generation are direct competitors, their connections are also obvious. Some of them still keep shares in the Vitasoy Group. In addition, all the soft drinks served in these restaurants are supplied solely by the Vitasoy Group (*Capital* 1991; Choi 1990).

In 1994, the Vitasoy Group went public and became a listed company on the Hong Kong Stock Exchange. With sufficient financial backing and following a series of restructurings, the Vitasoy Group further enhanced its competitiveness in the market and experienced another stage of substantial growth. Today, both the Vitasoy Group and their fast-food business connections are preparing for the third and fourth generation to play a leading role in its management and development (Lee 1998; So 1998).

Lee Kam Kee is one company specializing in the sauce and condiment business. Oyster sauce was accidentally invented in 1888 by Lee Kam-tong in Namsui, Guangdong. The sauce was found to be delicious and soon became highly popular with consumers. Lee Kam Kee soon became a household name. In 1920, Lee Kam-tong moved its factory from Namsui to Macau, and its sales outlets covered all of Guangdong Province, including Hong Kong and Macau.

Later in the 1920s, Kam-tong retired. His sons, Siu-nam and Siu-tan, took the leading posts. Under the helm of Siu-nam, Lee Kam Kee developed new products such as bean sauce, chicken sauce, soy sauce and onion and ginger sauce. Its market outlets also extended overseas to Southeast Asia, North America and Northern Europe.

Lee Kam Kee faced internal family conflict from the 1960s to 1970s. Although some family members were forced to leave under unhappy circumstances, Lee Kam Kee was still kept under the leadership of the Lees. At the same time, a third-generation family member, Man-tat, became the leader of the family enterprise. Lee Kam Kee nearly monopolized the sauce and condiments market.

Starting from the late 1980s, the well-educated fourth generation, like Wai-sum, Wai-chung, Wai-hung and Wai-man, joined the management team. With their contribution, Lee Kam Kee expanded further. Now, Lee Kam Kee still overwhelmingly dominates the condiments market. They sell over 60 types of sauce in around 60 countries, with total sales of nearly $1 billion dollars per year. In 1995 they won the Best Hong Kong Business Award. The fourth generation also seems ambitious to further upgrade their brand name and expand their market share in the future (*Capital* 1995; To 1996; Chan 1993).

In the Chinese medicine business, Ma Pak Leung, Eu Yan Sang and Lee Chung Shing Tong are successful names. The Ma Pak Leung (Pharmaceutical Shop) was set up by Ma Pak-leung in 1822 in Foshan. Pak-leung was a famous doctor in the Qing dynasty who had a keen interest in developing Chinese herbal medicine. 'Chut Lee Powder', a supplement for infants, was the company's main product. Pak-leung's sons and grandsons followed in Pak-leung's footsteps and kept on developing many new types of drugs.

In 1910 the company attended a drugs and pharmacy exhibition in Southeast Asia and won international recognition. According to their 'drug price list' in 1923, the company produced over 180 kinds of drugs. Ma Pak Leung was regarded as one of the key drug manufacturers and suppliers in the 1920s. In 1928, in order to diversify their direct sale outlets, they set up branches in Macau, Shantou, Hangzhou, Shanghai and Hong Kong. Later, they also spread to Bangkok, Singapore and Burma. Ma Pak Leung recorded tremendous business growth.

Today, Ma Pak Leung is headed by the sixth generation. The new leadership has not only introduced Western-style management, but has also modernized their manufacturing methods. In order to meet international standards, the company has also conformed to an internationally recognized system: Good Manufacturing Products (GMP), a standard of quality manufacturing that is similar to ISO 9000. They hope that with such improvements, they can upgrade the image of Chinese herbal medicine throughout the world (Ma Pak Leung Company 2000).

Eu Yan Sang is a key brand in Chinese medicine. It was founded by Eu Kong in 1879 in Perak, Penang (Malaysia), specializing in producing and retailing traditional Chinese medicine. From the late nineteenth century to the early twentieth century, due to political unrest in China and colonization in East and Southeast Asia, many Chinese left the mainland to seek their fortune in Southeast Asian countries. The Chinese immigrants naturally created a 'market enclave' for Chinese medicine. The 'Bak Foong Pill', a supplement for women, and 'Bo Ying Compound', a supplement for infants, were two of their major products that became popular. Eu Kong earned his 'first bucket of gold' and soon became a wealthy merchant.

The premature death of the company's founder saw the family business pass to his son, Eu Tong-sen, at the early age of 14. Eu Tong-sen grew up as an important leader who not only brought the family business back from the brink of despair on the death of his father, but also expanded it greatly to include other profitable areas, like tin mining and rubber plantations. Later, he also started to diversify his business into real estate, banking and money remittance businesses. Beside business diversification, Tong-sen also began to spread geographically, into areas such as Hong Kong (1909), Singapore (1910) and South China (from the 1920s to 1949).

In the late 1930s, Eu Tong-sen declared his intention to retire and his eldest son, K.C. Eu succeeded to the leading post. The death of Eu Tong-sen in 1941 marked the complete transfer of leadership to the third generation. Beside K.C. Eu, other third-generation members like Richard K.M. Eu, John K.D. Eu and Andrew K.W. Eu also joined the family business and took up key management posts. They even listed their company in 1973 in Singapore. Under the management of the third generation, there was no sign of stagnation or decline of the family business. Although the family flagship business was once taken over by the Lum Chang Group and there was conflict among some family members, they ultimately managed to buy back the company and solved their dispute internally.

In 1988, after the retirement of the third generation, like K.C. Eu, the fourth generation, such as Richard Y.M. Eu, David Y.T. Eu and Joseph Eu, came onto the scene. They were all well-educated people and their contribution further enabled the family business to keep growing. Yeung (2000a: 8) writes,

> Today, Eu Yan Sang has over 30 branches in Hong Kong, Singapore and Malaysia. It controls modern manufacturing facilities in Hong Kong and Malaysia, and exports its products worldwide to over 2,000 supermarkets, retail shops and pharmacies in Australia, Canada, China, Hong Kong, Malaysia, New Zealand, Singapore, Taiwan, the UK, and the US.

Starting from 1993, the family has also tried to train the fifth generation for future leadership. So today the fifth-generation members have become the pillars of the family business (Yeung 2000a; S.P.Y. Chung 1999; Lau and Wong 2000; Pick 1980).

Lee Chung Shing Tong (LCST) is another key brand in Chinese medicine. This firm was founded by Lee Siu-kay in 1896. Lee Siu-kay was born in Foshan, Guangdong and was a trained Chinese medical practitioner. In the early nineteenth century, sanitary and hygiene conditions were poor. Diarrhoea, stomach ache and indigestion were common. Lee Siu-kay used herbal medicine to produce the 'Po-Chai-Pill' (PCP), a drug that could effectively cure diarrhoea and digestion problems. PCP quickly became popular and Lee Siu-kay earned his 'first bucket of gold'. LCST became one of the best-known medical shops in Guangzhou.

In 1932, Lee Siu-kay died. His son, Lee Shek-ho, took over the leadership and the business still prospered. Unfortunately, their business was interrupted when Japanese troops invaded China. Lee Shek-ho and his family fled to Hong Kong in 1938. There was a serious shortage of medicine before and after the War. The total sales volume of PCP increased each year and the company earned a large profit every year.

The third generation of LCST joined the family business in the late 1950s. Under their leadership, LCST moved their manufacturing plant from Bonham Strand to North Point, where not only the plant size was far larger, the assembly line was also relatively advanced for that time. They also introduced Western-style manufacturing and packaging methods. As the Hong Kong population grew rapidly, their sales volume also grew from year to year.

The fourth generation – for example, Lee Chak-sun – took over the family business in the 1970s. Chak-sun tried to upgrade the quality of PCP and expand their market outlet overseas. Today PCP is sold all over the world. The fifth generation joined the family enterprise in the 1980s. In order to promote PCP to the world market, they paid great attention to scientific research. This generation wants to create a new image for Chinese medicine (Chow 1998).

Ying Kee was founded by Chan Chiu-ying in 1881 in Guangzhou. The company name Ying Kee (which means 'Ying's firm') in fact was derived from his name, Ying. Chiu-ying was a tea expert who had a special procedure for selecting tea, blending it and marketing it. Before long, the Ying Kee Tea Shop became a famous tea shop in Guangzhou. Following in the first generation's footsteps, the second-generation leader didn't make too many changes in their company's tea-making methods or the way they did business. Ying Kee kept growing, and in the early nineteenth century it had a leading role in the tea market.

In 1950 the third generation fled from the mainland to Hong Kong. Although the local tea market was weaker than in the mainland, Ying Kee eyed the overseas market. They tried to sell their tea to other tea-drinking regions like Japan, Korea, Taiwan and Southeast Asia. Throughout the 1980s, Ying Kee kept its firm position in the tea-trading business.

In the 1980s, the fourth generation joined the management of the company. Under the new leadership, tea packaging and quality were further upgraded. Chan Shu-yuen, the fourth-generation leader, confirmed that they still strictly follow their progenitors' method in selecting and making first-class tea. He believed there was a huge market for Chinese tea (Chan 2000).

Kin Tai Long (also known as Kin Tye Lung) is one of the oldest rice firms in Hong Kong. It was founded by Chan Wun-wing, a Chaozhou sailor, in Western District in 1851. Wun-wing bought rice, mainly from Southeast Asia, and sold it to Shantou, Guangzhou and Shanghai. Since Chan Wun-wing had good personal networks in Thailand, Burma and Singapore, and had also established his own shipping company, the business became even more prosperous and gradually became the market leader in the region. In addition, Kin Tai Long also became a prominent name in Nam Pak Hong, a famous market area in Western District.

Wun-wing died and his sons took up the family business and followed their father's conservative management philosophy. Kin Tai Long remained one of the leading firms in the field. When the third generation picked up the leadership, they expanded their businesses to canned and dry foodstuffs. However, the major business was still rice importation.

Wars and social unrest didn't terminate Kin Tai Long's rice trade. Its role became even more important during times of turmoil. In the 1950s, when the colonial government announced that it planned to register all imported rice, Kin Tai Long was appointed as one of the 29 rice importers. Its rice importation quota (total quantity of rice allowed to be imported each year) was one of the highest (*Commerce and Industry* 1967–9).

In the 1960s, Kin Tai Long also extended their businesses to general trading, but the result was not satisfactory. In the 1980s, Chan Ping-cheung, the fourth-generation leader, expanded their businesses to the property market. They built their own commercial premises, the Kin Tai Long Building, at No. 27–9, Bonham Strand West, Western District. Although there was a revolutionary change in the rice retail market after the introduction of 'five-kilogram bag rice' by David K.C. Lam in the early 1980s, there was no change to the importation business. Kin Tai Long still played a dominant role in the field. In 1989, Chan Cheuk-chow, the fifth-generation leader announced that he was planning to retire and that the sixth generation was preparing to take over the family business (Chan 1994; Choi 2001).

In 2003 the Hong Kong government announced plans to abolish the rice importation quota system by introducing free competition in the rice market. Since the fifth generation thought the rice business would no longer be as profitable as in the past, they chose to fold up the business they had engaged in for over 150 years, and just to put their business focus on general trading.

Kwong Sang Hong is a pioneer of cosmetic products in Hong Kong. It was founded by Fung Fook-tin in Hong Kong in 1898. Its main line of business was cosmetic products. From the late nineteenth to the early twentieth century, cosmetic products were exclusively targeted at upper-class women. Fung Fook-tin, however, regarded middle- and lower-class women as a huge potential market. He therefore developed his own brand name: the 'Double Girls' trademark. His business acumen paid off and he was successful. Kwong Sang Hong emerged as a market leader in the cosmetic business.

Later, the company expanded their products from perfume to facial creams, talcum powder, hair cream and many other products. Kwong Sang Hong earned large profits and started to increase production volume. They bought land to build their factory and diversified their business to property and other investments. In October 1941, Kwong Sang Hong was listed on the Hong Kong Stock Market and became a blue-chip company. It was called the short 'golden period' of its development. However, this period did not last long.

The fall of Hong Kong into Japanese hands in December 1941 brought serious financial difficulties to Kwong Sang Hong. Many of their properties were either destroyed or confiscated by Japanese troops. War and the following economic recession weakened the international and local cosmetics markets. The liberation of the mainland also meant the total loss of its huge investment in China and its market. Kwong Sang Hong entered its 'dark age'.

The gradual recovery of the Hong Kong economy in the 1960s made Kwong Sang Hong come to life again. In 1975, Kwong Sang Hong commenced their redevelopment plan. Old factories were demolished for rebuilding. 'Double

Girls' products were re-positioned in the market. Its business triggered off another stage of rapid growth.

In 1989 Kwong Sang Hong was taken over by Peregrine Holdings Limited, a Chinese-funded investment giant that went bankrupt in 1997. Its market even expanded to Europe and South America (B.Y. Fung 1997; Kwong Sang Hong Limited 1990). Today, Kwong Sang Hong is in the hands of the Lau Luen-hung family. Its business has also shifted from manufacturing of cosmetic products to financial investment and property development.

Looking at these family stories we can clearly see that there are ups and downs during the course of development. Some family business still maintain their strong competitiveness and vitality (the Vitasoy Group, Lee Kam Kee and Eu Yang Sang); some have been taken over by outsiders (Kwong Sang Hong and Yeo Hiap Seng); some have undergone massive restructuring (Ying Kee, Lee Kam Kee, Lee Chung Sing Tong and Eu Yan Sang); while some still keep their traditional ways of management (Ma Pak Leung and Kin Tai Long). There are conflicts and competitions both internally and externally. However, their businesses are still intact even after a century of operations.

Apart from the above-mentioned first sub-group, the second sub-group's families invest extensively and enjoy very large amounts of wealth. Although the scale and variety of their businesses are different, their development is quite similar. Their way of handling family and business crises also looks alike.

First and foremost, let us discuss the Ho Tung family. This family was founded by Ho Tung, an illegitimate Eurasian, whose mother (only her surname 'Sze' was known) was Chinese, while his father (C.H.M. Bosman) was European. Ho Tung 'invented' the surname 'Ho' for himself as his father's surname was pronounced 'Ho Szeman' in Cantonese, and adopted the Chinese identity and way of life of his mother. Ho Tung's mother was believed to be a boat woman who played an influential role in Ho Tung's childhood. Ho Tung was brought up and educated at the Central School (now known as Queen's College). Upon graduation, he joined China Customs in Canton. Two years later he quit the job and joined Jardine, Matheson & Company as a salesman. Since he could speak both fluent English and Cantonese, and had good knowledge in Western and Chinese culture, he won the appreciation and trust of Jardine's *taipans* (big bosses) and was soon appointed 'chief comprador'. His shrewdness and business acumen made him a millionaire within a very short period of time.

After Ho Tung, his brothers Ho Fook and Ho Kom-tong, sons Ho Shai-wing (adopted), Ho Shai-kim, and his numerous brothers-in-law and nephews also joined Jardines or other key foreign firms like the Hong Kong and Shanghai Banking Corporation (HSBC), E.D. Sasson and Company, Mercantile Bank, Arnold and Company, Hong Kong and Kowloon Wharf and Godown Company, Banco Nacional Ultramarina, and Nippon Yusen Kaisha as compradors. Gradually, the family established a closely knitted 'comprador network' in the colony and extended their influence from business to politics.

At the turn of the twentieth century, the name of Ho Tung was well-known not only in Hong Kong and the Chinese mainland, but also over the world.

Around that time, Ho Tung started to diversify his business to other markets, such as shipping, banking, land and property, as well as gold and silver trading. He also published a local newspaper, the *Hong Kong Industrial and Commercial News*. Ho Tung had successfully transformed his family comprador-related business into a transnational conglomerate.

Ho Tung died in 1956. Since his two older sons were unable to take over the leadership role (Ho Shai-wing died in 1946 and Ho Shai-kim died in 1957), his other son, General Ho Shai-lai took over the family business. However, Ho Shai-lai was a trained soldier and was lukewarm about managing the business. During his leadership, although the business did not experience any remarkable expansion, there was no sign of decline or instability. Ho Tung's family was still one of the wealthiest in Hong Kong. Since Ho Shai-lai showed little confidence in the future of Hong Kong, when the Sino-British Declaration was proclaimed in 1984, the third generation, under the leadership of Ho Shai-lai's son, Ho Hung Ngai, closed down the *Hong Kong Industrial and Commercial News*, the flagship company of the family. Clearly, the family preferred to retreat from Hong Kong or to keep a low profile.

Apart from Ho Shai-wing, Ho Shai-kim and Ho Shai-lai, one more person needs to be mentioned: George Ho, the illegitimate son of Ho Tung. Although Ho Tung himself never admitted this fact, he bequeathed George Ho a substantial amount of money, directly or indirectly (even more than his adopted son, Ho Shai-wing). Instead of joining the family flagship company, George Ho started his own business, Commercial Radio Hong Kong Limited. Through Ho Tung's personal connections, George Ho obtained a radio broadcasting licence and gradually become an influential tycoon in the colony. Today, the family is planning for the fifth generation to take over the helm (I. Cheng 1976, 1997; Zheng and Wong 2007, 2008).

The Li Shek-pang family is another case I will use for illustration. Li Karsheng, founder of the family, came to Hong Kong during the Taiping Uprising. He set up a trading firm, Sui Shing Hong in Western District. Although he was quite successful in business and earned a lot of money, his sojourner mentality prompted him to move back to his home town, Waitun in Guangdong Province. He built new houses and took concubines there. After his death, his sons, Kinchoi and Shek-pang, came to Hong Kong to take up leadership of the firm. Li Shek-pang was only five years old when he came to Hong Kong. He helped his brother in the shop and later enrolled at St Joseph's College. Even in his youth, Shek-pang understood that English was vital for success in a British colony where it was the official medium of instruction. He therefore studied hard in school. After finishing junior secondary school, Shek-pang joined his brother in managing Sui Shing Hong. Shek-pang was sensitive to numbers and shrewd in business. Under his management, Sui Shing Hong grew rapidly. Some years later, he set up more companies, Wo Fat Sing, to focus on shipping, and Nam Wo Hong, to specialize in the rice business. His sons, Koon-chun and later Tsefong joined the family business. The third generation also joined such people as Kan Tong-po, Chow Shouson, Mok Ching-kong and Fung Ping-shan to found the Bank of East Asia in 1919. The bank expanded gradually and the wealth of the Li family increased in parallel.

In the 1930s Li Fook-shu and Li Fook-wo joined the family firm, as well as the Bank of East Asia. The fourth generation was mostly well educated. Their entry into the company marked the rapid growth of the family business. The Li dynasty diversified their businesses from rice and shipping to entertainment, insurance, banking, property and public utilities. The entry of David K.P. Li marked the transmission of the family business from the fourth to the fifth generation. Following in his progenitors' footsteps, David Li carefully expanded their bank business overseas and to mainland China.

Starting from Li Fook-shu, many of the Li's members, such as Li Fook-wo, Andrew Li Kwok-nung, David Li and Arthur Li, have been appointed as legislative councillors or executive councillors by the early Hong Kong Colonial Government or the present Special Administrative Government. Now, the family is preparing to let the sixth generation, such as Adrian M.K. Li and Brian M.B. Li, take up the leading roles (Ching 1999; *Capital* 1988c; Hung and Bun 1988).

Like the Li Shek-pang family, Lee Leung-yick and his father also fled to Hong Kong during the Taiping Uprising. Motivated by the 'gold-rush' in the USA, Leung-yick went to San Francisco in the 1880s, but he did not stay there long. Some years later he came back to Hong Kong and set up Lai Cheung Lung, which specialized in wedding and men's wear. He also set up Kam Hing Hong, which sold ladies' underwear. Opium, at that time a legal business, was another key trade that the Lees were involved in.

Since Leung-yick earned huge profits from the opium trade, he also reinvested heavily in that field. The entry of his second son, Lee Hysan, into the business also marked an expansion of the family business. Since Lee Hysan received his education both in the USA and at Queen's College in Hong Kong, he had a good command of English and this enabled him to communicate with his Western trading partners without difficulty. Under the leadership of Lee Hysan, the family not only went deeper and expanded the opium trade from Hong Kong to Macau, but also invested in other businesses such as shipping and property. Unfortunately, he was assassinated in 1928.

Richard Charles (R.C.) Lee, his eldest son, was recalled from Oxford University to take up the family business. Graduating with a Master's degree in civil engineering, R.C. Lee brought the Lee family business to a higher stage of development. He also tried to emerge from the shadow of the 'dirty opium scum' business by actively participating in charity, social and political affairs. He was appointed as a legislative councillor (in 1953) and executive councillor (1961) by the colonial government. In fact, his personal connections were not confined to Hong Kong, but also extended to high-ranking leaders in the Communist Party like Chou Enlai, Li Xiannian, Yang Shangkun and Ye Jianying.

The death of R.C. Lee in 1983 marked the taking over of the fourth generation, Lee Hon-chiu. Under the new leadership, the Lees' business further diversified into entertainment, communications and public utilities. The family is now preparing fifth-generation members like Lee Ding-cheong, Lee Tze-hau and Lee Tak-yan to take a leading role (*The China Mail* 17 April 1928, 30 April 1928; *Capital* 1989a; Ho 1991b; Poy 1995, 1998).

The Fung Pak-liu family is another famous family in Hong Kong. Fung Fung Pak-liu's father, Fung Kit-sze came from Heshan in Guangdong and sent Pak-liu to study at Queen's College in Hong Kong. Pak-liu's performance in school was outstanding. He earned a Junior Morrison Scholarship and was sent to the US for one year. In 1906, Pak-liu, together with a friend called Li Daoming, set up a trading company, 'Li & Fung'. They focused on silk, fireworks and porcelain trading. Since Pak-liu had good connections both in China and the USA, their businesses grew rapidly. Unfortunately, the Second World War broke out and interrupted their businesses. On the eve of the war, Li Daoming sold his entire share to the Fungs. Li & Fung therefore became wholly owned by the Fung family. Mo-ying and Hon-chu, sons of Pak-liu, joined the company about that time. Under the new leadership, Li & Fung expanded greatly.

In 1973 Li & Fung became a publicly listed company. At the same time, Victor K.K. Fung and William K.L. Fung joined the management team. The third generation was well educated. They brought new concepts and the Western style of management to the company. Li & Fung further expanded to toys, retail shops, entertainment and property. In 1989, due to political turmoil in mainland China, the Hong Kong economy suffered a serious setback, and Li & Fung was privatized. In 1992 Fung's brother restructured the company and went public again. They gained tremendous profit from this 'management-buy-out', restructuring and re-listing process. Now the family is planning to pass the leadership on to the fourth generation. Li & Fung has been elected as a blue-chip company on the Hang Seng Index in Hong Kong (Chiu 1996; *Capital* 1995; Lui 2000a, 2000b; Li & Fung Limited 1982).

Another wealthy family is the Chau Wing Tai family. In 1886, Chau Wing-tai left Dongguang, Guangdong to come to Hong Kong, where he opened a grocery store that specialized in selling ceremonial goods. Although the business did not bring Wing-tai much profit, his emphasis on his children's education actually laid the groundwork for the family's prosperity.

Wing-tai had three sons, Siu-kay, Yam-kiu and Cheuk-fan. Wing-tai sent them to Queen's College to study different languages – English as well as Chinese. In fact, it was these three sons that brought the family glory and wealth. With a good education, the three brothers expanded their businesses from groceries to insurance, shipping and money shops. By then the Chau family had become one of Hong Kong's influential families.

Chau Tsun-nin and Chau Shek-nin were the key members of the third generation. Graduating from famous Western universities, both Tsun-nin (University of Oxford, UK) and Shek-nin (University of Vienna, Austria) were trained professionals. Under their leadership, the Chaus' business grew remarkably. Tsun-nin was appointed a legislative councillor (1931–41 and 1946–53) and an executive councillor (1946–53), while Shek-nin followed in his elder brother's footsteps and also served as a legislative councillor (1946–53) and an executive councillor (1953–9).

Cham-lam, Cham-sun, Cham-wang, Kai-bong, Kai-yin and Kai-him were fourth-generation members of the Chau family who took over the management in the 1970s. Although the fourth generation was criticized because of their 'extravagant lifestyle' and conservatism in investment, the Chau family still remained one of the most influential families in Hong Kong.

In the late 1990s the fifth generation, such as Chau Ka-wan, Ka-lai and Ka-ho, joined the family management team. It is believed they are preparing for the formation of new family leadership. In recent years, in order to alleviate the risk of political uncertainty in Hong Kong, they have diversified their investment to other countries such the UK, USA, Canada, Australia and South Asia (*Capital* 1988a; Yuet 1992; Ho 1991b; Mak 1992; Chau 1926).

Hui Oi-chow family is another wealthy family in Hong Kong. The founding father, Hui Oi-chow, was a first-generation shipping tycoon in Hong Kong. After finishing primary school, he joined his father in Guangzhou to learn to do business. Several years later (in 1895), he started his own business in whole-selling edible oil, charcoal and food. Oi-chow was a shrewd and meticulous businessman. He was also hardworking, frugal and generous. His business grew successfully and he soon became a wealthy businessman. In the 1920s he expanded his business to shipping by founding Shun Cheong Shipping, which later emerged as one of the leading shipping companies in Southeast Asia.

During the Japanese invasion in 1937, Hui Oi-chow donated huge sums of money to the Nationalist Army to allow the purchase of weapons. Later, when the Japanese troops landed in Guangzhou Bay, he ordered his crews to sink two of his ships to avoid these ships being seized by the enemy. He was called thus call a 'patriotic businessman'. After the end of the Second World War, he moved his office to Hong Kong and bought a large amount of land in a prime location while the property market was in the doldrums. He died in 1966.

Sze-fun and Sai-fun, the second and third sons of Oi-chow, took up the leadership post and brought the business to another stage of expansion. Seeing that the shipping business was on the decline in the mid-1960s, the Hui brothers gradually shifted their businesses to real estate development. Central Holdings, the flagship of the family, was listed in the early 1970s when the local stock market was buoyant. Hanley Building, Prince's building, Asia Building, Central Building, Wan Chai Centre, Oi Kwan Building and Purple Villas were key properties owned by the Huis. In the 1980s there was a serious recession in the shipping business. Seeing that gloomy future, the family decided to transfer their shipping business to property development.

The third generation, such as Chun-ling, Chun-keung, Chun-ye and Chun-ping, joined the family business in the early 1980s. Today, although Hui Sai-fun is still the chairman of Central Holdings, most of the daily management has been passed to the third and fourth generations. The ability of the new generation will be tested in the coming years (*Capital* 1989b; Ho 1991b; Yu 1999).

Fung Ping-shan, a prominent name in early Chinese society in Hong Kong, was born in Xinhui, Guangdong and received his informal primary education in his home town. At 15, he gave up study and chose to leave China for Thailand, where his uncle had opened a retail store. He helped his uncle in the shop. However, a few years later, he found there was little room for career development and therefore returned to China. Instead of staying in Xinhui, he went to

Sichuan and opened On Kee Trading Company, which exported cereals, oil and dry food to Southeast Asia. His sharp business acumen earned him large profits and his business expanded rapidly.

In 1913, Fung Ping-shan moved his office to Hong Kong and quickly emerged as one of the leading businessmen in the colony. The most important firm he set up at that time was Siu Fung Hong [Trading Firm], which specialized in buying rubber and rice from Thailand and other Southeast Asian countries and selling to the Chinese mainland. He was well-known in Nam Pak Hong and his business also later extended to money shops (*qianzhuang*). The Wai Kat Money Shop and Yee On Money Shop were two of his companies that were famous during that period.

In 1919 Ping-shan, together with Kan Tung-po and two members from the Li Shek-pang family (Li Koon-chun and Li Tse-fong), set up the Bank of East Asia. His status in the community reached its apex at that time. The death of Fung Ping-shan in the early 1930s marked the transmission of leadership to the second generation. Fung Ping-fun and Fung Ping-wah, the twin sons of Fung Ping-shan, became the new leaders of the family enterprise. Inheriting his father's business talent, Ping-fun brought the family business to another stage of expansion. He diversified the business to department stores, property development, insurance and entertainment. Fung Ping-fun was appointed a legislative councillor in the 1960s.

The third generation, like Kenneth Hing-cheung, Cyril Hing-chiu and Lawrence Hing-lun, joined the family business in the 1970s. Fung Ping-fun let his sons have free rein in managing the enterprise in the early 1980s. Unfortunately, due to over-expansion, Hing-cheung and Hing-chiu almost brought great disaster to the family enterprise. With the help of Fung Ping-fun, the family gradually recovered. At present, the family has a low profile in the community (Ho 1991b; Qi 1981, 1984; Chan 1983; Tsui 1986).

Tang Chi-ngong was born in Nanhai, Guangdong, and came to Hong Kong in the late nineteenth century. Shortly after settling down in Hong Kong, Chi-ngong opened a money shop in Central with friends. Seeing the business prosper, Chi-ngong started another firm, the Tang Tin Fook Money Shop, on his own at the turn of the new century. In 1916 his son, Tang Shiu-kin, was asked to help in the shop. Like his father, Shiu-kin was shrewd and meticulous in business. The money shop business expanded steadily.

In 1933 their business experienced another stage of expansion. Tang Shiu-kin, who was known as a great philanthropist, founded the Kowloon Motor Bus Company (KMB) with some other businessmen. KMB was the major transportation giant that mainly served the Kowloon peninsula and New Territories region. Because of his great commitment to social welfare and social services, Shiu-kin was knighted by Queen Elizabeth II in 1964.

The third and fourth generation managed to keep the family business along the right track. David Tang Wing-cheung, the fourth generation of the family, was another famous figure in Hong Kong. He took over the helm in the 1980s and started his own business, Shanghai Tang (*Capital* 1990a, 1990b, J. Wong 1981). Like his grandfather, Wing-cheung also received a knighthood from the

British royal family in 2008 as a token of recognition of his contribution to the community. The Tang family is still one of the largest families in Hong Kong.

The Wing On Kwok family is another key family. The founding brothers, James Gocklock [Kwok Lock], Philip Gockchin [Kwok Chun] and William Gockson [Kwok Shun], went to Australia in 1883 during a gold rush. At the beginning, they engaged in fresh fruit trading. The three brothers worked hard and lived frugally. After they had earned their 'first bucket of gold', they moved to Hong Kong and set up its first department store, the Wing On Department Store, in August 1907. Under the leadership of Kwok's brother, Wing On experienced tremendous growth. Within a short period of time, they opened branches all over Hong Kong and then expanded to Shanghai and Guangzhou. They also spread to other businesses such as property, insurance, textiles and garments. They set up Wing On Bank in the 1920s.

The 1920s also marked the entry of the second generation into management. The sons, Lam-po, Lam-shan, Lam-but and Lam-yong, all worked in Wing On at some point. With the introduction of Western concepts of management and new methods in marketing, Wing On became a popular place to shop. The Kwoks' wealth expanded in parallel.

The death of the founding generation signified the entrance of the third generation into the family business. Philip C.K. Kwok, Chi-bun, Chi-leung, Chi-hong and Chi-yan represented a class of well-educated new leaders of the company. Although the new leadership committed some mistakes in the early transmission stage, such as being charged with fraud over the Wing On Bank issue, and the hostile take-over of the New World Group, they managed to weather these crises and recovered rapidly. Beginning from the late 1980s, the family has prepared for the fourth generation to take a significant role in the business (*Capital* 1988b; Ho 1991b; Chuang 1990; Wing On Holdings Limited 1981; Wing On Life Insurance 1975; Kwok 1980).

From the above stories, we can see that the growth and expansion path of these family businesses generally follows the developmental process of the Hong Kong economy. One of the critical factors for their success is the family leaders' ability to seize chances before the economy took off, and overcome crises when the economy was in downturn. In addition, their highly adept skill in managing business and social networks also made them the most competitive players in their assorted fields. Because of all these factors, their family businesses could expand when the Hong Kong economy grew, while still remaining agile when the Hong Kong economy was in the doldrums.

Note

1 I would like to offer wholehearted thanks to the executive director and the general manager of the company for their valuable comments and kind assistance during the half-year on-the-job participant observation.

3 The transfer of economic capital

Sibling conflict over power and control, the carving up of family estates, or the design for inheritance and succession of wealthy families in Hong Kong is always a talking point in the community (*Oriental Daily* 28 January 1996; Law and Chan 2000; Wong and Wang 1999; *South China Morning Post* 5 April 2007; *Sing Tao Daily* 19 February 2008). As Victor K.K. Fung (1997: 224), a third-generation leader of the Li & Fung Group, points out:

> A lot of family enterprises and partnerships were started after the war, and they are now getting to the stage where the entrepreneurial patriarch has either passed on or needs to transfer control to the next levels of family control.

The message Victor Fung conveys is one of the key problems that has perplexed many Chinese family businesses. In fact, such issues are usually regarded as sensitive questions that become 'taboo' topics in many families. Conservative founders may consider that talking about family conflicts and inheritance are disrespectful, or regard it as a kind of struggle for power. Although many families are aware of this problem and most of them have already prepared for the division of estate or the transmission of leadership, some still overlook its importance and make little effort in preparing for a proper transfer. Kets de Vries (1988: 168) comments, 'Succession is a very sensitive topic, and beside that, even when a real willingness to deal with the matter exists, its planning remained at best a very inexact science.' In other words, inheritance and succession are vital issues, but many family businesses neglect to deal with them in advance. The main task of this chapter is to look at the transmission of physical capital, while the transmission of intangible capital (human capital and social capital) will be dealt with in the following two chapters.

Fight for the family estate

Family businesses and their inter-generational conflicts are rich fodder for Hong Kong scriptwriters. Highly popular local TV soap drama series such as *The Heart of Greed*, *The Gem of Life* and *Best Selling Secrets* all feature an elderly patriarch presiding over a sprawling family business with internal dissention and struggles for business control bubbling under the surface.

When we talk about inheritance, the transfer of economic capital is generally regarded as less complicated when compared to other kinds of capital. However, it should not be overlooked or considered a simple matter. Very frequently, disputes erupt because of less careful arrangement or dispersal of family property. Some of these families even choose to lodge their disputes in the probate court when they find they cannot settle the matter by themselves. That is why traditionally estate litigation was perceived as the main factor toppling family businesses.

Why can family members not solve their conflicts internally, but feel it necessary to take their case to the court? In addition to huge litigation fees, they put their businesses at great risk and jeopardize their blood-ties relationship. Some scholars bluntly state: 'It [estate litigation] resembles the "last straw" reported in breakups in other close relationships' (Titus *et al.* 1978: 240). Does estate litigation really shorten the life of a family business?

In Hong Kong, no concrete data about the sources of estate litigation can be found. In the USA, however, according to Rosenfeld's (1998) research, most litigation is due to changes in family structure, the impact of divorce and remarriage, chronic illness, and the change of roles and lifestyle of elderly people (Table 3.1). Industrialization, urbanization and modernization have radically transformed the family structure. Traditional social values and norms were also challenged. Family ties became less close and marriages less secure. When Rosenfeld asked one of his interviewees (a group of family estate probate officers and lawyers) about the reason for estate litigation, his respondent said:

> I suppose it's a breakdown in family. Families are not so effective at controlling kids as they once were. Siblings just go to war. They have no loyalty to each other or to their family. There are fewer sibling bonds.
>
> (ibid.: 177–8)

In fact, Rosenfeld further discovered that his respondent's heavy caseload consists mostly of siblings either as proponents or contestants in will disputation.

Table 3.1 Social and demographic context of estate litigation

Case category	*Number of cases (%)*
Changes in family structure	60 (42.8)
Impact of divorce and remarriage	45 (32.1)
Impact of chronic illness and long-term care	21 (15.0)
New roles and lifestyles of elderly people	6 (4.3)
Homophobia/AIDS epidemic	5 (3.5)
Other	3 (2.3)
Total	140 (100.0)

Source: Rosenfeld 1998: 177.

An increasing rate of divorce and remarriage complicates the family structure and blurs the right of inheritance. The impact of chronic illness or long-term care of the elderly drives them to revise their will and therefore generates room for future disagreement. Occasionally, when the elderly change their will late in their life, conflicts will be triggered. As a result, Rosenfeld concludes that estate litigation occurs more frequently in families where the social structure is ambiguous, or where the line of communication has broken down.

As mentioned previously, Rosenfeld's research only focuses on American society. Does it also reflect the overall trend in Hong Kong? In order to examine this question, I collected all estate litigation cases that appeared in a local newspaper, the *Ming Pao Daily News* (MPDN), from 1 January 1997 to 31 December 2000. A summary of the major information, such as the name of the plaintiff, case number, their relationship and the source of dispute, are cited as shown in Table 3.2.

From the specified period of four years, there are a total of 64 cases of estate litigation reported by MPDN. Among them, some have lasted for a number of years (in the case number, the last two digits indicate the year that the case was lodged in the court). Some disputes concern very famous families, including some of the families we cited as examples in this study. Some, however, are actually very minor disputes, such as a dishonoured cheque or claims for a small amount, for instance, HK$15,000. For consistency, all of them are listed exactly as they appeared in the newspaper.

From the data, it shows that a great proportion of the litigation (62.4 per cent) relates to family property arrangements, while 14.1 per cent of disputes involve the validity of agreements. Some family members may dispute agreements or previously signed contracts. Contracts such as those for the purchasing and selling of flats, houses, or provision of living expenses, are frequently quoted. Disputes over the right of inheritance (such as illegitimate sons or mistresses) are another category of estate litigation (10.9 per cent). Some family members may query the principle or criteria for distribution of the family estate. They challenge why some sons get a greater proportion while some get less. Some female members argue that they have the right to the deceased's property while others disagree. An unclear right of inheritance arises from a complicated family structure – for example, when the founders have had more than one wife or where adopted children are involved. Children from a second wife or concubine may also want a piece of their father's property. Litigation is also filed because of unclear terms in the will (9.4 per cent). Family members may query the validity of the will or the psychological state of the person when he or she prepared the will. Struggles for leadership and disputes over use of company trademarks share the remaining 1.6 per cent of these cases (Table 3.3).

From the above data, we can see that most family conflicts are due to unclear stipulations of the terms of the will. Ambiguity leads different parties to interpret the meaning differently. Such unclear stipulations become complicated when the father has more than one partner, such as a second wife or mistress. A great

Table 3.2 Summary of estate litigation in Hong Kong: 1997–2000

Family	*Relationship*	*Case No.*	*Source of Dispute*
Ho Kwong-hing	Brother *vs* brother	HCA8342/97	Dispute over family property
Cheung Kwok-lun	Adopted brother *vs* brother	HCA3104/95	Dispute over family property
Yan Chim-kee	Brother *vs* brothers	HCA14502/96	Struggle for leadership of family firm
Chow Lin-wah	Stepmother *vs* son	Civ App 61/97	Dispute over family property
Lau Wai-chau	Nephews *vs* nephews	HCA8917/92	Debate over the validity of founder's will
Lee Kin-wo	Aunt *vs* nephew	HCA9522/97	Dispute over the validity of will
Eric Ho Tung	Son *vs* father	HCA9920/00	Debate over violation of agreement
Siu Kwok-man	Sister *vs* brother	MP2071/91	Dispute over the right of inheritance
Wong Haking	Brothers *vs* brothers/sisters	HCA17008/98	Dispute over rebuilding family house (agreement)
Shum Tai-hing	Mother *vs* daughter-in-law	MP3470/95	Dispute over family property
Wang Shan-mui	Grandmother *vs* granddaughter	HCA6027/93	Dispute over family property
Mui Po-chu	Daughter *vs* father	HCA11507/97	Dispute over family property
Kwan Chi-on	Son *vs* stepmother and concubine	n/a	Dispute over right of inheritance
Lai Kam	Sister *vs* brother	MP3090/96	Dispute over family property
Ma Kam-chuan	Aunt *vs* nephews	MP5112/98	Asking for return of shares
Chan Ting-chun	Brothers *vs* brothers	MP2315/95	Dispute over right of inheritance (intestacy)
Chan Sai-lung	Sister *vs* brother	P2/93	Argument over the validity of will
Lee Pui-wan	Sister *vs* sister-in-law	A3979/94	Dispute over purchasing property (agreement)
Yau Kwong-han	Brother *vs* sister	App. 2607/97	Dispute over mother's property
Leung Hey	Principal wife *vs* concubine/son	HCA1960/95	Dispute over family property
Tin Ying-sin	Nephew *vs* uncle	HCA14534/96	Dispute over family property
Charles Fong Yee	Daughters *vs* sons	MP1016/81	Dispute over right of equal inheritance
Ho Yong-hong	Father *vs* son	HCA15909/99	Dispute over family property
Ng Yiu-ming	Brother *vs* sister	HCA7462/98	Dispute over trademark
Low Hung-kwan	Sister *vs* brother	WSC 8494	Dispute over family property
Chan Doi-kwai	Mother *vs* daughter-in-law	MP7803/98	Dispute over family property
Lau Oi-king	Mother-in-law *vs* son	DCJ15310/99	Dispute over $15,000 of estate
Wang Tin-yam	Father *vs* daughter-in-law	HCMP4157/00	Validity of will (agreement)

Tang Siu-ngai	Sons/daughter *vs* mother	HCA1424/97	Dispute over family property
Chan Sau-wah	Principal wife *vs* concubine	HCAP9/96	Dispute over family property
Cheung Man	Mother *vs* adopted daughter	HCAP4/96	Dispute over right of inheritance
Hiranand	Brother *vs* sister	HCA18678/99	Dispute over family property
Wong Shu-chi	Brother *vs* brother	HCA5333/99	Dispute over family property
Tsang Chi-fong	Brother *vs* brother	HCA10134/93	Dispute over family property
Lau Kie-shang	Uncle *vs* nephew	WSC17507/97	Dispute over contract
Yau Kam-to	Parents-in-law *vs* son	HCA428/98	Dispute over daughter's property
Tung Hau-ning	Brother/Sister *vs* brother	DCC1084/97	Dispute over fake will
Chan Chiu-lam	Principal wife *vs* concubine	P6/91	Dispute over husband's property
Chau Chiu-ho	Wife *vs* mistress	HCA7558/96	Dispute over husband's property
Chan Ping-wing	Mother *vs* son	HCA7083/98	Dispute over validity of will
Ting Piu-tak	Mother-in-law *vs* daughter	HCA8113/90	Dispute over sons' property
Ming Cheung-fook	Brother *vs* brother/sister	Civ App. 22/98	Dispute over validity of will
Chan Chang-hey	Brother *vs* brother	HCA12972/95	Dispute over mother's property
Li Ah-yan	Brother *vs* brother	HCA10000/98	Dispute over family property
Wang Sau-kin	Brother *vs* brother	HCA10631/98	Dispute over family property
Cheng Muk-chung	Brother *vs* brother	HCA3467/97	Dishonoured cheque (agreement)
Wang Wan	Principal wife *vs* concubine	AG1797/98	Dispute over husband's property
Liu Ling	Stepson *vs* stepmother	MP4222/98	Dispute over right of inheritance
Tang Kwan-po	Son *vs* mother/sons	HCA 14608/98	Dispute over father's property
Yung Hing	Mother *vs* son	HCA14669/98	Dispute over property
Kwan Dik-on	Brother *vs* brothers	DCC301/98	Dispute over right of inheritance
Yip Mo-ching	Sister *vs* sisters	HCA18674/98	Dispute over property
Yip Hung-ying	Principal wife *vs* concubine	MP3459/95	Dispute over husband's property
Yip Kwai	Ex-husband *vs* wife	HCMC5/97	Dispute over property
Yu Siu-ngum	Brother *vs* sister	HCA11148/97	Dispute over property
Chow Shuk-kwan	Mother *vs* daughter-in-law	HCA2684/95	Dispute over property
Yi Ying-hang	Principal wife *vs* concubine	MP3459/95	Dispute over husband's property
Fu Yuk-ching	Sister *vs* brother	HCA3817/96	Dispute over property

continued

Table 3.2 Continued

Family	*Relationship*	*Case No.*	*Source of Dispute*
Cheung Cheong	Cousin *vs* cousin	HCA8006/93	Dispute over property
Lam Yee-lai	Wife *vs* ex-husband	HCC4639	Dispute over property
Choi Ching-ching	Brother *vs* brother's mistress	HCAP13/97	Dispute over validity of will
Leung Po-chu	Brother *vs* sister	HCA12866/97	Dispute over property
Chan Ting-lam	'Brother' *vs* sister	HCAP9/97	Dispute over right of inheritance
Chan Leung-nung	Sons *vs* stepmother	HCA9776/00	Dispute over apportion of dividend (agreement)

Sources: *Ming Pao Daily News* 1 January 1997 to 31 December 2000.

Notes

1 All cases reported in *the Ming Pao Daily News* from 1 January 1997 to 31 December 2000.
2 All cases related to fight for family property were included, regardless of whether they were Chinese or non-Chinese.
3 Number indicating pre-1997 implies that those cases lasted for a number of years.
4 All Chinese names here are Romanized according to local Cantonese usage. No Pinyin is given in the glossary.

Table 3.3 Categories of estate litigation in Hong Kong: 1997–2000

Categories	*Number of cases (%)*
Dispute over family property arrangements	40 (62.4)
Violation of agreement	9 (14.1)
Dispute over right of inheritance	7 (10.9)
Debate over the validity of the will	6 (9.4)
Dispute over trademark	1 (1.6)
Struggle for business leadership and control	1 (1.6)
Total	64 (100.0)

Source: Adapted from Table 3.2.

percentage of the cases are related to a small amount of property and little effect is reported on the family businesses. Thus, it is unreasonable to say that estate litigation causes the downfall of the family businesses.

Apart from giving the family a bad name, the side effects of estate litigation have clearly been vastly exaggerated. Traditionally, taking a family dispute to court is regarded as a 'lose–lose game' and is a bad omen for the family. Some even treat it as taboo, a disgrace or 'losing face'. However, I would argue that to bring family disputes before the court is not always negative. First, a court jurisdiction can legitimate the line of inheritance and give guidelines for future disagreements. Second, it can serve the function of 'pruning the family tree'. Through a court ruling, illegitimate members can be excluded from the line of inheritance. For legitimate members, they can have unchallengeable ownership of their family property and thus can concentrate their attention on the business. Third, it can establish a rational and formal mechanism for solving family conflict. In other words, estate litigation is not the main reason that brings down a family business, and litigation itself should not be regarded as totally negative and destructive.

Family and business: divided or united?

When talking about family business, many people will think that when the estate is divided and family members disperse, their businesses will eventually fold. In fact, many scholars have tried to argue from this angle that a family may divide either when the founder dies (Freedman 1957, 1979), or when siblings marry (Cohen 1970, 1976). In this study, many respondents confirmed that they had divided their family estate before the passing away of the family head. F9 told me his arrangement:

> A large family will divide eventually [*jiada bifen*]. No one will challenge it. I think dividing the family estate can enhance each member's freedom and reduces conflict. Even though our estate had been divided, we still keep very close connections. For instance, during important festivals or family rituals, we will have dinner together.

In answering the question of why family business did not follow the similar process of division like family estate, F4's son explained, 'The business was founded by my grandfather, its fortune represented the family's reputation and well-being in the community. We should not ruin or dishonour it.' F7 also had a similar perception and elaborated this point as follows:

> Each member had certain proportion of shares. My father and uncles agreed to divide the family estate after the sudden death of my grandfather. However, they decided to keep the business intact. Each branch [*fang*] had their representative on the management board. Many of my cousins and nephews are professionals. They seldom get involved in management. We have the responsibility to keep it and prevent it from being dissipated.

Family business has been regarded as a 'symbol' of the whole family. It can be likened to the 'ancestral hall' (*zuci*), 'family reputation' (*jiasheng*) or 'ancestral grave' (*zufen*). All descendants have the right to access the family fortune and therefore have equal responsibility to pay tribute to it and to defend it. Traditionally, division of the family estate was treated as natural. If family members did not want to keep the business or if they wanted to divide it, they would be treated as 'prodigal' or incapable, and they would be looked down upon in society. Clearly, the dividing force that appeared in family (estate) does not equally show in business (equity).

The blood-ties among family members are crucial for business solidarity and cooperation. In order to test these ties, let me cite some cases for illustration. The sudden death of the family head, usually a patriarch, but sometimes also a matriarch, is viewed as a serious crisis for the family and the business. If the relationship between members is not strong enough, they could break up when a crisis arises. Brown's (1993: 264) comment is worthy of careful study. He writes, 'For family firms, the sudden death of the founding patriarch creates special difficulties in the ownership and business arenas.' Undeniably, siblings' struggle for leadership and ownership may suddenly surge up from this issue and ultimately plague the business (Levinson 1971).

In this research, it is found that the unexpected death of F7's grandfather, F2's father and brother, Lee Hysan, Eu Kong and Lam But-chung are frequently cited examples both in business circles and in the academic circles (Table 3.4). How did these families get over the crisis and keep their businesses from going into decline?

When F7's grandfather died, his father and uncle were in England. The sudden death also coincided with the rumour of a bank-run on the family-owned bank. His father was summoned to take over the leadership. Since his grandfather had three wives (a principal wife and two concubines), the issue became complex. Both the family and the business were on the brink of break-up. His father promptly asked other influential Chaozhou dignitaries for assistance. Then, he also sought help from other banks to squash the rumour. All his uncles were called to unite under his father's leadership. With their businesses partners'

Table 3.4 Cases of the sudden death of the founder

Case	*Crisis*
F7's grandfather	When his grandfather died, his father and uncle were still studying in the UK
Lee Hysan	When Hysan was assassinated, R.C. Lee and H.W. Lee were studying in the UK
Eu Kong	When Eu Kong died, his son Eu Tong-sen was a child in mainland China
Lam But-chung	When But-chung died, Kuan-chuang had only been in the business for one year
F2's brother and father	When F2's elder brother died in Hong Kong, F2 was in Chaozhou. One year later, his father also died

Sources: Interviews 1997–2000; Ho 1991b; Yeung 2000a.

assistance and all his uncles' mutual trust and cooperation, the family weathered the crisis.

In the study, F2 shared with the researcher his story. He said that his elder brother, the former 'heir-to-be', died prematurely in Hong Kong. He was recalled to take up his place. Struck by his brother's sudden death and also the business in difficulty, his father developed a serious illness and died around one year later. F2 found it hard to pick up the business at the beginning. He admitted that he had thought about giving up at that time. His uncles and friends encouraged him to keep the business as it was his father's and brother's effort. He sold some of the family key property to generate cash to settle some accounts to regain his suppliers' confidence. He also worked hard to re-establish his own business network and personal ties, and finally brought the business out from the quagmire. Several years later, when he looked back, he said he could take a deep sigh.

Similarly, when Lee Hysan, the founding father of Hysan Development Limited, was assassinated in 1928, his two sons, R.C. Lee and H.W. Lee were still studying in UK. They were called back to tackle the turmoil and take over the leadership. R.C. Lee united all his brothers and ushered the family business to another level of expansion. Later, he even diversified the family businesses into other areas and successfully brought the family out from under the negative image of being an opium trader.

Another Chaozhou case was Lam But-chung. When Lam But-chung, founder of the Golden Resources Group, passed away, his son David K.C. Lam had just joined the business and was preparing to take over the leadership. The Lams were nervous at first. With the help of his father's brothers and the effort of each Lam family member, the family got through the crisis and David Lam eventually became the 'rice king' when he later introduced revolutionary packaging to the rice trade.

In Taiwan, Numazaki (1991: 234) found another example concerning heirs summoned to take up the leadership post when the founder suddenly died:

> [The] sudden death of Huang Jijun, founder of the San Yang Industry Group, his eldest son, Shihui was summoned back from abroad to inherit the group and succeed to his father's position, despite the fact that he had no management experience, he was a physician and had practiced medicine in the U.S. and Japan for more than twenty years.

In fact, after Huang Shihui took over the leadership, the San Yang Industry Group was still prosperous and the Huangs still played a key role in Taiwan. In short, all these cases clearly show that even though there are crises and family property can be divided, family business does not necessarily break up. In fact, in order to protect their interests, family members may try every possible means to keep their businesses steady, despite rapid changes in circumstances. Clearly, sibling cooperation can have very positive effect if managed properly.

A follow-up question is: Will equal inheritance issues among sons that disintegrates the family also dissipate the business? In this research, it is found that there is a weak correlation between these two variables. First, division of family property does not necessarily lead to the separation of the family business. Even though the property and shares may divide among heirs, they may not necessarily withdraw them from the company. Usually, they prefer to keep the business intact. Such decisions may be due to careful and rational calculation. In a competitive business environment, keeping their family as a single entity offers a better competitive edge. F4 shared with me his thoughts on the fact that family shares and property had been divided to each sibling before his father passed away. After much consideration, their family members decided unanimously to keep their businesses united instead of dividing it. He said,

> We preferred to uphold the family ownership. Although my father had assigned each son a certain proportion of the business, we had consensus that the business should be kept intact. You know, if capital was divided and was withdrawn, it would be very difficult to accumulate it again. The present world stresses capital domination or economy of scale. No member of the family would like to see a weak business organization. A strong and prosperous business benefits each member more.

The message F4 delivered here is a good example that can be used to illustrate the process of rationalization as suggested by Max Weber. In Weber's view, rationality or rational economic action is one of the key factors that affect the development of modern capitalism. In the introduction to Weber's book, *Theory of Social and Economic Organization*, Parsons defines rationality:

> An act is rational in so far as (a) it is oriented to clearly formulate an unambiguous goal, or a set of values which are clearly formulated and logically consistent; (b) the means chosen are, according to the best available knowledge, adapted to the realization of the goal.
>
> (Weber 1947: 13)

Another influential Weberian, Swedberg, adds that 'rationality in the economy means first and foremost calculability ... things are done in a methodical manner; in rational capitalism capital accounting is used and there is a great measure of depersonalization in economic life' (ibid.: 281). In addition, Weber also tries to argue that rational and logically consistent behaviour is more predictable, efficient and therefore more favourable to corporate management and continuity.

Looking from this perspective, we can see that in order to enhance their own interest, they choose to maintain their family businesses intact after rational and careful calculation. To be more specific, after rational counting and evaluation, they may see that a united business entity can give each family member better advantages – thus they choose to keep their family business intact.

F21 shared that same point of view as F4 and said that his brothers and sisters agreed at a family meeting to keep the business unified. He suggested that a united and larger business would bring more advantages than many separate, smaller sub-units. Both F4 and F21 have over six brothers and sisters, and several dozen nephews and cousins. In such large families, sibling disagreement and conflict is enormous and inevitable. However, they still vetoed the division of the family business in favour of maintaining a united, family-controlled enterprise.

In explaining this phenomenon, Cohen (1976: 144–99) hits the mark. He writes of, 'A deep interest in the joint holdings, for it is important to all of them that the maintenance of the common body of holdings be compatible with their own interest.' In other words, after careful consideration, family members may consider that a united business can generate more interest to each member. In fact, Weber (1947: 252–3) has clearly indicated that a modern company structure that emphasizes transferable shares is a typical example of formal rationality:

> It is particularly important that the capital at the disposal of the enterprise should be clearly distinguished from the private wealth of the owners, and should not be subject to division or dispersion through inheritance. For large-scale enterprises, this condition tends to approach an optimum from a formal point of view in the fields of transport, manufacture, and mining, when they are organized in corporate form with free transferable shares and limited company.

Separation of family property or company shares does not imply loss of control of the company. Some scholars argue that if the family property is equally assigned to each son, its property will be levelled off from generation to generation (Chau 1991; Qi 1984, 1985). Such an argument is based on a static assumption about family property and overlooks modern economic structure and the volatility of the stock market. Family business can expand from time to time, and its property can grow continuously. The expansion can be remarkable when a family company lists on the stock market. Family wealth can expand exponentially. The control of a certain proportion of shares can enable a single family to exercise control over a multinational corporation with multi-billion dollar assets.

Looking from another perspective, I argue that a united family business does not inhibit individual members' freedom and career development. Some families may assign their members to manage their businesses while encouraging others to develop their own careers. Such a practice not only can reduce sibling conflict, but can spread social and business uncertainty. From these 26 Chaozhou families, we can see that most of them have members working in various professions.

In the past, it was a common criticism that internal conflict plagued family business. After in-depth research, I find such an argument underestimates the strong internal force for unity and consolidation. As found through this research, not all family conflict is negative. Some conflict can facilitate sibling competition and business cooperation (Freedman 1991; Jehn 1997). As a unit of economic competition, family business at least can excel over other organizations in term of mutual trust, mutual cooperation, resource mobilization and risk bearing.

Arrangement for succession

In the case that most family members prefer to keep their businesses united, how can they arrange their property and shares to ensure a smooth succession? Traditionally, family property was transferred along the male line or the so-called patriliny. In a modern society, does this mechanism still prevail? What is the general perception about equal inheritance and succession? Is there any succession plan in Chinese family business? All these questions are the key areas that will be investigated in the subsequent paragraphs.

Let me begin with the preparation for inheritance. In the past, drafting a will for arranging the family estate was regarded as taboo and was not a popular practice in Chinese culture (Smith 1995). As a result, when parents died intestate, there would often be a struggle over the estate. In the modern world, the usage of wills in estate division is common. Whether the respondents are prepared to use such methods is one of the main concerns of the study.

When the interviewees were asked, 'Has your family prepared a will for the division of the family estate?' the majority of them did give me a positive response. Over 80.8 per cent of respondents replied that their family had already drafted one (Table 3.5). This shows a mature and rational perception on the need for a will. Some had even divided the estate as well as company shares when their patriarchs were still alive. They suggested that such arrangements would lessen the chance of sibling disputes. F10 commented as follows:

> When I read newspaper articles about siblings fighting for family property in court, I feel upset. In my mind, it was their father's fault. If he had divided the property before he died, or had prepared a will, there would be no room for disagreement. No one can take his property into the nether-

> world. Why did he not divide it before he died? In order to avoid this kind of dispute, I divided up my property some years ago. I had also asked my sons' opinion before making my decision.

Another senior respondent (F11) said,

> When my father divided the family estate, he called most of the dignitaries in the community as witnesses. Although he had written down certain arrangements, it was not that formal. But there was no disagreement among us. When it was my turn to prepare *fengjia* [division], I chose a will. It was formal and legally valid.

Although there is no longitudinal data about people's perceptions on wills, qualitative analysis shows that most people have a mature attitude about them. In addition, it can be inferred that the respondents preferred to rely more on formal documents rather than traditional ways of settlement.

Referring to the question of inheritance, although an overwhelming majority of families considered that there could be 'no equality', there was an indication that they tried to achieve a state of 'fairness'. In the study, it is found that inheritance among sons is more or less equal, while daughters are generally excluded from the line of inheritance. Most of the interviewees agreed that they would (and many of them have actually done so) divide their family estate and company shares equally among male heirs. On principle, each son gets 'one share'. There are, however, some minor variations. For instance, the eldest son may get a little bit more, like 'one and a half shares'. Such differences, according to one of the founding fathers, were not due to the birth order, but were due to the greater contribution of the eldest son who had helped in building the family firm by giving up the opportunity for further study when he was young. He said, 'When the eldest son was very young, he had to give up his education to his younger brothers and worked in the family firm. I thought this arrangement was a kind of compensation.'

Another exception is for children who have not yet finished their study or who have not yet married – in this case a half share more was also assigned. Some parents regard such arrangements as compensating for their children's education and marriage expenses. In the eyes of outsiders, such arrangements may violate the principle of equality. However, if one looks at it from another angle, one will realize that such practices are a minor adjustment for achieving the ultimate goal of 'fairness and equality'.

Compared with sons, most of the daughters are not entitled to family property as expected, especially in the male-dominant Chaozhou community. The only thing they could get from their parents is a dowry when they marry. In this study, there were only two families who had offered a certain proportion of company shares to their daughters. F21's father assigned to his three sons 'one share each', while for his two daughters 'a half share'. When F21 was asked to evaluate why his father could give each daughter a half share, he simply said, 'It was

Table 3.5 Respondents' views on inheritance and succession

Questions	*Number (%)*
Has your family prepared any will for the division of the family estate? (N = 26)	
Yes	21 (80.8)
No	5 (19.2)
Does each family member get an equal share? (N = 26)	
Yes	3 (11.5)
No	23 (88.5)
Does each son get an equal share? (N = 26)	
Yes	18 (69.2)
No	8 (30.8)
Does your family also divide the estate/business to daughters? (N = 26)	
Yes	2 (7.7)
No	24 (92.3)
Do you think your father's or your own arrangement is fair to each child? (N = 35)	
Yes	21 (60.0)
No	14 (40.0)
If someday you draft your own will, will you give each child an equal share? (N = 16)	
Yes	5 (31.2)
No	11 (68.8)
Has your father assigned a family member to take over the leadership of the business after he retires or dies? (N = 19)	
Yes	19 (100.0)
No	0 (0.0)
What are the criteria for choosing a successor? (N = 35)	
Ability/educational qualification	15 (42.9)
Filial piety	1 (2.9)
Interest in business	16 (45.7)
Birth order	1 (2.9)
Conduct, personal character and others	2 (5.7)
Does your family have any formal succession plan for the business? (N = 26)	
Yes	9 (34.6)
No	17 (65.4)
How do you monitor the succession process? (N = 26)	
Direct supervision	18 (69.2)
Indirect supervision	6 (23.1)
Prefer to let the successor have a free hand	2 (7.7)
How many years have you worked in the family firm before taking up a leadership post? (N = 17)	
0–2 years	1 (5.9)
3–5 years	6 35.3)
6–10 years	8 (47.1)
Over 10 years	2 (11.8)

Source: Interview 1997–2000.

Note
"N" represents the number of respondents interviewed. The question only addressed the relevant interviewees.

due to the contribution of my two sisters.' According to F21, his two younger sisters helped in the family factory after finishing their primary education. They served in the family firm for over 30 years and made a great contribution to its success. Even after they had married, they still worked in the firm.

Another example is F22. When F22 started up his secretarial and taxation services business, his two daughters were his two key assistants. F22's two sons, who studied in the UK and later moved to Australia, showed little interest in the family business and chose to become professionals upon graduation from university. F22 therefore gave shares to his two daughters. However, he preferred not to disclose the proportion of shares. Generally speaking, if female members do not make a great contribution, they will rarely get a share. It is completely different for the male members of a family.

When a follow-up question relating to why daughters were generally excluded from the line of inheritance was put to the male respondents, they gave quite consistent answers. In principle, they disagreed that there was any discrimination against female members. However, in reality, they suggested that such a practice was sensible and inevitable. First, they thought daughters would eventually marry and move away from the family. They would bear the surname of their husbands and were more or less regarded as 'outsiders'. If company shares were assigned to daughters, family ownership would be diluted and more conflicts would be triggered. Second, parents preferred to give daughters property on a 'one and for all' basis, but not company shares. The property they gave usually was in the form of a dowry.

There are two female respondents in the research sample. When the same question was asked, their answers did not deviate too much from the male respondents. Although they disapproved of the traditional practice, they still accepted that in Chinese culture it was natural and inevitable. F19's daughter, a senior chartered public accountant and partner in a world-leading accounting firm (Deloitte Touche Tohmatsu), even consented to her father's arrangement in giving most of the family assets to her brother, the only son in the family. She said,

> Although my other sisters may have different opinion, I speak on my own. I have no objection to my father's decision. If my father also gave each daughter shares, the management would be very complicated. The family business would no longer be controlled by my father's family. Even though my father did not give me any share, he gave me a sizable dowry. He also provided me with a good education and other assistance. After I graduated from university, I joined my present accounting firm on the recommendation of my father's business friend. Some years later, I was invited as a partner. I thought all these were 'given' by my father. So, you can see, on the surface, I received no company shares from my father. In reality, I received what I was entitled to.

When F26's wife was asked about the practice of equal inheritance, her reply did not differ from the male respondents. She speculated that her husband would assign most of the company shares to their two sons. She reiterated that she did not want to complicate the inheritance problem, but rather followed tradition. If her daughter was allowed access to the family business, it would invite further disagreement from other parties (she did not mention which party she was referring to) and make inheritance more complicated. Instead, F26's wife agreed that she would give a large dowry to her daughter when she married. From this perspective, we can see that although inheritance among sons can more or less be treated as 'equal', it is seldom the case between sons and daughters. Daughters are regarded as 'temporary' family members who will eventually marry and bear the surname of another family. Such perception clearly conforms with Wolf's (1972) research finding about Chinese women's role in rural Taiwan.

The inequality between males and females is not a unique feature of Chinese culture. Even in the West, 'equal inheritance' among sons and daughters is in name only. Many scholars find that in the USA, UK or other European countries, real property is usually transmitted only to sons, without preference for birth order. Daughters are generally excluded from the line of inheritance (Deen 1972; Auwers 1978; Traver 1952; Gundersen 1998).

Having discussed the principle of equal inheritance, now let us turn to the preparation process. Succession is regarded as a turning point for business continuity. As Kets de Vries (1988: 165) comments: 'Succession at the top can have a ripple effect throughout an entire organization bringing with it some profound strategic and structural changes.... Poor succession planning has been called a major contributing factor to business failure.'

In their paper, *Dynamics of Growth and Succession in Entrepreneurial Organization*, Cunningham and Ho (1994) point out that the transfer of control in the family and the growth of businesses often run parallel to each other. In their case study of four Chinese family-owned businesses, they find all of them had no formal plan for succession. Two of them took up the businesses after the death of the founders. One was forced to take up even when he was not interested. Only one was 'trained from childhood'. They concluded that most of them did not understand the operation and management of their businesses before taking up the leading role. It was therefore the lack of a formal plan for succession that made the transfer of business very difficult. Is this argument valid? And, does it reflect the reality?

First, when second- and third-generation interviewees were asked if their father had picked a successor for the business before their retirement, the answer was clearly positive. All of them replied that the leadership role had been assigned beforehand. Then, a follow-up question was asked about the criteria in choosing a successor. The question was addressed to all respondents. About 45.7 per cent of them suggested personal interest in the business as the most important criteria. Personal ability and educational qualifications ranked only slightly lower (42.9 per cent). Other factors, such as personal conduct, character, birth order and filial piety, scored much lower.

The founder can choose his successor at an early age. He may first observe the behaviour of his offspring to see who has an interest in the family business.

If some children show little interest, he may simply let them choose their own career. On some occasions, if the patriarch has only a few sons, he may 'force' his son(s) to take up the family business irrespective of his/their preference. F1 is just such a case. Although F1's only son wanted to work in a US-based petroleum company as its regional executive director, when his father asked him for help, he had to change his plans.

One thing is very interesting. When successors are chosen, the founder may like them to start at the bottom, even working as office boys, clerks or ordinary workers. They think their successors should learn all about the operation of the business, instead of assigning them a management post at the beginning. There is no time frame for the successor to work as a 'trainee or assistant'. After a certain period (usually several months to one year) of work, when the founders feel their successors have gained enough experience, they may be assigned to key positions.

In order to establish the successor's leadership status, the founders may also bring the successor to social gatherings or business activities. The heirs may be introduced to business partners or dignitaries in the community. Through such activities, the image of the 'heir-to-be' can gradually be established. In addition, leadership may also be inculcated by encouraging their son to participate in social and business activities (for details, please refer to Chapter 5).

There are two salient facts that can be concluded from this data. First, when selecting the family leader, parents place greater value on objective factors (personal interest, educational qualifications and ability) rather than subjective elements (filial piety or birth order). In other words, a merit base for selecting a successor applies (Table 3.4). Second, in order to avoid a struggle for leadership, parents will appoint the new leader while he is still at a young age. Such a practice can reduce the chance of internal conflict among siblings.

In this study, it is found that the real picture does not follow what Cunningham and Ho have suggested. Although on the surface, when the question of whether there was any formal succession plan in the interviewees' firms was asked, most of them (65.4 per cent) gave negative answer. It does not mean there is no 'succession plan' at all. When the question is rephrased and a similar question was put to them, the genuine picture comes out. For instance, when I asked the interviewees 'How many years have you worked in the family firm before taking up a leadership post?' There was only one respondent who took up the family business within two years. Over 82.4 per cent of them had worked in the family firm for 3–10 years. About 11.8 per cent of them had even worked for over ten years. From their working history, one can easily learn that some of them have started from the bottom and obtained formal job training before being appointed to a key position. Such a long working track record could enhance their familiarization and understanding of their firm's culture, organizational structure and business connections.

In order to illustrate this argument, the succession process of the Fung Pak-liu family can be cited as reference. Fung Hong-chu, second son of Fung Pak-liu, joined Li & Fung, the flagship company of the family, in 1931 as a junior clerk.

He was promoted to supervisor and then branch manager in 1935. After the end of the war in Hong Kong in 1945, Fung Hong-chu rose to become managing director, a key management post. After the death of his elder brother, Fung Hong-chu became the chairman of the Li & Fung Group in 1975. Fung Hong-chu's sons, Victor Fung and William Fung, also followed a similar succession path. Comparatively speaking, Victor Fung and William Fung were luckier than their father as they did not need to work as junior clerks. Having got his doctoral degree at Harvard University, Victor Fung worked at Citibank (USA) in 1970. Two years later, he joined his alma mater (Harvard Business School) and became an assistant professor. In 1974, he left Harvard and joined Li & Fung. He was appointed manager of Li & Fung Trading, one of the subsidiaries of the Li & Fung Group. He worked for three more years and then, in 1977, was promoted to managing director of the subsidiary. Four years later, he was appointed as managing director of the group. Victor Fung became the group deputy chairman in 1985. In 1996, he succeeded his father and became the chairman, the paramount leader of the group, when his father announced his intention to retire. William Fung also experienced quite a similar process of advancement as Victor Fung (Table 3.6). In fact, the succession process of other large families more or less follows the Fungs' experience.

From this story, one can see that there is no such thing as a formal succession plan. However, if looking at the actual work that has been done, the picture clearly shows the opposite. Many of the successors have worked in the family firms for a period of time before taking up the helm. What are the implications from this 'self-contradictory' evidence?

Even a well-planned succession will be meaningless if there is no monitoring mechanism. In this study, it is found that many of the patriarchs would closely

Table 3.6 Work history of the Fung Pak-liu family

Name	*Year*	*Work history*
Fung Hong-chu	1931	Junior clerk
	1935	Manager (trading section)
	1945	Managing director (trading section)
	1975	Chairman (group)
	1996	Retired
Victor Fung	1970	Officer (Citibank, USA)
	1972	Assistant professor (Harvard Business School)
	1974	Manager (trading section)
	1977	Managing director (trading section)
	1981	Managing director (group)
	1985	Deputy chairman (group)
	1996	Chairman
William Fung	1972	Manager (textile section)
	1975	Managing director (trading section)
	1982	Managing director (properties section)
	1986	Chief executive officer (group)

Sources: Li & Fung Limited 1982; Chiu 1996; C.W. Lui 2000a, 2000b.

supervise their children after they had taken over the leadership. Over 73.1 per cent of the respondents claimed that they would directly monitor their heir's behaviour. They would still hold a prominent position, such as chairman or honorary consultant in the company. About 19.2 per cent preferred indirect supervision. They would resign from all formal positions and only gave advice when they saw the situation was critical. An insignificant proportion (7.7 per cent) of respondents favoured giving free rein to their children. They showed great confidence in their heirs and gave them full support. Such data reflects a reality that even though the patriarch has announced his intention of retirement, he still keeps visiting his company and gives advice. Chan and Chiang (1994: 125) write,

> At seventy-four, Chew Choo Keng is now semi-retired after an unfortunate stroke in 1989 which forced him to slow down his lifestyle. Leaving his business now to his eldest son and his two daughters, Chew follows a routine of daily early morning walks at the MacRitchie Reservoir before he goes to his office at nine where he still attends to some business matters.

Clearly, unless the patriarch suffers serious illness or dies, he may still keep a close eye on his business even when in poor health.

From such stories, a succession process of choosing a candidate, job training and network building to the transfer of ownership and leadership and the later stage of monitoring can be clearly depicted. However, one may ask why the founder does not spell out clearly the succession plan at the beginning, or systemize the selection criteria and monitoring mechanism? It is not difficult to answer. Since Chinese culture stresses personal connections rather than formal documents or contracts, a verbal promise is enough. A black and white contract is considered only applicable to outsiders or less trustworthy people. For a well-trusted and close person, one's word is gold. Very often, the patriarch's verbal acknowledgement is the 'plan'. This is consistent with the paternalistic style of management.

On the other hand, we must admit that a vague and not so clearly announced succession plan can give the founder greater power to exercise. For the successor, the 'unclear appointment' generates anxiety and uncertainty. Thus, he needs to pay great attention to his father or to be more filial. If he does not meet his father's expectations, he may be 'dethroned'. Such a threat can motivate the successors to work harder, be more faithful and show greater filial piety.

The case of Lam Pak-yan (generally called Uncle Lam, founder of the Lai Sun Group) can be used to illustrate this point. Uncle Lam always said that Peter Lam, his youngest son, brought him good luck. When Peter Lam was born, his business grew remarkably. Later, after finishing his education, Peter joined the Lai Sun Group, the flagship company of the Lam family, and was crowned as the 'heir-apparent'. Uncle Lam also frequently criticized his eldest son, Lam Kin-ming, saying he was incompetent. In 1998 Uncle Lam was embroiled in a land sale scandal in Taiwan and was detained there for approximately one year.

Coinciding with the Asian financial turmoil, Lai Sun Group suffered a serious financial crisis. Peter Lam was forced to sell a large proportion of shares in Asian Television Broadcasting Limited, one of the local television broadcasting companies that was controlled by the Lams, without prior consent from Uncle Lam. Uncle Lam was furious and publicly criticized Peter Lam as 'prodigal' (Kwan *et al.* 1998). He also altered his opinion about his eldest son, Lam Kin-ming, pleasing the latter, who then became active in the management team. Eventually, Uncle Lam could leave Taiwan and took up the leadership once again when he came back to Hong Kong in February 1999 (Sze and Fu 1999; Kwan and Leung 1999).

Although Lam Kin-ming's role became more important in the management of the company, Uncle Lam's attitude remained ambivalent. He still queried Lam Kin-ming's competence and ability as heir. He once again publicly commented that both sons were not helpful, so he turned to his nephew and adoptive son Lam Kin-hong, a London University law school graduate, who had helped him in Taiwan. It was reported that Uncle Lam even wanted to pass the baton to Lam Kin-hong (*Apple Daily* 11 September 2000; Lo and Wong 2000). However, Uncle Lam later also harshly criticized Lam Kin-hong and expressed disappointment in him. Echoing Uncle Lam's comment, Pearl Lam, Uncle Lam's daughter, openly criticized Lam Kin-hong by saying that he was only an employee of Lai Sun Group, not a 'son' of Lam Pak-yan. Clearly, Uncle Lam's 'unclear appointment' of successors created strong anxiety among his sons and daughter and further perplexed the matter of inheritance.

Exercising family control

From many family members' point of view, maintaining family ownership and control is always regarded as the most important issue. This problem becomes acute when the family business goes public and when professional non-family members are absorbed into the senior management. In this research, I found that there are two major mechanisms deployed for securing family domination.

Imposing internal regulations for resale of company shares is the major and most effective means of exercising family ownership. Wong (1988: 155) found that most Shanghai cotton spinners in Hong Kong have an internal regulation for the reselling of company shares:

> Most family-owned mills have company regulations designed to keep their capital intact. Shares cannot be freely sold to outsiders. If family members want to give up company ownership, they must first offer the shares to existing shareholders 'at fair value'. Company regulations usually provide a further safeguard empowering the board of directors to refuse to register shares.

These regulations are used to secure the control of the firm in the hands of the family. In this research, I found such a practice is also common among the

Chaozhou entrepreneurs. F9's family is a famous example. Before the death of F9's uncle, the patriarch had clearly stated in his will that if any of the family members wanted to sell his share, he should first approach other family members. If there was no family members interested, then one could sell to non-family members with the prior consent of all family shareholders. In addition, only sons had the right to hold the company shares. They feared that if family shares were given to daughters or sons-in-law, non-family members might dilute family control in the company. Such an arrangement made the transfer of shares very difficult, although not necessarily impossible.

According to F9, the reason for adding this rule to the will was to prevent any hostile takeovers. It was learnt that there was a hostile takeover decades ago. In the 1970s, F9's family banking business was prosperous. They earned a good profit both in banking and property investment. Seeing the potential, a Fujianese-owned listed company masterminded a takeover of their company in 1976. The company secretly absorbed quite a large number of shares on the stock market. Share prices shot up. Some family members were not aware of this problem and sold their shares at a high price. Later, F9's family learnt that if they let the Fujianese acquire more shares, their majority stake in the company would be threatened. F9's uncle therefore counter-offered a far higher price to buy back most of the shares. Although F9's family eventually won the battle, they paid a huge price for doing so. Having learnt their lesson, F9's uncles and his father added a codicil on their will to limit the transfer of family shares. Because of this stipulation, shares in the company became nearly inactive on the market.

Another example is F7's family. In an interview, one of the family members told me that a significant proportion of their bank's share was not allowed to be sold to non-family members. The proportion of shares he mentioned was the threshold that can ensure their domination in the family-controlled bank. Obviously, restrictions on reselling family shares is considered as the 'shield' that defends the family business from being attacked by outsiders.

Beside restrictions on reselling family shares, certain key management positions are excluded from non-family members, such as chairman, managing directors and a certain proportion of seats on the board of directors. Many scholars have pointed out that the management of Chinese firms is over-dominated by family members (Redding 1988, 1991; Yeung 2000b). In this research, such practices can clearly be seen. From the 26 interviewed families, all chairman and managing director posts are held by family members, mainly the founder, or sometimes second-generation leaders. In addition, heads of functional departments, such as accounts and finance, advertising and marketing, production and operation, administration and personnel, are sometimes held by family members. Non-family members are usually recruited to the second tier as supervisors, assistant managers or deputy directors. A common practice is that the father is the chairman and the sons are heads of various departments. From the study, it is confirmed that very few non-family members join the management team. Only F4 and F7 are exceptional. Since these two family firms are publicly listed on the stock market, their books are open to public monitoring. Accepting professionals to the board of directors can project a good image to the public. Tong (1991: 196) cites Kwek Hong Png's family in Singapore as an example of this point:

> The founder Kwek Hong Png [sic] still holds the chairmanship for the holding companies and all the subsidiaries. His son and chosen successor, Leng Beng, sits on all the boards as an executive director. He is also the managing director of most of these companies. With his father's retirement from Hong Leong Finance Limited in 1984, Leng Beng has stepped in as chairman. His younger brother, Leng Joo, has also gradually been appointed to the various boards. Hong Png's brother used to sit on most of the boards too. Now, their sons have stepped into their places. It is interesting to note that even though Hong Leong has grown into a business conglomerate, the 'hands-on' style of management of a Chinese 'towkay' [the boss] is still evident.

Such practices, as Redding and Yeung have indicated, can be detrimental to business development. A rigid and sluggish channel of promotion, or discriminatory criteria, will inevitably hurt employees' feelings, lower working morale and company commitment. However, in this study, it was found that the appointment of family members is done very carefully. Usually, sons or daughters who are assigned for particular positions have good academic qualifications or experience. Thus, I think although there is a negative effect, its impact may be over-exaggerated.

In fact, thc absorption of the younger generation may make company reformation more likely. Many firms have tried to introduce Western management concepts and absorb non-family professionals into their management team when new leaders are appointed. A clear finding is that if reformation is initiated by the new family leader, trust and support may be greater, and the chance of success may also be higher. If the new leader is from outside, the opposite is often the case. In other words, although nepotism and over-reliance on family members may create some management problems, the positive aspects should not be totally discounted.

In fact, the fall of Lehman Brothers Holdings Inc. in 2008 and many other originally family-controlled enterprises under non-family professional CEO-type leadership in the recent credit disaster in the USA drives many people around the globe to ponder deeply about the philosophy of separation of ownership and management. Although there are undeniably 'dark sides' of family business, its consciousness of profit-seeking *and* risk-bearing shows us that it can more effectively avoid irresponsible over-expansion. As a basic form of economic organization, we must also admit that family business is highly dynamic, competitive, and can be regarded as one of the dominant forces in most economies.

The essence of family ownership

Family ownership is the main idea raised in this chapter. Maintaining family control is a key element of the business. In fact, ownership is one of the key concepts in Marxist theory. Karl Marx argues that in capitalist society, the origin of exploitation and class conflict is the nature of ownership, or to be more specific, private ownership. He suggests that capitalists control the forces of production. These forces of production themselves produce nothing. Only labour, whose providers contribute their effort, create wealth. Since capitalists own the forces of production and the appropriation of profit is accorded to private ownership, all 'surplus value' or profit goes into the hands of the capitalists. A contradictory relationship between the forces of production and the relation of production is created and conflict is activated. Marx predicts such inherent conflict will eventually lead to the downfall of the capitalist system (Bottomore and Rubel 1963).

The major concern of this book is not to debate with Marxists about the nature of ownership and modern capitalism. The idea is that family ownership is the starting point of the whole discussion. Many conflicts emerge because of the seizure of ownership and the loss of family ownership means that the business organization is no longer controlled by a single family, such as the cases of Kwong Sang Hong and Yeo Hiap Seng. Since ownership can ensure that a family harvests the profit and bears the loss, having no family control implies the business is no longer 'accountable' to the family. The ownership mechanism implies that family members are supposed to pay close attention to their company's management, investments, planning and market domination.

Maintaining family ownership is considered to be of the utmost importance in Chinese culture. In order to achieve this goal, business owners could rationally 'institutionalize' a series of measures, such as preventing outsiders from serving in the most senior posts in the company, restricting the reselling of shares, or even excluding female members from the line of inheritance to the family business equity. However, proper transfer of ownership itself does not imply business continuity and prosperity. As Chan and Chiang (1994: 340) write, 'Despite their rich endowments, many heirs squandered away their inherited wealth. Doing business is a passion, a life commitment. When the passion ceases, so will the business.' In other words, for ensuring effective succession, the patriarchs not only need to pay special attention to the transmission of ownership, but also to ensuring their descendants learn sufficient knowledge and skills, and more importantly, to building effective networks before taking over the leading jobs.

A vast property means nothing if the family leader does not show his leadership and cannot mobilize existing networks to safeguard the family business. For the sake of simplicity, I use a metaphor to illustrate the interplay of ownership, leadership and business networks. Ownership is like a stage in a theatre. It is the foundation of the business. Leaders are the actors and actresses. Passion and commitment to business is the entrepreneurship. The networks can be regarded as the performing skill that each performer displays. If one of these elements is missing, it means that the play cannot be a success. The same applies to business.

To sum up, in this chapter, I find that although estate litigation does takes place sometimes, it doesn't mean that the transmission in Chinese family business is always a contested affair. As a basic social unit, it is quite natural to expect that family spreads out from generation to generation. However, as a basic economic unit, it is common to see that family business is more resistant to splitting in order to retain its vitality, agility and competitiveness in the market.

Similarly, although Chinese family businesses are frequently criticized for lacking formal succession plans, this research has found that the opposite is the case. In order to retain their family fortune, many large family businesses have paid extra attention to their heirs' training, not only in giving them as much education as possible, but also in requiring them to have down-to-earth work experience. Some of them even ask their highly educated heirs to work from the bottom-up to make sure that their heirs know every detail about the family businesses. Of course, we must admit that such 'succession plans' are generally not clearly spelt out, but exist only in the patriarch's mind.

As expected, female members are generally excluded from the line of inheritance, particularly in family business. Such an arrangement further reflects the patrilineal feature of Chinese culture. In short, we can see that the transmission of economic capital is less complicated. However, since its right of ownership or usage is exclusive, disputes can easily erupt if it is not clearly arranged. This explains why fights over the family estate may sometimes occur.

4 The transfer of human capital

Unlike the transfer of economic capital, the transmission of human capital is subtle and complex. However, it is one of the most important factors that affects business continuity, stability and prosperity. Whether in the East or the West, education is generally perceived as the key human capital that not only maintains family status, but also fuels family business expansion. It is also regarded as one of the key indicators of earning power (Brittain 1977).

Apart from education, leadership is regarded as another key element of human capital. Unlike education, although the influence of leadership on the development of family and business is more far-reaching and critical, it is more difficult to transfer from one generation to the next. In addition, it is also believed that the result of the transmission is less certain and more unpredictable. In this chapter, light will be shed on these two key types of human capital to see how they affect the fate of family business.

Education and leadership as human capital

As we all know, the advantage of education has always been acknowledged. In Chinese tradition, education is generally perceived as serving two major functions: to obtain adequate knowledge for daily use (*dushu shizi*); and to take the civil examination and earn a place in officialdom (*kaoqu guongming*). The civil examination was the major route for social mobility. In Pan and Fei's (1947) research, during the Ming and Qing dynasties, education was stressed as the most important means for social advancement. After years of unremitting effort, when one was appointed by the emperor to the particular post, the whole family would be honoured. The path 'from education to officialdom' was regarded as the main channel for upward social mobility. In this sense, education means social status. Tales were frequently told of the whole family living thriftily and frugally to support their sons while they were studying for the civil examination (Ho 1976).

Compared to the past, the path of social mobility has widened. Joining the government bureaucracy is no longer considered the only way for advancement. Other routes, such as forming one's own business, earning a professional qualification or joining large corporations, can also bring good prospects. However, a great emphasis on education still remains top of the list in modern society. Postiglione (1999a, 1999b) argues that better-off Chinese parents are 'more than willing to dip into their savings to spend on their children's higher education.'

In Western countries, education is also equally stressed. Many scholars regard education as a form of human capital investment (Becker 1964; Schultz 1971). It can generate 'future income' for their children, as well as for the family. Other scholars even argue that 'parents seek to provide the "best" education opportunities possible' to their children (McNamee and Miller 1998). Warner and Abegglen (1955) also say that '[e]ducation is now the royal road to success and positions of power and prestige at the higher rungs of big business'. Clearly, in parents' eyes, education not only serves the function of enabling their children to acquire knowledge, but also serves as a kind of long-term investment for the whole family.

Although education plays an important role in enhancing family competitiveness in society, it is believed to be less critical when compared to other types of human capital, such as leadership or entrepreneurship. As mentioned in previous chapters, leadership and entrepreneurship are believed to be the critical factors that affect family business development and continuity. In fact, in other similar studies, it is clearly found that leadership and entrepreneurship have some kind of overlap (Smilor and Sexton 1996).

Generally, Weber's concept of leadership covers all aspects, from family and business to sociopolitical arenas, while Schumpeter's idea of entrepreneurship only narrowly applies in business and economic circles. Since Schumpeter was a close friend of Weber, I speculate that the concept of entrepreneurship may be derived from or under the influence of the concept of charismatic leadership. In fact, there are some similarities between these two concepts.

First, both qualities are innate gifts. Weber points out that charismatic leaders are 'endowed with supernatural, superhuman, or at least specially exceptional powers or qualities'. Schumpeter suggests a similar definition and says that entrepreneurs should have a dream and ambition to found a kingdom, the will to conquer, the impulse to fight, and the joy of creating. All these personality traits are also 'endowed by nature'.

Second, both elements are unstable and fluid. Weber (1978: 1114) himself has suggested that charismatic leadership is naturally unstable. The holder may lose his charisma instantly. Mommsen (1974: 78) tries to elaborate this point.

> Indeed, the emotional and personal character of the relationship between the leader and his retinue was, in his [Weber's] opinion, the main reason for the peculiar instability of 'charismatic rule'. A charismatic leader has to prove his qualification for leadership anew every day, and a good deal of success is therefore essential for maintaining his position. It is somewhat irritating to note that, in the last resort, success is the main, although possibly not the only, criterion by which a leader may be judged charismatic. A leader who fails, who does not live up to the expectations which he himself has created in the minds of his retinue, is likely to lose his charismatic appeal all of a sudden. His retinues disbands, his followers desert him.

Clearly, Weber (1947: 334) has indicated that because of its unstable nature, no one can retain his leadership spirit all the time: 'It cannot remain stable, but becomes either traditionalized or rationalized, or a combination of both.' Entrepreneurship is also unstable. It will disappear if one cannot keep abreast with the constantly changing environment. Schumpeter (1934: 78) writes,

> Everyone is an entrepreneur only when he actually 'carries out new combinations' and loses that character as soon as he builds up his business, when he settles down to running it as he has built up as other people run their businesses. This is the rule, of course, and hence it is just as rare for anyone always to remain an entrepreneur throughout the decades of his active life as it is for a businessman never to have a moment in which he is an entrepreneur, to however modest a degree. Because being an entrepreneur is not a profession and as a rule not a lasting condition, entrepreneurs do not form a social class in the technical sense, as for example, landowners or capitalists or workmen do.

So, we can see that Schumpeter also argues that every entrepreneur can become an ordinary individual once he has lost the innovative spirit.

Third, both leadership and entrepreneurship emphasize creativity and innovation. Weber sees charismatic leadership as a 'revolutionary break-through brought about by the determined action of charismatic personalities and their retinues in the face of a traditionalist environment. Such a dynamic break-through, as a rule, results in the establishment of a kind of charismatic rule' (Mommsen 1974: 80).

Schumpeter advocates that the core of entrepreneurship is the concept of innovation. Everyone is an entrepreneur only when he actually 'carries out new combinations and loses that character as soon as he builds up his business'. In other words, the heart of entrepreneurship is a creative and innovative mentality. Losing this kind of spirit relegates an entrepreneur simply to the status of manager.

Fourth, Weberian charismatic leadership and Schumpeterian innovative entrepreneurship can not be easily transmitted. Only ordinary leadership skill can be learnt or cultivated. Weber (1978: 1143) elaborates:

> Once charisma qualification has become an impersonal quality, which can be transmitted through various and at first purely magic means, it has begun its transformation from a personal gift that can be tested but not transmitted and acquired, into a capacity that, in principle, can be taught and learned. Thus charismatic qualification can become an object of education, even though at first not in the form of rational or empirical instruction, since heroic and magical capacities are regarded as inborn; only if they are latent can they be activated through a regeneration of the whole personality.

Regarding entrepreneurship, although not transmittable by its very nature, some of its skill can also be learned: 'Entrepreneurship can be taught but not the mindset or spirit. Nevertheless, it can be cultivated, nurtured and developed while skills certainly can be taught or developed' (Kao 1995: 143).

To sum up, we can cite Mommsen's astute comment on the nature of leadership and entrepreneurship as a concluding remark. He writes, 'A dynamic economy could not get along without the economic leadership qualities of private entrepreneurs' (Mommsen 1974: 79). In other words, he not only agrees that there are certain aspects of overlapping between these two concepts, but also points out that both elements are very critical for sustaining business development. Subsequent paragraphs will deal with educational attainment and the development of the family business.

Educational attainment of the Chaozhou families

In the interviews, I dug deeply into the respondents' educational background, specialization and their family members' attainment and found that the Chaozhou families placed great value on their children's education. In addition, it is also found that their family's educational achievements run parallel with their family's economic emergence.

From the survey data, we can clearly see that most of the studied Chaozhou families have experienced a gradual improvement in education. Nearly all of the founders came from poor family backgrounds and their educational level is relatively low. Many of them only attended informal classes, and some were even illiterate. Educational attainment improves in the second, third and later generations. Although some second-generation family members may be asked to work in the family firm at an early age, many of them in fact have obtained university degrees. Some of their degrees are obtained from local universities while some are from abroad. Quite a high proportion of them even get higher degrees. Clearly, their family educational level increases as their wealth and size expands.

Based on the survey data on the educational advancement of the 26 Chaozhou families (Table 4.1), a six-stage model can be generalized. In stage one, the first-generation entrepreneurs only attend informal classes or primary school. Since they come from a poor family background, it was a great burden for their families to provide them even the most rudimentary of education. They are only taught basic knowledge such as elementary writing, arithmetic and conduct, and are forced to leave school in early childhood to earn money to support their families. In retrospect, many of the patriarchs express regret that they did not study more when young. Thus, they hope their children do not follow in their footsteps.

In stage two, some family members, usually the second generation, may gain a secondary education. This reflects that the family has made some improvement both socially and economically. However, due to the lack of reliable workers, some members are requested to help in the family shop or factory as 'cheap labour', even though they are young and eager to continue their studies. For example, F3 and F14 were asked to leave school earlier due to this when they were young.

Table 4.1 Educational attainment of the studied Chaozhou families

Family member	*Name of institution*	*Field of study and degree obtained*
F1	Hanjian Teachers' College	Graduated
F1's son	University of Toronto	Chemical engineering
	Princeton University	PhD (organic chemistry)
F2's father	n/a	Informal education
F2	n/a	Secondary level
F2's first son	A university in the USA	Electronic engineering
F2's second son	A university in the USA	Mechanical engineering
F2's third son	A university in the USA	MBA
F2's fourth son	A university in the USA	Economics
F3's father	n/a	Informal primary education
F3	n/a	Junior secondary school
F3's second brother	n/a	Secondary level
F3's third brother	n/a	n/a
F3's fourth brother	Monash University, Australia	Economics
F3's son	University of London	Accounts and finance
F3's nephew	n/a	University graduated
F4's father	n/a	Primary level
F4	n/a	Secondary level
	New York Banking Academy	Banking and finance (certificate)
F4's brother	A university in Thailand	University graduated
F4's first son	n/a	MBA
F4's second son	Ponoma University, USA	Arts
F4's nephew	MIT	Master's (chemical engineering), MBA
F5's grandfather	Informal school in Chaozhou	Informal elementary class
F5's father	n/a	Junior secondary school
F5	A school in Hong Kong	Secondary level
F5's first son	University of Waterloo	Computer engineering
F5's second son	University of British Columbia	Science
F5's third son	University of Waterloo	MBA
F5's daughter	University of Waterloo	Nutrition and food
F6	University of Golden Gate	Mechanical engineering
	University of Hong Kong	MBA
F6's son	n/a	High school in the USA
F7's grandfather	n/a	Primary school
F7's father	Tung Chi University	Economics
F7's first uncle	University of London	Law
F7's second uncle	College of Arts and Sciences in Guangdong	Arts and sciences
F7's third uncle	University of Oxford	Medicine
F7's fourth uncle	University of London	Law
F7	University of York	Accounting
F7's brother	University of Oxford	Law
F8's father	n/a	Primary level
F8	Columbia University	MBA
F8's first brother	University of California, Berkeley	MBA

continued

Table 4.1 Continued

Family member	*Name of institution*	*Field of study and degree obtained*
F8's second brother	University of Toronto	Engineering (Masters)
F9's first uncle	n/a	Primary level
F9's second uncle	n/a	Secondary level
F9's father	n/a	Secondary level
F9	Harvard University	Law
F9's first brother	Harvard University	Architecture
F9's second brother	University of Ohio	Medicine
F9's third brother	Princeton University	Psychology
F9's fourth brother	University of British Columbia	MBA
F10's father	n/a	Secondary level
F10	A school in Hong Kong	Secondary level
F10's first son	University of Surrey, UK	Social Sciences
F10's second son	A university in Canada	University graduated
F10's third son	University of Toronto	MBA
F11's father	A school in Shanghai	Secondary level
F11	Fudan University	Philosophy (interrupted by war)
F11's first son	Stanford University	Bachelor of accounting
F11's second son	Stanford University	Bachelor of electronic engineering
F11's daughter	University of Hong Kong	Master of philosophy (sociology)
F12	n/a	Primary level
F12's first son	University of Hong Kong	Art
F12's second son	National University of Singapore	International business
F13's father	n/a	Illiterate
F13	Shantou Middle School	Junior secondary level
F13's first brother	Fudan University	Economics
F13's second brother	University of Cambridge	Law
F13's first son	University of Oxford	Accounting
	University of Oxford	Master's (economics)
F13's second son	MIT	Engineering
F14	n/a	Primary level
F14's first son	Stanford University	PhD (medicine)
F14's second son	A university in Canada	PhD (civil engineering)
F14's third son	University of Pennsylvania	Business administration
F14's first daughter	Harvard University	PhD (clinical psychology)
	Harvard University	Professor in clinical psychology
F14's second daughter	University of Oregon	Arts
F15's father	n/a	Secondary level
F15's first brother	Yale University	PhD (physics)
	Yale University	Professor in physics
F15's second brother	University of Hong Kong	Economics
F15's third brother	University of New South Wales	Civil engineering
F15	n/a	Secondary level
F15's first son	University of New South Wales	Law
F15's second son	A university in Australia	Social sciences

Family member	*Name of institution*	*Field of study and degree obtained*
F16's father	A school in Shantou	Primary level
F16's uncle	A school in Shantou	Secondary level
F16	n/a	Secondary level
F16's brother	University of Hong Kong	Accounts and finance
F16's first son	University of Pittsburgh	Civil engineering
F16's second son	University of Toronto	Computer science
F17	A secondary school in Shantou	Secondary level
F17's son	University of Toronto	Economics
F17's first daughter	Hong Kong City University	Language and translation
F17's second daughter	University of Toronto	Arts
F17's third daughter	n/a	University level
F18	n/a	Secondary level
F18's first son	Hong Kong Polytechnic	Textile and manufacturing (diploma)
F18's second son	University of Hong Kong	Arts
F18's third son	University of Hong Kong	Accounts and finance
F19's father	A primary school in Chaozhou	Primary level
F19	n/a	Secondary level
F19's first brother	University of Hong Kong	Law
F19's second brother	University of Stanford	Law
F19's son	UCLA	Economics
F19's daughter	Stanford University	Accounts and finance
F20's father	n/a	Primary level
F20	A school in Chaozhou	Junior secondary school
	A school in Hong Kong	Evening school
F20's first son	University of Toronto	MBA
F20's second son	University of Toronto	Computer engineering
F20's third son	University of Toronto	Business
F20's daughter	Monash University	Art and design
F21's father	A school in Shantou	Junior primary school level
F21	A school in Hong Kong	Secondary (form five) level
F21's first brother	University of Hong Kong	Economics
F21's second brother	University of Waterloo	Computer science
F21's third brother	University of Toronto	Design
F22	A primary school in Chaozhou	Junior secondary level
F22's first son	University of Australia	MBA
F22's second son	University of York	MBA
F22's first daughter	Hang Seng Community College	Commerce and accounts (diploma)
F22's second daughter	University of Lancaster	Social work
F23's father	n/a	Informal class
F23's brother	Wah Yan College	Secondary level
F23	Wah Yan College	Matriculate level
	Johnston, Stoke and Master	Admitted solicitor by training
F23's son	University of Hong Kong	Medicine
F23's daughter	A university in Hawaii	Law faculty
F24	A secondary school in Vietnam	Secondary level
F24's son	University of York	MBA

continued

Table 4.1 Continued

Family member	*Name of institution*	*Field of study and degree obtained*
F24's daughter	City University of Hong Kong	Graphic design
F25	n/a	Secondary level
F25's first son	University of Georgia	Computer science
F25's second son	University of Georgia	Management
F25's daughter	University of Hawaii	Hotel management
F26's father	n/a	Primary level
F26	Hong Kong Polytechnic	Manufacturing (diploma)
F26's first son	A university in New Zealand	MBA
F26's second son	High school in New Zealand	Still in school
F26's daughter	A university in New Zealand	Social sciences

Source: Interviews 1997–2000.

In stage three, some family members may go to university. This is a turning point as it signifies that the family business is operating in a proper and successful way. The family may save enough money and have the financial ability to send their offspring to university. However, they can only afford one or two members in local universities. F7 and F11, who obtained their university degrees abroad, are very exceptional cases. It not only implies that their families have accumulated sufficient wealth, but also signifies that their businesses have been transformed from small retailing concerns to large conglomerate businesses.

During stage four, both the size of the family and the capacity of the business have expanded remarkably. They now have the ability to send their sons or grandsons to study abroad. In order to give them a good-quality education, they prefer to send them to famous universities, such as Oxford and Cambridge in the UK or Yale, Stanford and MIT in the USA. The achievement in business drives the patriarchs to ponder deeply about the methods needed to sustain the family business, ensuring its continuous growth, and more importantly, succession. Investment in education always has a positive outcome and most of the families would like to invest in their family members, including female members, at this stage.

Apart from gradual elevation of education level, educational quality is also upgraded gradually as the family's wealth goes up. In stage five, family members can not only obtain qualifications from famous universities in Western countries, they can also gain higher degrees, such as Master's or doctorates. F4's, F9's and F14's families are examples of this.

Diversification and specialization is the sixth stage of educational advancement. Each family member is assigned to study a particular field. Such a practice creates a sense of interdependence among family members. Since each member needs the other members' professional expertise and advice, sibling division of labour becomes feasible and possible. Increased educational level helps them to solve conflicts in more effective and rational ways, therefore avoiding disharmonious conflict.

In order to have a clearer picture of the remarkable educational attainment of the Chaozhou families, let me make a comparison with the general population of Hong Kong. According to the Census and Statistics Department's reports, in 1961 only 1.41 per cent of the total population had received a university education. In 1971 the proportion rose slightly to 1.67 per cent. Later, in 1981, it reached 2.25 per cent, and in 1991 4.30 per cent. In 1981 and 1991 the Department's report also listed postgraduate education, and this proportion was 0.27 per cent and 0.33 per cent in 1981 and 1991, respectively (Census and Statistics Department 1969, 1972, 1982, 1992). Clearly, if we compare these ratios with the studied Chaozhou families, the later group's advancement is truly remarkable.

Educational attainment of the long-established families

However, if we compared the studied Chaozhou families with long-established families, the latter becomes far more outstanding. The heavy investment in education in these families confirms the traditional wisdom that improvement in education can enhance the socio-economic position of the family. To facilitate detailed discussion, the Ho Tung Family, Li Shek-pang family and Wing On Kwok family are cited as examples.

There are no firm details concerning the educational background of Ho Szeman, father of Ho Tung. Based on his background and the nature of his job, it is estimated that his educational level would have been around junior secondary. Since Ho Tung and his brothers, Ho Fook and Ho Kom-tong, graduated from Queen's College, an elite English school in Hong Kong, we can reasonably say that their educational attainment was far higher than the average of the population at the time. Equipped with such good educational qualifications, they surpassed their competitors both in the business and political arenas.

The second generation's educational level increased as their wealth expanded. Edward, Eva, Irene, Grace and Jean graduated from the University of Hong Kong. Florence was a Lingnan University alumnus. Ho Shai-lai was a general who was trained in colleges in the UK, France and USA. Ho Tung's illegitimate son, George Ho, was an alumnus of the University of California, Los Angeles. Many of the second generation also held university degrees.

Among the third generation members, Eric Ho-tung was a Georgetown University graduate, Ho Hung-ngai graduated from Columbia University, Ho Hung-chim obtained a doctoral degree from London University and Joseph Ho-tung graduated from Stanford University. Stanley Ho went to the University of Hong Kong in 1941, but his study was interrupted by the Japanese Occupation in 1942.

The fourth generation, like Ho Yau-chung, Pansy Ho and Daisy Ho, obtained their Master's degrees in Business Administration in the USA. Robert Ho was a legal practitioner working in the USA. Lawrence Ho was also a university graduate (Table 4.2).

The Li Shek-pang family is a typical example that demonstrates clearly the path of educational advancement. Like the Ho Tung family, the Li family is also

Table 4.2 Educational attainment of the Ho Tung family

Family member	*Name of institution*	*Field of study and degree obtained*
Ho Tung	Hong Kong Queen's College	Secondary
Ho Fook	Hong Kong Queen's College	Secondary
Ho Kom-tong	Hong Kong Queen's College	Secondary
Ho Shai-kim	Hong Kong University	Economics
Ho Shai-lai	Royal Military Academy, Woolwich	Military training
	Ecole d'Application d'Artillerie, Fontainebleau	Military training
	Command and General Staff School, Fort Leavenworth	Military training
Ho Irene	Hong Kong University	Art
Ho Eva	Hong Kong University	n/a
Ho Shai-yiu	n/a	University level
Ho George	UCLA	n/a
Eric Ho-tung	Georgetown University	Banking and finance
Joseph Ho-tung	Stanford University	Law
Ho Hung-ngai	Columbia University	Journalism and communication
Ho Hung-chim	University of Hong Kong and University of London	Radiotherapy and oncology PhD (Medicine)
Ho Hung-sun	University of Hong Kong	Interrupted by war
Ho Yau-long	A university in Canada	Business and Economics
Ho Lawrence	n/a	Lawyer in the USA
Ho Yau-chung	A university in the USA	MBA

Sources: I. Cheng 1976, 1997; Zheng and Wong 2007, 2008.

a large and well-established Hong Kong family. Many members play crucial roles in different areas. At only five years of age, Li Shek-pang came to Hong Kong to join his elder brother. With the help of a priest, Shek-pang enrolled at St Joseph's College, a famous secondary school in Hong Kong. After finishing his junior secondary school, he worked in his brother's shipping company. Later he founded his own enterprise. Although Shek-pang wanted his son to study further, he had to abandon his plans when he needed his eldest son, Koon-khun, to assist him in his business. This eased a 'labour shortage' and made his other sons' (Tse-fong, Lan-sang, Siu-pang and Chok-chung) education possible. Tse-fong was the first member of the Li family to get a Bachelor's degree. It marked the turning point in the family's educational achievement.

Educational achievement was far more remarkable in the third generation. Many of them (for example, Fook-shu and Fook-kwan) got their university degrees in Hong Kong. Others obtained their degrees from abroad, such as Fook-sean, Fook-cheung and Fook-kow. Some others even obtained higher degrees – such as Fook-siu, who obtained an MBA at Wharton Business School; Fook-chiu, who received a doctoral degree from the University of Hawaii; and Fook-kuen, who obtained his PhD from the University of Toronto.

Their educational achievement did not stop there. The fourth generation's performance went even higher. David Li graduated from Cambridge University with a Bachelor's degree in law and a Master's degree in art. Arthur Li also graduated from Cambridge, where he got a Bachelor's degree in medicine and a doctoral degree in surgery. Andrew Li also graduated from Cambridge, gaining a Bachelor's degree in art and a Master's degree in law. Other members, like Li Kwok-lun and Li Kwok-cheong, were also Cambridge alumni.

Li Man-kiu, Li Man-bun, Li Man-ying and Li Man-chuen represent the fifth generation of the Li family. Some of them have already graduated and joined the family-controlled bank, while some of them are still studying at Cambridge. In all likelihood, their educational attainment will be similarly outstanding (Table 4.3).

Like the Li and Ho Tung families, Wing On Kwok's family also did remarkably in education. Kwok Pui-fun was a farmer in Zhongshan who urged his sons to seek their fortune in the outside world. Although there was little formally known about the educational background of the founding brothers, it was thought that since they helped their father on the farm from an early age, they might only have reached primary or junior secondary level.

Most of the second generation of the Kwoks studied at Lingnan College. Some of them then studied overseas. For instance, Kwok Lam-po went to Manchester University in the UK, while Lamson Kwok studied at Stanford. The educational level had thus been raised.

A noticeable improvement in education came with the third generation. Many third-generation members earned doctoral degrees, including Philip Kwok, Chi-hon, Chi-piu and Chi-ho. Other members like Chi-leung, Chi-bun and Chi-yat obtained Master's degrees. Clearly, nearly all of the fourth-generation members were at least bachelor degree holders (Table 4.4).

For these super-wealthy families, their educational achievement more or less follows the proposed six-stage model. At stage one, we can clearly see that since most of the founders come from a poor family background, they would have had little chance for an education. For example, the Kwok brothers, Kwok Lock, Kwok Chun and Kwok Shun, were forced to halt their studies at an early age and left for Australia to seek their fortune.

At stage two, since the family business is at the 'striving' stage, some members are forced to help. For instance, Li Koon-chun was asked to help in the family firms, Nam Wo Hong and Wo Fat Sing, when he was only 15 years old. Although Li Shek-pang agreed in principle that it would be better for Koon-chun to have more education, he changed his mind when he really needed an extra pair of hands. He even took a pragmatic view in persuading Koon-chun that joining the family business could also give him a kind of education.

Educational achievement marks a distinctive change at stage three. As their family businesses expand gradually, pressure for 'family labour' reduces greatly, while resources for children's education increase substantially. Li Tse-fong, R.C. Lee, Fung Hong-hing, Hui Sze-fun and Kwok Lam-po represent the first members of their families to earn a university degree. Later on, these university graduates take over as heads of their families and lead their businesses to another stage of development.

Table 4.3 Educational attainment of the Li Shek-pang family

Family member	*Name of institutions*	*Field of study and degree obtained*
Li Shek-pang	St Joseph's College	Junior secondary
Li Koon-chun	St Joseph's College	Secondary level
Li Tse-fong	University of Hong Kong	Art
Li Lan-sang	n/a	Secondary level
Li Siu-pang	n/a	Secondary level
Li Chok-chung	n/a	Secondary level
Li Fook-shu	University of Hong Kong	Art
	University of London	Master's (accounting)
Li Fook-sean	University of Hong Kong	Art
	University of London	Law
Li Fook-wo	Boston University	Law
	New York University	MBA
Li Fook-sum	Institute of Chartered Accounts	Chartered Public Account
Li Fook-siu	University of Hong Kong	Art
	Wittenberg College	MBA
Li Fook-cheung	MIT	Engineering
Li Fook-kow	MIT	Master's (engineering)
Li Fook-kwan	University of Toronto	PhD (music)
Li Fook-tai	University of Hong Kong	Art
	University of Denver	MBA
Li Fook-pui	St John University, China	Political sciences
	University of Pennsylvania	MBA
Li Fook-luen	n/a	Dentist
Li Fook-chiu	University of Hong Kong	Medicine
	University of Hawaii	PhD (gynaecology)
Li Fook-hai	University of Hawaii	n/a
Li Fook-kuen	University of Hong Kong	Medicine
	St John's University, China	Medicine
Li David	University of Cambridge	Law and economics
	University of Cambridge	MBA
Li Arthur	University of Cambridge	PhD (surgery)
Li Kwok-lun	University of Cambridge	Medicine
Li Andrew	University of Cambridge	Art
	University of Cambridge	Master's (law)
Li Kwok-wai	University of Boston	MBA
Li Kwok-cheong	University of Cambridge	Medicine
Li Man-kiu	University of Cambridge	Business administration
Li Man-bun	University of Cambridge	Still studying
Li Man-ying	University of Cambridge	Still studying
Li Man-Chuen	University of Cambridge	Still studying

Sources: Ching 1999; *Capital* 1998c; Hung and Bun 1988; Poon 1995.

At stage four, both family size and business capacity expand remarkably. At this stage, they can have the financial ability to send their sons or grandsons to study abroad. In order to give their children a good-quality education, some of them prefer sending their offspring to famous universities such as Oxford and Cambridge in the UK, or Yale, Stanford and MIT in the USA. Female members also get equal opportunities for an education at this stage.

Table 4.4 Educational attainment of the Wing On Kwok family

Family member	*Name of institution*	*Field of study and degree obtained*
Kwok Lock	n/a	Primary level
Kwok Chin	n/a	Primary level
Kwok Shun	n/a	Primary level
Kwok Lamson	Lingnan College, China	n/a
Kwok Lambert	Lingnan College, China	Business
Kwok Lam-po	Lingnan College, China	n/a
	Manchester University	Dying and spinning
Kwok Lam-yeung	Lingnan College, China	n/a
Kwok Lam-shan	Lingnan College	n/a
	Stanford University	Master's
Kwok Philip	MIT	Physics
	Harvard University	PhD (physics)
Kwok Chi-hon	Yale University	PhD (economics)
Kwok Chi-bun	MIT	Master's
Kwok Chi-shun	MIT	Engineering
Kwok Chi-leung	University of Pennsylvania	MBA
Kwok Chi-hang	Stanford University	Law
Kwok Chi-piu	University of Chicago	PhD (biology)
Kwok Chi-yat	University of San Diecana	Master's (economics)
Kwok Chi-yan	UCLA	Pharmacy
Kwok Chi-ho	California Technology College	PhD (physics/chemistry)

Sources: *Capita* 1988b; Qi 1980; M.C. Ho 1991b; Kwok 1980; Wing On Holdings Limited 1981; Wing On Life Insurance 1975.

At stage five, nearly all of the children would have earned basic university degrees, while others have even obtained higher degrees. For instance, there are a total of five sons from the third generation of the Kwok family with doctoral degrees. Such a remarkable achievement explains why these wealthy long-established families could maintain their economic, social and political status in society from generation to generation. High educational qualifications ensure that the family enterprise has a larger stock of human capital and therefore an adequate supply of well-qualified, reliable and trusted talent.

Diversification and specialization are shown clearly at stage six. Different members are usually assigned to study different streams. For example, in Li Shek-pang's family, Fook-shu studied accounting and became a chartered accountant, and later chairman of the Bank of East Asia. Fook-sean studied law and became a high court justice. Fook-siu studied business at Wharton Business School and later became the founder of the Far East Exchange. Fook-cheung is a trained engineer and Fook-kwan is a professor in music who taught at the Hawaii University. Fook-chiu studied medicine and is an expert in gynaecology. Other families, like the Chau Wing-tai and the Wing On Kwok, also show similar patterns of educational diversification and specialization.

In short, not just the Chaozhou families put strong emphasis on raising their children's education level, long-established Hong Kong families also do so. Since these families have more than sufficient resources, they can afford to hire private teachers for their children, or send them overseas if necessary. In addition, these families also have an increased possibility of upgrading their children's educational quality or in diversifying their children's educational 'investment'. Through such a mechanism, the chance of sustaining family wealth or perpetuating social status can be enhanced.

Education and family business

The remarkable educational achievement of the studied families drives me to ask the following questions: Why do people from long-established and wealthy families do better at school when compared with the general public? Is it due to biological factors, economic factors or social factors? How can this educational achievement extend their influence in their business?

Although there are divergent views on educational performance, one thing is clear. They unanimously reject the biological explanation. Since all these families come from the same cultural background, this factor can be kept as a constant. Socio-economic background is suggested as the core factor that affects educational attainment (Jensen 1973; Boudon 1974). In order to motivate their children to study harder, many respondents 'formulated their own reward and punishment system'. In the fieldwork, some interesting examples were found. During an interview, F1's son said:

> I am the only son. I know that my parents adore me. My father, although a graduate of teachers' college, still kept the traditional mindset of favouring sons over daughters. I have two elder sisters, but I know I am 'the star of the family'. My father frequently told me stories when I was a child. Although he was quite busy, he still kept checking my homework regularly. When he found that I had made a mistake, for instance, writing a Chinese character incorrectly, he would teach me how to do it properly and the 'secret tactic' to avoid committing the same mistake again. When I got a good result in an examination, he would take me to the cinema or drive me to the countryside for sightseeing. I loved that and even now, I still dream about it. After I went to secondary school, I studied very hard even without father's direct guidance. He became even busier at that time. Later, when I went to study in Canada, my father asked me to write him a letter in Chinese at least twice a month. He told me that since I was Chinese, I should emphasize some important Chinese values. I found these teaching methods were good and I also used the same methods to teach my children. Today, when my children do well in extra-curricular activities, I will also take them sightseeing as a reward. It is rewarding for both my children and me.

Although F1's son still adheres to his father's method in teaching his children, he mentioned to me that one thing is different – he treats his sons and daughters equally and pays similar attention on them. Another respondent, F9, told me the story of his education:

> Father always emphasized that if one did not get a good education, one's life would be ruined. He was a well-disciplined man and stressed self-motivation. I remembered that one day I left school to go on a date. It was only puppy love but unfortunately my father learnt about it. He beat me heavily. It was due to my mother's intercession that I had narrowly escaped this 'punishment'. Father reprimanded me that if I did not learn from that lesson, he would kick me out the family. Since father needed to help my uncle, he had to leave school when he was young. Even then, he still showed great regret about this. He mentioned that he actually wanted to be a writer and really loved school. He put high priority on our education and asked my mother, who graduated from St Paul Girls' College in the 1940s, to take care of our education. When we were young, my mother taught us English. She also taught us how to memorize new words and idioms efficiently. She brought us lots of English storybooks and checked our homework regularly. I recollected that she paid particular attention to our English. She would give us candy if we studied hard. She also told us English stories and sometimes took us to see English movies. Mother played an influential role on our learning. Later, when my younger brother and I went to the States to attend high school, mother accompanied us. She stayed in the U.S. for a whole year to look after us until we were fully accustomed to the new environment. My father also asked a private teacher to teach us mathematics and science. When I graduated from university, my parents flew in to attend my graduation ceremony. It was the first time I saw my father's proud eyes on me.

There are other similar examples from the long-established families. For instance, the Cheung Chuk-shan family states emphatically that if any family member wants to continue their study, their costs and school fees would be borne by the 'family educational trust fund'. When any of them achieves something academically, they will conduct a formal ceremony in the ancestral hall. That is, when family members are about to enter university or when any of them are accepted by a university, the patriarchs/matriarchs will represent the whole family and will offer incense to their ancestors and the gods to acknowledge the achievements (Chuk 1996). Through such practices, we can see that the family stresses the importance of education.

The Li Shek-pang family have their own method for keeping their children motivated to study. When the family became better off, Shek-pang wanted his eldest son, Koon-chun, who left school early, to further his studies. He tried to persuade him of the importance of education, especially English, an important language in the colony of Hong Kong. Koon-chun, however, was adamant and refused to accept. As a last resort, Shek-pang simply offered Koon-chun several thousand dollars in cash – a huge sum of money at that time – as a reward if he was willing to go to evening school. This method worked. Koon-chun went back to school. Later, he became an influential businessman and a Justice of the Peace. Coincidentally, Koon-chun's eldest son, Fook-shu, used a similar method to urge his son, David Li, to take a particular subject. Fook-shu wanted David to study accounting and hoped that he could take up an important post in the Bank of East Asia. Originally, David declined to do so. Fook-shu then offered a financial incentive of £5,000 and a new car if David passed an accounting examination. Tempted by this reward, he studied hard and finally gained his accounting qualification at Cambridge University (Ching 1999). From these stories, one can easily sense the importance of education in the eyes of the patriarch.

In order to influence their sons' decisions about their education, the patriarchs may have different methods. For instance, Chau Kai-bong had his heart set on studying art and film producing. His father, Sir Shek-nin Chau, however, preferred him to study law and hoped that he could join the family business. Kai-bong was not willing to give up his dreams at first, but he 'fell into the trap' when his father bought him a luxury car. Kai-bong finally joined the Middle Temple in England and later was admitted as a solicitor (Ho 1991b).

Some special features can be highlighted here. Many parents pay great attention to their children's education by either directly teaching their children or employing family tutors to do so. They also put strong emphasis on their children's performance in school. As the family becomes better off, the investment in their children's education increases in parallel. For instance, sons and daughters may have the equal chance to receive education. In fact, many female members also perform brilliantly academically. For example, Ho Tung's daughters, Eva, Irene, Grace and Jean; Cheung Chuk-shan's granddaughters, Miu-ching, Miu-ping, Wai-yin, Wai-chenga and Wai-ming; and the daughters of F14, F17 and F22 are good examples. Clearly, we can see that good educational performance and qualifications further implies better life chances in the next round of competition.

In the eyes of the founding entrepreneurs, education for their posterity is regarded as 'the whole family's welfare'. They usually encourage their progeny to study more. In addition, they also deliberately assign them to study different fields and subjects. It is generally believed that through such mechanisms, family members can excel in various areas. The following are some examples.

During the interviews, although some respondents claimed that they were liberal, open-minded, and their children were 'free to choose' their field of study, many of their children's decisions more or less followed their patriarch's expectations. There is impressive evidence that their children's field of study is largely related to the family businesses. By combining Table 2.1 with Table 4.1 in correlating their family businesses and educational attainment, a clear picture can be shown (Table 4.5).

In Table 4.5, we can see an overall picture showing a strong correlation between the specialization of their family businesses and their fields of study. Amongst these 26 families, nearly all of them have sons or daughters who took business, management or business-related subjects, such as accounting, economics or banking and finance. For instances, F1's business focused on producing poultry feed, thus his son studied organic chemistry. F1 frequently asked his son nutrition and health questions. Since his son wanted to improve the quality

Table 4.5 Family businesses and children's field of study: a correlation

Family	*Major field of businesses*	*Major field of study or professional training*
F1	Poultry feed production	Organic chemistry
F2	Semi-conductor, property investment	Engineering, business administration, economics
F3	Rice trading, mobile ice-cream business	Economics
F4	Rice importation, godown, banking and insurance	Financial and banking training, business administration
F5	Imitation jewellery, taxi services, property	Business administration
F6	I-C manufacturing, property	Mechanical engineering, business administration
F7	Banking, financial investment, insurance	Economics, accounting
F8	Clock and watch manufacture, property	Business administration, mechanical engineering
F9	Gold trading, banking, insurance, property	Business administration
F10	Jeans manufacture, property	Business administration
F11	Shipping, button manufacture, household appliances trading, cement trading	Accounting
F12	Rice importation and wholesaling, warehousing	International business
F13	Rice wholesaling, textiles and garments, property	Economics, accounting
F14	Cotton fabric, restaurant, property	Business administration, civil engineering
F15	Rice importation, gold trading, financial services	Economics
F16	Rice trading, deposit-taking company, property	Civil engineering, finance and accounting
F17	Plastic flowers, decorations product, property	Economics
F18	Dry food trading, property	Accounting and finance
F19	Rice importation, property	Economics, accounting and auditing
F20	Garments and textiles, property	Business administration, accounting
F21	Decoration products, leather clothing, property	Economics, design
F22	Secretarial and taxation services	Auditing and accounting, business administration
F23	Solicitors and notary services	Law
F24	Feather garments, property	Business administration
F25	Textiles, camera production	Business and management
F26	Garments and textiles, tourism, property	Textile manufacturing, business administration

Sources: Interviews 1997–2000; Table 2.1 and Table 4.1.

of poultry feed, he was asked to supervise a research and development team in the company when he first joined the family business.

To sum up, although parents' teaching methods may be different, their aim of instigating their children's interest in business is similar. This phenomenon implies at least two salient facts: First, parents' expectations and influence creates a strong influence on their children's field of study. Second, children's desire and willingness to take up the family business is related to their familiarity in the field, their leadership skills and the business networks they have already built up.

Parental instruction, persuasion and rewards are some of the methods used to direct their children's career. Some parents directly ask their sons to study a particular subject in believing that 'it is good for the family's development' or for their sons' career. Many patriarchs see education as a long-term investment. In *Lineage Record of the Chau Family*, it clearly states,

> [Chau] Wing-tai had three sons, Man-fai [also known as Chau Siu-kay), Yat-fai (also known as Chau Yam-kiu], and Tai-fai [also known as Chau Cheuk-fan]. Wing-tai considered that as international transport and business was becoming more prosperous, foreign languages would also become increasingly important. He then assigned Man-fai and Yat-fai to study Western languages, Tai-fai to learn Chinese. As a result, they would keep abreast with the changing world. Because of the specialization in study amongst his sons, the Chau family gradually emerged as an aristocratic family in Hong Kong.
>
> (Chau 1926: 2)

Some parents use a less authoritarian approach. In order to influence their son's decision, they offer gifts or rewards to encourage them to choose those streams that they wish them to pursue. For example, F14 bought his son a car to attract him to the business. Other parents may deliberately talk to their sons about the business when they are still young. It can motivate their children's interest towards the family business. This kind of 'socialization' is influential in their children's decisions on education.

Although parental influence is critical and far-reaching, their children's own decisions should not be underestimated. Starting from childhood, their parents might have told them stories about business. They have also gained some knowledge related to running a business, so that when they grow up, they might want to learn something concrete. Their family business, in fact, gave them a chance to test their business theories. In addition, a sense of personal commitment and responsibility towards their family should not be ruled out. David Li and Arthur Li's cases are good examples.

> Soon, the children of Daisy and Fook-shu, grew up. Their eldest daughter Jeanette become a doctor and specialized in radiology... David and Arthur, wanted to be doctors, too. However, Koon-chun felt that there should not be

> too many doctors in the family and advised David to follow in his father's footsteps in the family and became an accountant. Arthur could not be persuaded. Since childhood he had wanted to be a doctor, and so he did, become one of the best surgeons of his day.
>
> (Ching 1999: 139)

Arthur Li insisted on making his own decisions and became a professor of medicine. David Li followed his father's footsteps. Why were these two brothers' decisions completely different? A more appropriate explanation is that David, the eldest son from the biggest branch, was socialized to shoulder the responsibility of taking up the family business when he was still a baby. Thus, he showed greater enthusiasm and was more eager to accept his father's arrangements. David joined the Bank of East Asia and became chairman. This completely different career path reflects that, apart from parental influence, children still possess some discretion in their choices.

Throughout this chapter, it is found that investment and diversification in education is enormous in many families. Such practice increases the 'species' and therefore enhances family stability and continuity. Research in evolutionary biology confirms Darwin's observation that diversity is the key to adaptation. This principle can also be applied to Chinese family businesses. If different family members can be directed to study different fields, it is believed that their family businesses' competitiveness and adaptability can be enhanced.

On the other hand, diversification of education can also indirectly reduce the potentiality for conflict, since some members of the family may study professional subjects and eventually become professionals. Then, fewer family members compete for leadership or management positions. Thus, internal family conflict may be greatly reduced.

Another influential function is the screening involved in marital selection (Brittain 1977: 2). Educational background is one of the key factors in mate selection. Generally speaking, young people with similar educational and economic backgrounds tend to gravitate together and eventually marry (for detailed discussion, please refer to Chapter 5).

As an alternative explanation, Brittain (ibid.: 23–4) goes further and argues that good educational attainment can affect people's socio-economic opportunities in the next round of competition. He states,

> A man's chances of economic success are strongly influenced by his start in life, as provided by his parents.... The most obvious way in which status is transmitted is through the inheritance of educational opportunity.... The inheritance of educational attainment is a significant factor in economic status transmission.

In other words, good education can help a family business to expand. In addition, the new 'educationally upgraded' generation can also bring new concepts and management ideas to the family firms. Such a reformation can increase their business' competitive edge and image. When Philip Kwok was asked if his stepping down from the chairmanship of the Wing On Group in the 1980s would topple the development of the group, he simply replied, 'There are lots of well-educated people in the Kwok family. We are not worried about a decline in leadership' (Ho 1991a: 232).

With an increase in education level, a family's social networks can be extended exponentially: 'It is clear that a man's birth into the business and professional echelons enormously increased the probabilities of his subsequently holding similar positions' (Warner and Abegglen 1955: 42). Such improvement can further ensure wealth accumulation in the next generation. In other words, we can summarize certain findings as follows: first, the higher the educational achievement, the larger the size of business; second, as more members are absorbed into management, a high frequency of reformations occurs; and third, the greater the number of children, the greater the diversification into various professions.

Establishing leadership

After a comparison and elaboration on education and family business, now let us turn to another critical element of human capital: leadership. Apart from heavy investment in children's education, many families also try to develop the younger generation's leadership skill so that when the baton is passed on, their family businesses remain prosperous. Since we are focusing on learnable leadership skills, inborn charismatic leadership is excluded from the subsequent discussion.

In the previous chapter, we learnt that the sudden deaths of Fu Kong, Lee Hysan, Lam But-chung, F7's grandfather and F2's brother and father were considered serious crises in their family businesses. In fact, these crises are critical events to test the leadership abilities of each individual. The heirs of these five families forged their new leadership during a crisis and emerged as influential figures in the community. After the crisis, these families not only brought their businesses out from trouble, but also triggered another stage of expansion. F4 told his story:

> Personally, I was a close friend of F7's father and Lam Kuan-chuang. My father had helped these two families to overcome their crises. At first, although these two men were worried, they did not give up. They tried their best to seek support from their business partners and friends. They overcame the difficulties eventually. I know they learnt a lot. I admire their endurance and fighting spirit.

In fact, we can use a famous saying from Mencius, a great philosopher in the Warring States Period (453–221 BC) to further illustrate this point.

> Thus, when Heaven is about to confer a great office on any man, it first exercises his mind with suffering, and his sinews and bones with toil. It

> exposes his body on hunger, and subjects him to extreme poverty. It confounds his undertakings. By all these methods it stimulates his mind, hardens his nature, and supplies his incompetencies. Men for the most part err, and are afterwards able to reform. They are distressed in mind and perplexed in their thoughts, and then they arise to vigorous reformation. When things have been evidenced in men's looks, and set forth in their words, then they understand them.... From these things we see how life springs from sorrow and calamity, and death from ease and pleasure.
>
> (*The Works of Mencius* 1949: 447)

Although many of my respondents agree with Weber that a crisis can test leadership, in this study, I find most of them chose to prevent it rather than letting it run its course. It is unlikely that they would initiate a crisis to test their children's leadership abilities – understandably, as if they cannot control the crisis, their family business will crumble. Thus, even though many founders know that handling crises forges leadership, they dare not to let it occur. In other words, 'crisis-tested leadership' is not a commonly used method for establishing leadership.

Unlike crisis-generated leadership, education-initiated leadership can be rationally planned in advance and is therefore frequently adopted. Bacon says 'knowledge is power'. Good educational achievement can enhance one's social power or expertise and thus can be regarded as a major indicator of leadership. Knowledge-dominant leadership is very important in those fields in which know-how is a prerequisite. Seeing that knowledge is part of the source of leadership. Many parents try to improve their children's knowledge by giving them more education. F11 commented,

> If you want your son to be a leader, give them more education. If you want them to pick up the business, also give them more education. Nothing is securer then knowledge. You leave them money, it could drain away quickly. Only give them education, or a professional qualification, they will thank you when they have problems.

As mentioned earlier, the educational achievement of the studied families is remarkable. Although higher educational attainment cannot definitely ensure a stronger leadership, its positive effects cannot be ruled out. With better education, one's leadership image can be strengthened. In addition, improvement in education can also enhance the family with a secure supply of qualified personnel. Selvin (1960: 95) concludes from his research that 'it is therefore not surprising that education has a pronounced effect on a trainee's behavior [leadership training]'. He even suggests that 'education means more than intellectual activity and the acquisition of knowledge. It is closely related to social class.' His finding further supports the idea that knowledge is one of the conditions of leadership. This also explains why many family leaders put strong emphasis on their children's education.

Achievement can generate leadership. If one has achieved in certain areas, one's ability and leadership in that field can generally be confirmed. In fact, achievement can also attest to one's ability to face challenges. Many leaders' status is reinforced when they achieve something. This explains why new leaders prefer to carry out progressive or ambitious projects. The case of Henry K.S. Cheng is a good example. On reaching 70 Cheng Yu-tong, the founder of the New World Group, passed the baton to his son, Henry Cheng. When Henry first took over, he was regarded as 'green and inexperienced', and he himself realized that he had a less than favourable image. Shortly after taking over the leadership, he conducted a series of expansionary investments, hoping to walk out from his father's shadow. He mobilized a total of $6 billion in takeover projects. Such projects included using $0.76 billion to buy Key-lap Enterprises, $0.54 billion to buy in further controlling shares of the Wing On Group (eventually failed), $0.48 billion to buy the Renaissance Harbour View Hotel, and $4.2 billion to take over the Miramar Hotel Group, all within a short period of time (Sito 2000). Clearly, by launching these projects, he hoped he could establish his authority and leadership.

Social status is another key indicator for leadership building. By definition, social status means 'social position or rank in relation to others, or relative rank in a hierarchy of prestige' (*The Webster's Third New International Dictionary* 1986). Higher social status implies higher social prestige and greater influence in the community. Social status more or less relates to social power. In order to train their children's leadership, many patriarchs encourage their children to participate in social service and charitable work (for details, please refer to Chapter 5). F4, a senior banker, showed us his strong emphasis on his sons' participation in community and social services. He said,

> Achievement, social status and leadership are interconnected. When you achieve something [either in education, social service, politics or business], your social status rises, and your leadership status is confirmed. To my mind, leadership is not inborn. If you want to build your leadership, you have to train up yourself. Participating in or organizing social activities is good experience. I therefore encourage my sons to do so.

Although F4's perception is not flawless, it at least reflects that there is a learnable aspect of leadership. In fact, he is not the only one who voiced this opinion. Ward's (1987a: 198) comment also clearly reflects his affirmative stance.

> The would-be president must be familiar with everything from formal management analysis techniques to business etiquette. He or she must be prepared to assume leadership roles in the business, the family, and the community. Often, the best way to acquire these capabilities is from peers: presidents and the president-to-be. Many trade associations sponsor young executive groups for this express purpose. A popular alternative is the Young Presidents Organization. Based in New York City, this group holds

> workshops, seminars, and meetings and in general offers young presidents the opportunity to fraternize with one another.

The formation of the Youth Committee of the CCC is believed to accomplish such a goal. Another similar example is the Overseas Students' Union of Yan Chai Hospital. Through organizing or participating in these social activities, children of similar backgrounds can interact with each other. In fact, the source of leadership is not confined to the above-mentioned aspects. Other factors, such as morality and religious status, are equally important. In his book, *Leadership and Values*, Silin (1976: 62) argues that a business leader is recognized by subordinates as a morally superior man:

> An individual who leads because of his overwhelming superiority based not simply on technical competence, but also on a certain mystical quality of understanding.... The leader ... will work for the good of the group rather than for his own interest.

Silin realizes that a person's social status can upgrade his moral superiority and therefore enhance his leadership. Skinner (1958), on the other hand, suggests that in the Chinese value system, leadership is a function of six important elements. They are: (1) attainment of wealth; (2) quest for respect/prestige; (3) quest for power/authority; (4) attainment of skills; (5) religious values; and (6) quest for rectitude and enlightenment. In fact, these six elements largely cover Weber's (1947) six types of charisma transmission – tradition, revelation, designation, recognition, heredity and ritual.

In this research, except for the religious factor, I find that most of the studied families have covered these elements when training their children for leadership. To sum up, it seems quite clear that one of the most important factors in maintaining a family business is not simply reassigning ownership, but also establishing the successor's credibility as having strong leadership. Without strong leadership, it is believe that even great wealth can be drained away easily and quickly.

Passing the leadership baton

Since most patriarchs know the importance of leadership in affecting the fate of the family and business, they usually pay strong emphasis to the passing of it from one generation to the next. In the past, people thought that the process happened naturally and therefore pay little attention to the issue. However, without proper arrangement of the transmission of leadership, trouble usually appears. Leach (1991: 13) states:

> It is not simply a move from one generation to the next – it is a revolution in which the culture of the organization is reconstructed by the young people who bring them new ideas about how the business should be run, how it is to develop, new loyalties, new staff, and so on.

Even when the new leader has been clearly designated and the succession process is deliberately planned, problems may still arise. In the following paragraphs, let me discuss the process of leadership transferral by applying my participatory observation and citing some typical cases.

When talking about the preparation for new leadership, the first question that worries most founders is the ability and skill of the new leader. Conger and Kanungo (1998: 30) comment that 'Successors may not possess the strategic skills and other abilities crucial to ensure the firm's future leadership.' In order to solve this problem, many respondents tried to develop their children's entrepreneurial characteristics while they were young. Some bring their sons to business meetings, some tell them stories about management and business-related issues, while some ask their children to take business-related subjects at school. Although their methods are different, their aim is the same. They want to stimulate their children's interest in business, so that they can fill in their shoes some day. One of the respondents, F5, shared with me his story during our interview:

> My grandpa always told me stories about business philosophy and life. These stories formulated my leadership spirit when I was young. Some of the most important ideas he conveyed to me are: 'do not be too greedy, otherwise swindlers will make use of your greediness and cheat you' or 'a leader must think wider and look higher, otherwise, his business will shrink and wither'. All these are useful values that formulated my business ethic.

In addition to business values, other traditional values are also inculcated and transmitted. Some of them believe in harmony, fraternity and unity. In the past it was not unusual to hear that 'sibling conflict leads to disunity and dissipation of the family business'. In order to avoid this, many patriarchal entrepreneurs teach their offspring how to maintain a good and harmonious relationship with one another. They urge them to live amicably, work together and cooperate with each other. F15's feeling about his parents' teaching is just such an example.

> My father always tells us to love and help each other. I have five brothers. Due to my father's influence, we get on well, our relationship is therefore very good. I have also passed this value on to my sons. I have asked them to maintain good relations with my nephews. We have the same ancestor. Blood is thicker than water. As far as I can see there has never been any serious dispute amongst them. That is why our business is still intact. Even though we had *'fengjia'* [divided the family estate] decades ago, and some of my brothers and nephews have migrated to the USA and UK, we still keep in close contact. They also wholeheartedly delegate us to run the family business.

Apart from giving their children a good education, some patriarchs show strong enthusiasm in socializing their children's leadership in business through informal on-the-job training. They use different methods to arouse their offspring's interest at an early age.

> Tycoons in Hong Kong have their special ways in training up their children. When his two sons were very young, Li Ka-shing held regular family meeting to discuss with them about business matter.... When Frank W.K. Tsao, one of the influential shipping tycoons, was a student, his father had made him to undergo an intensive training program.... Lui Chi-wah, a construction tycoon, on the contrary, asked his sons to go to the construction site to work from the lowest level.
>
> (Ho 1991b: 156)

Chan and Chiang's (1994: 331) story of Tan Kok Kheng, the fifth son of Tan Kak Kee, is insightful:

> On the eve of my first day at work, I was told not to be driven by his chauffeur to work. Instead, I had to walk for half a mile from my home at Meyer Road, near Katong Park, to Tanjong Katong Road to catch a six-seater small 'mosquito' bus to work. For six months, I did this unfailingly, much to the amusement of my fellow workers who occasionally sneered at me, calling out at me sarcastically towkay kia [the boss's son]. Underlying my father's seemingly mean move was chihku, literally meaning eating bitterness, or enduring hardship. This was a common and traditional practice among Chinese immigrants in Southeast Asia to prepare their children by toughening them up before they began their careers.

In fact, we should bear in mind that even when the new leader is announced, the patriarch may still hold the paramount leadership role. Silin (1976: 177) comments:

> Succession to headship and other status in enterprises is generally left unclear. Leaders, especially the boss, do not designate successors but choose to keep the issue cloudy. Among other things, such actions prevent potential successors from developing an independent power base.

Another point that we need to bear in mind is about the transferability of leadership. Although Weber argues that the Chinese equal inheritance system is favourable for heredity charisma transmission, the process is not clearly stated. In fact, this process takes time and patience. To a certain extent, if the process is not carefully monitored, it can also be quite problematic.

From the time the new leader commences his training to the formal announcement of his taking over, and then to the actual retirement of the predecessor, many patriarchs still keep their eyes on their successor's performance. Apart from direct supervision, some of the patriarchs may assign some loyal senior staff to guide the new leaders in managing the business. When the patriarchs retire or die, these senior staff may become mentors to the young leaders. This often occurs in wealthy families as their businesses are usually larger in size and more established, so a smooth transmission is therefore highly emphasized.

However, internal resistance is one of the major problems that may occur. Frequently, when the new leader is too ambitious and too hasty in establishing his own status, he may institute drastic measures and overlook the original organizational structure. Then, friction will inevitably emerge. In my fieldwork, the interviewees seldom discussed their personal experiences on taking over the leadership. Instead, they talked quite a lot about other people's stories. For instance, one of the often-told stories in their circle is about an influential Chaozhou rice importing company in the 1970s. When the father announced his intention to retire because of his poor health, his son was asked to take over the helm. The son was over-confident and paid little attention to his older employees' opinions. As a result, two of his jobbers (one of them his sworn uncle, his father's sworn brother) left the firm. These two men later started their own wholesaling firms. In rice business, jobbers play an important role in procuring rice. The resignation of these key personnel nearly toppled the company.

A successful transfer of leadership requires that many hurdles be overcome. From my respondents' stories, we can learn that many parents paid great attention in establishing their children's leadership. They tried to reduce any friction or resistance that could arise when transferring leadership, and establishing their children's leadership is an important factor in this. Making the power transferral smooth is another. Theoretically, a rational, well-planned and successfully conducted reformation can enhance the image of the new leadership, while an unsuccessful one can seriously weaken the transmission. It is true that not all family businesses can overcome all these hurdles and therefore keep their business from one generation to the next.

The essence of leadership

In this chapter I have discussed the transfer of human capital with a special emphasize on education and leadership. From my research data, we can see that many of our studied families place strong emphasis on their children's education in order to raise their human capital. However, as we all know, education is easier to inculcate, while leadership is harder to establish. One of the core factors that make leadership very difficult to establish is its inborn nature. It is generally believed that leadership is tested instead of learnt from a textbook. Thus, even though many families have spent lots of time and money in forging the new generation's leadership, only very few of them can achieve the satisfactory result they desired.

It goes without saying that leadership is the prime mover for the family business. Losing this leadership can imply a failure in business: 'It is a commonplace observation that leadership plays an important role in the creation, survival, growth, and decay of organizations' (Conger and Kanungo 1998: 3). Seymour (1993: 263) further concludes, 'When the firm lacks an adequate succession plan or the next generation has not been trained for leadership, the result may be business failure or the loss of family continuity in the firm.' In other words, the vital part of leadership transferral is to maintain a spirit of innovation and creativeness. Unlike the manager, who is responsible for coping with organizational complexity, the leader is responsible for coping with dynamic change (Kotter 1990). If family heads cannot tackle the problem of establishing new leadership during succession, their businesses will become less competitive and less stable.

In their book, *Charismatic Leadership in Organizations*, Conger and Kanungo (1998: 8) suggest that the essential characteristics of leadership are: (1) challenging the status quo; (2) having a creative vision for the future of the organization; and (3) promoting appropriate changes in followers' values, attitudes and behaviours by using empowering strategies and tactics. To simplify the matter, we can see that the key idea of leadership is to 'challenge, create and change'. If the new leadership cannot keep on challenging the existing system by taking creative measures in managing all these changes, the likelihood of maintaining the family business will be low, and as a result, their businesses may sooner or later be driven out of the market.

To sum up, in this chapter, we can clearly see that both the studied Chaozhou and other long-established families in fact have invested tremendously in human capital, particularly in education, with a strong intention that through such a mechanism, their family fortunes can be kept from generation to generation. However, although education level can be raised as more resources are 'invested', entrepreneurship and leadership can't be easily inculcated even though much effort is made. Thus, there is still great uncertainty over whether family business can be passed on continuously.

5 The transfer of social capital

In addition to the transfer of economic capital and human capital, social capital is regarded as another critical element that determines the success or failure of family business transmission. Unlike physical capital, such as land, real estate, machinery, jewellery and vehicles that can be simply transferred by reassigning ownership, personal ties and social connections are complex and abstract, and therefore cannot be transmitted by using similar procedures. Similarly, unlike educational attainment and professional qualifications, which can be obtained through formal examination, personal connections are relatively harder to cultivate or transmit. In order to make the succession process smooth and successful, many patriarchs try to transmit their social capital to their children as much as possible.

Generally speaking, during early childhood, the founding patriarch may try to involve their children in the family business, either by their direct participation, or involving them in social gatherings. If they want to pass the leadership to the next generation, they must first cultivate their successors' interest in business and give them working experience, personal connections and business networks. To use a Chinese expression, one should establish his *jianghu diwei*, which means his social status in the community, so that he would have the sufficient 'standing or authority' to lead the enterprise.

Personal connections as social capital

We should first discuss the inculcating of personal connections. As there is no such thing as a perfect market, personal connections 'emerge naturally' for reducing transaction cost and business risk (Williamson 1975; Landa 1983). Literally, personal connections mean special ties with different persons. Since such connections can 'facilitate certain actions of individuals who are within the structure' (Coleman 1990: 302), it falls clearly into the category of social capital. Although it is difficult to obtain solid data for quantifying interpersonal connections, one can use special social connections to illustrate how it is built and how it functions. Generally, the sworn relation, affiliation to certain associations and old school networks are typical examples of personal connections.

The 'sworn relationship' or *jieyi*, literally meaning 'forming a righteous and just relationship', is a kind of social relation forged for a particular purpose.

When people want to build a sworn relationship, they may formally conduct a ritual ceremony, such as taking an oath before God or informally making a pledge to each other that they will keep their oath. A sworn relationship can be father/mother–son/daughter, brother–brother and sister–sister. The story of Liu Bei, Kwan Yu and Chang Fei in the Three Kingdoms period (AD 220–65) is a frequently quoted example. Silin (1976: 52) writes: 'Sworn brothers are expected to treat each other as brothers and to lend support to one another's families in time of financial and ritual need.' The sense of mutual support is very obvious.

Since *jieyi* is a very personal and informal thing, few people like to disclose it publicly. During my interviews, quite a large number of interviewees preferred to keep this as 'private and personal'. However, there are some useful examples that can be used for discussion. For instance, F26 and one of the directors of the CCC are close friends. They frequently meet together. Before F26's son left Hong Kong to study in Australia, his friend and his son swore to become 'father and son'. In the oath-taking ceremony, his friend gave a jade pendant to his son, while his son presented him a golden hare (the sworn-father was born in the Year of the Hare, one of the 12 animals of the Chinese zodiac) in return. Through this kind of special connection, F26 and his friend's relationship became closer.

Another case concerns F5's son and F20's son. F5's son and F20's son are members of the Youth Committee of the CCC. They had a close and intimate relationship from the time they were former classmates in primary and secondary school. Later, they were sent abroad to study at different universities. After finishing their education, they returned and joined their family businesses, and got in contact again. Coincidentally, at both parents' recommendations, they joined the Youth Committee. According to F5, his son later made an oath with F20's son and they became 'sworn brothers'. Both families attended their oath-taking ceremony and hoped that 'this pair of brothers would help each other in time of need, and share tears and laughter in their life'. The sworn relationship signified that both families were eager to forge a well-connected relationship.

There are lots of other examples. 'Starting from the age of sixteen, Chiang Kai-shek [Jiang Jieshi] started to build his personal connections via *jieyi*. During the warlord Period in the 1920s, Chiang had made a total of 30 sworn brothers' (Bao 1997: 1). Although Chiang's case is an exceptional one, there are some other examples that can be used to indicate the influential connections of *jieyi*.

One more example is Ellen Li (mother-in-law of Philip Kwok, who is a member of the Wing On Kwok family), the first Chinese woman legislative councillor in Hong Kong. In July 1987 she held a formal oath-taking ceremony and declared to take 18 sworn daughters altogether. In the oath-taking ceremony the sworn mother and daughters pledged to share with one another the ups and downs of life. In fact, all of the 18 ladies were wives of famous people in Hong Kong (Table 5.1). Some of them were Peggy Pei (former legislative councillor, chairwoman of the Family Planning Association, and wife of Gilbert Lam), Kathy Kwok (wife of Thomas Lee, former secretary of home affairs), Junie Cheng (granddaughter of Ho Tung), Ivy Kwok (wife of Gordon Wu), Helena

Table 5.1 Names of the sworn daughters of Ellen Li

God-daughter's name	*God-daughter's husbands' name*
Victoria Sin	Mr Sun
Gloria Chan	Mr Wong
Junie Cheng	Mr Dandiker
Rene Chan	–
Peggy Pei	Mr Gilbert Lam
Vivian Chan	Mr Peter Chan
Denise Lo	–
Lily Lo	Mr Choy
Kathy Kwok	Mr Thomas Lee
May Yuan	Mr Chow Kwan-lim
May Ma	Mr Wilson Chan
Rita Tong	Mr Liu Lit-chun
Kitty Yip	Mr David Lee
Sally Chan	Mr Chan Tak-kwong
Helena Kwong	Mr Cheung Yuk-leong
Nancy Chan	Mr Hans Tang
Vivian Fong	Mr Patrick Poon
Lucy Chan	Mr Stephen Lau
Susan Tam	Mr Wong Wah-sang
Erminia Hung	Mr Chow Huk-wing
Maria Wong	Mr Peter Chan
Marina Mok	Mr Gallent Ho
Eva Fung	Mr Woo Wing-fai
Ivy Kwok	Mr Gordon Wu

Sources: Li 1993, 1998.

Note
All names are direct quotations. No pinyin is given in the glossary.

Kwong (wife of Cheung Yuk-leung, member of the Cheung Chuk-shan family) and Marina Mok (wife of Gallent Ho).

Another example is Sir Shiu-kin Tang, who is a sworn son of Hui Oi-chow. Such special connections reflect the intertwined relationship between the Huis and the Tangs (Ho 1991b). One more example is Tam Oi-ling, the daughter-in-law of Cheung Chuk-shan, who is a sworn daughter of Mrs Fung Ping-fun (Fung Ping-shan family). Tam Oi-ling's aunt, Woo Po-king, is in fact the wife of Li Fook-shu (Li Shek-pang family). Cheng Ka-shing, son of Cheng Yu-tong, one of the most influential tycoons in Hong Kong, is a sworn son of Kathy Chiu. Kathy's father is the famous filmmaker and tycoon, Chiu Sheung-chow. Cheng Yu-tong is the sworn father of Ming Mei-lin. Mei-lin's father, Ming Ka-fook, is a famous property developer in Hong Kong (*Apple Daily* 3 September 1999).[1] Through these kinds of connections, intertwined social networks can be formed.

Social and commercial associations are another kind of connection that is believed to be useful for upgrading one's social capital. Such organizations include townsmen associations, clansmen associations, professional associations and commercial associations. These connections can improve their mutual understanding, enhance sentiment and facilitate information flow. In their book, *Stepping Out:The Making of Chinese Entrepreneurs*, Chan and Chiang (1994: 339) try to support this point by quoting one of their respondents' stories for reference.

> I joined the Ee Hoe Hean Club .. and concurrently also joined See Teong Wah's club called the Goh Loo. The latter was called the 'bankers' institute' because most of the directors of all the Chinese banks, Ho Hong Bank, Overseas Chinese bank, Commercial Bank – were members of the Goh Loo Club. The chairman of the Goh Loo Club was concurrently chairman of the Overseas Chinese Bank.... I joined the Club because the members were all bankers. Also it was next to the Weekly Entertainment Club whose members were all Babas, which I had the intention to join.... I joined about twelve clubs in one year. I eventually joined the Singapore Garden Club which included people like Song Ong Sian, Lim Boon Keng and all that.

Being members of the same association, their interactions can be enhanced. Through repeated interaction, their relationship can become stronger and more intimate. Such a relationship can further reinforce their social position in society. Omohundro (1983: 68) argues: 'Taking on something of the character of a lineage and a sworn brotherhood society, the sib association encourages closeness between men of the same surname and provides a court of appeal when business disputes involving its members arise.'

In this study, the CCC can be used as an example to illustrate the establishment of personal connections. As its name suggests, all members are of Chaozhou origin. They share a common language, culture and identity. Based on such common background, they further share with one another market information and experience in doing business, lend support to each other during times of trouble, and therefore can forge a close-knit social web. F2's comment offers an insightful idea about such a linkage: 'In the CCC, we know each other very well. We are all close friends. Now, more young people have joined. They are sons or grandsons of some senior directors. I hope they would also cultivate close relations like us.'

Clearly, in many patriarchs' eyes, encouraging children to participate in social and business activities can bring certain palpable advantages, such as greater exposure to society and business as well as better life experiences. Both are key elements for leadership building.

Extending the connections

In order to transmit their social capital from one generation to the next, many large family businesses have also initiated a mechanism of interlocking directorship – a powerful and frequently used method in extending lateral business linkages. What is interlocking directorship? It means that members of the board of directors of one company act as directors, either executive or non-executive, of other companies, while other companies' directors also join that company in exchange (Wong 1991). Scott and Griff (1984) point out that an interlock is created when two companies have a director in common. If a director sits on two or more boards, he or she is called a 'multiple director'. This is also called a 'tight interlock'. Through such linkages, business interests can be enhanced and a 'high level of cohesion among the dominant stratum of business leaders' will be created (ibid.). That explains why Useem (1984) sees interlocking directorates as an instrument for reinforcing inter-corporate resource exchanges.

Levine and Roy (1979) offer substantial empirical support for the strong connection of directors among companies. They found that among a total of 8,623 directors in the UK, 82 per cent only sit on one board, 18 per cent sit on two or more boards, and 2 per cent sit on seven or more boards. The maximum achieved by one director in their study is 11. Although only one in six directors is an 'interlocker', this 18 per cent represents a dominant influence in the economy if calculated by the total capital they control. Thus, Levine and Roy comment that the distribution of membership is 'highly skewed' and 'the interlocking among the leading corporations is quite common'.

Levine and Roy's finding is confirmed by Lim (1981) in his research on the 100 largest corporations in Malaysia. Among his sample data of 579 directors, 79.1 per cent hold only one seat on one board, 19.2 per cent hold seats on 2–4 boards, while 1.7 per cent of directors hold seats on more than five boards. In other words, a certain percentage of directors are closely meshed with other companies. They form a web of shared interests.

In this research, one can also find this kind of interlocking. F4, the chairman of Bank A, joined another Chaozhou-funded bank, Bank B, as a member of its board of directors. Bank B was controlled by F7's family. F4 also joined another Chaozhou-financed bank, Bank C, to serve as an honorary advisor. Bank C was owned by F9's family. On the other hand, F7's father, president of Bank B, served as one of the directors of Bank A. F7's elder brother, the executive director of Bank B, was appointed as a director of Chase Manhattan Bank. F9's brother, the chairman of Bank C, also served as a director of Banks A and B. These three Chaozhou-controlled banks clearly formed an 'alliance'. The newly formed Bank Consortium Trust Company Limited was a very good example of this. In order to compete with the major market leaders – the HSBC, Standard Chartered Bank and the Bank of China – 11 local medium-scale Chinese banks joined together. Thus, they could share with each other market information and banking facilities. They also agreed that they could not compete with each other in their own specialized market. Such practice could more or less be regarded as a form of social closure (Weber 1978; Parkin 1979), or from another perspective, usurpation (Murphy 1988).

Admittedly, this 'alliance' can on the one hand improve their competitive edge, while on the other reduce their business risk. F7's father had clearly pointed out this feature. He commented that many family businesses tried to avoid hiring non-relatives, viewing them as 'outsiders', and also resisted interference from others. The core reason was that they were afraid of non-family members' domination in their businesses or the possibility of hostile takeovers. As a result, the family business relied solely on the contribution of family members and suffocated non-family members' chances of promotion.

Seeing external capital and professionals could enhance their competitiveness, some Chaozhou family businesses try to invite better-educated and well-experienced non-family members. The cases of F7 and F9 are good examples. In addition to interlocking, they also cooperate with other well-known banks. For instance, F7's family sold 7 per cent of their bank shares to a Japanese bank and 5 per cent to an American bank. They considered that a strategic sale could strengthen their financial backup and improve their international image. In fact, through such business policy, their reputation was enhanced and both Moody and Standard & Poor upgraded their bank's financial status. The family bank had already evolved from a traditional, sub-standard local bank to a modern, sophisticated international bank.

Apart from forming an 'alliance', F4's family and F7's family also joined with other merchants, most of them of Chaozhou origin, to form a corporation that specialized in warehouse services. This corporation owns warehouses in Yuen Long, Kwun Tong, and Kwai Chung, and played a vital role in the market. Carrinna Restaurant is another example that can be used to illustrate the interlocking directorship. When Carrinna Restaurant went bankrupt after the major shareholder, George Tan, was charged with fraud, it faced liquidation. Some Chaozhou entrepreneurs, led by Chim Pui-chung, a former legislative councillor who was jailed in 1998 (but re-elected in 2008), formed a company and took over Carrinna Restaurant. The new board of directors consisted of Chim Pui-chung, Ma Kai-cheung and several other Chaozhou merchants. Both F16 and F14 were members of that company. Under the new leadership, Carrinna Restaurant turned heavy losses into a promising profit and eventually recaptured its leading status in the Chaozhou food market. F14, a meticulous businessman, brought me to have lunch there and shared with me his experiences in exploring the restaurant market.

> I frequently meet with my Chaozhou friends. Nearly all of us are directors of the CCC. We play mahjogg [a kind of popular local game] together in Carrinna and then have dinner there. Sometimes, when I have to meet my business counterparts, I also dine there. I love Chaozhou food. One day, when I learnt that George Tan was arrested and later prosecuted, I was shocked. Inevitably, Carrinna Restaurant was also forced to wind-up. I felt it would be a pity since the restaurant itself was well-founded. I then approached my Chaozhou friends to see what would we do for it. Chim Pui-chung shared my views, and we came to a conclusion that Carrinna Restaurant would be profitable if we could manage it properly and efficiently. We thus formed a company and took it over. A series of reforms were conducted to trim costs, streamline the organization, and introduce a greater variety of foods. The quality of services was also upgraded. Our effort ultimately proved successful. We turned the Restaurant to a multi-million dollar business.

An interlocking directorship is typical business behaviour for securing mutual support and spreading risk. If two directors are interlocked, the relation may not be so complex. However, if the dyadic relation extends to other areas, like personal connections, social relationships and political linkages, it turns triadic or quadratic. A web-like network is then formed. Thus, family interests, business interests and social interests become embedded together. As a concluding remark, let me quote Lim's (1981: 49–50) observation for illustration:

> Large corporations, unlike small independent enterprises, are closely and intricately linked to one another by a variety of networks. Among the most common and important forms of links are interlocking stock ownership and interlocking directorates.... Interlocking ownership has become more sophisticated and complex. Although institutions seem to be owners of the stocks, many of these institutions are ultimately owned by a few wealthy families who control them through the process of pyramiding and through the use of nominee and trustee companies.

Apart from helping their children establish personal ties or putting them in certain key positions, many patriarchs also help to increase the next generation's social capital either by engaging them in marriage alliances or deploying them in the political arena. In the subsequent paragraphs, I will deal with these two special areas thoroughly.

Forming marriage alliances

Formation of marriage alliances is one example of visual social capital that we can see in many of our studied families. From a legal perspective, marriage is a union of a man and a woman as husband and wife. From a cultural perspective, however, marriage can further imply the union of two families, two clans or even two nations. In the past, marriage was an effective means of achieving social or political purposes. For instance, it was used to build a special relationship with another person or to upgrade connections with a special aim in mind. Such a phenomenon was more obvious in traditional days when arranged marriages were common. Some famous historical examples can be cited for reference. A princess of the Kingdom of Qin married a prince from the Kingdom of Jin to form a military alliance between these two states during the Spring and Autumn Period (770–476 BC). In the Tang dynasty (AD 618–907), Emperor Li Shu-ming arranged Princess Wen-sheng to marry the King of Tufan. Tufan then became a loyal mandatory state to the Tang dynasty and maintained close relations with China for hundreds of years. The story of Wang Zhao-jun was another frequently quoted arranged marriage for political reasons in the Han dynasty (206 BC–AD 220).

In the West, social relations forged through marriage were also common (Argyle 1994). Sabean (1976: 101) writes:

> Marriage, as a way of forming alliance between households, has been the subject of a recent study of a Normandy village since the eighteenth century. There are in addition many examples of reinforcement of kin ties by new marriages in successive generations. The whole system implies the circulation of goods and their control within a loosely knit extended kin group.

Clearly, as a means for forging social networks, marriage has always taken on this role in both in the East and West.

In this research, although some of the Chaozhou merchants have also tried to create social connections for their children through marriage, their opinion on whether their children should marry outside their own ethnic group or confine themselves to their own group is mixed. Some interviewees preferred their children to marry Chaozhou people in Hong Kong and suggested that since they shared the same sub-culture, values and language, it would be easier to communicate and live together. However, a large proportion of them hoped their children could marry non-Chaozhou people, and argued that 'inter-ethnic marriage' could bring greater advantages, so that they could extend their social relations with local people. This phenomenon matches quite well with other scholars' findings on this topic (Landon 1941; Guldin 1977).

Examples of those who had married within the group and those who had married out can be found in this study. F8's elder sister dated her cousin, John (a pseudonym), when they were young. Later, they married. John finally emerged as a highly influential business tycoon in Hong Kong. John's eldest son, Johnson married Sarah (also a pseudonym). Sarah was the daughter of a wealthy garment and textile manufacturer. With help from John, F8's business grew in parallel with the marriage. He finally became one of Hong Kong's leading tycoons.

F8's younger brother, who graduated from Toronto University, married F11's daughter. F11 and F8's father were close friends. Their children played together frequently when they were young. This marriage reinforced the connection between these two families. During the interview, F11 confirmed to me that he was satisfied with this marriage and also praised his son-in-law. Through marriage, F11 extended his connections with John. That relationship implicitly explained why F11 held a significant proportion of shares in a John-controlled cement company. Indeed, F11 himself also ran a joint-venture cement production company with his Japanese counterpart.

Another example of a marriage within the Chaozhou group is F1. F1's sister married F1's partner's elder brother and moved to Hong Kong in the early 1920s. Later, F1 came to Hong Kong and worked in his brother-in-law's company. With his sister's help, he started his own business in partnership with his in-law's younger brother. When F1 was asked to evaluate his relationship with his partner, he said:

> In the past 53 years, we have not had any serious confrontations or disagreements. Of course, we might have minor disagreements over some

> management decisions. In fact, this is natural. When we had a difference of opinion, we preferred to sit down and discuss it openly. All important decisions were made with each other's consent.

When the question 'Can the second generation still maintain a harmonious and amicable relationship like the previous generation?' was presented to F1 and his son, both of them replied that they have confidence in upholding their close connections. F1's son said,

> We played together when we were young. We studied in the same primary and secondary school recommended by the same well-known local educator. Although I went to Canada after finishing secondary school, and my cousin went to the States, we still kept in close contact. Then, we worked together in the company. We took charge of different departments and thus had different responsibilities. We met frequently. When we had disputes, we would discuss openly. I think, even when the old people are no longer around, we will maintain the status quo. I do not think we will separate our partnership.

From their intertwined relationship, one can clearly see that marriage is still regarded as the glue that holds these two families together.

In Hong Kong, another group of respondents favoured marriage with non-Chaozhou people. F9's brother married the daughter of a banker of Shandong origins. Since F9's family was also engaged in the banking business, their marriage reinforced their relations not only in the economic aspect but also in the social aspect. The Shandong banker's youngest son married a well-known publishing tycoon's daughter. F9's first sister married an industrialist's son, while his second sister married a famous lawyer. In fact, F9 himself was a solicitor. He therefore had a close relationship with his brother-in-law. Through their marriages, these four families were closely linked together.

According to Han (1980), for the first-generation Chinese immigrants, intermarriage among ethnic groups in Malaysia was rare. This phenomenon can be explained by several factors. Mutual feeling of superiority with each speech group is one reason. Little social contact is another reason. However, from the second generation onwards, due to the increase in social interaction between the two sexes and among different ethnic groups, and also the improvement in education, inter-speech group marriage becomes more common. The increasing amount of inter-marriage of Chaozhou people with other groups directly reflects the advancement of education, assimilation into the host community and their general acceptance in Hong Kong.

Many wealthy families also use marriage to extend their networks in order to cement their economic and social interests. The Ho Tung and Li Shek-pang families are two frequently quoted famous examples. Ho Tung was famous for his ability in building personal connections. He arranged for his adopted son, Ho Shai-wing, to marry Kitty Hung, the daughter of another well-known Eurasian family patriarch, Hung Kam-shing. The Hung family was known as the Anderson family in the local Eurasian community. One of its famous daughters was Catherine J. Symons (nee Anderson) who was the headmistress of Diocesan Girl's School (1953–85) and served as the first woman legislative councillor (1972–6). In 1977 she was even appointed as the first woman executive councillor in Hong Kong. Ho Tung's other son, General Ho Shai-lai, was also arranged to marry a member of the Hung family, Hesta Hung. These two marriages bound the Ho Tung and Hung family tightly together.

Ho Tung's eldest daughter, Victoria, was arranged to marry Lo Man-kam, son of Lo Cheung-shiu, of another famous Eurasian family. Victoria's younger sister, Grace, followed her sister's footsteps to marry Lo Man-ho, younger brother of Man-kam. In fact, Lo Cheung-shiu was the sworn father of Ho Shai-kim, another son of Ho Tung. Lo Cheung-shiu's sister, Lo Shiu-choi, was picked to marry Ho Fook, younger brother of Ho Tung. Lo Cheung-shiu's daughter, Doris, was arranged to marry Ho Fook's son, Ho Shai-kee. In this sense, the Lo and Ho Tung families were also clearly intertwined with one another.

Ho Tung's other daughter, Mary, was also arranged to marry Wong Shek-lam. Shek-lam's mother was Ho Sui-ting, younger sister of Ho Tung. Ho Sui-ting was arranged by Ho Tung to be the second wife of Wong Kam-fook, comprador of Hong Kong, Kowloon Wharf and Godown, to secure a relationship with each other. Ho Tung's eldest sister, name not known, married Choy Sing-nam, the first comprador of Jardines. Through Choy's recommendation, Ho Tung decided to leave the Chinese Maritime Customs and became a comprador. Ho Tung's grandson, Lo Tak-shing, a famous legislative and executive councillor, married Cheung Wai-yue, daughter of Cheung Yuk-kai (of the Cheung Chuk-shan family). As a result, the Ho Tung, Lo Cheung-shiu and Cheung Chuk-shan families were also linked together.

Ho Fook's second daughter, Bessy, was arranged to marry Cheung Pui-kai, younger brother of Ho Tung's wife, Clara. Ho Fook's other son, Ho Shai-kwong, was arranged to marry Flora Sin, daughter of another key Eurasian patriarch, Sin Tak-fun. Sin Tak-fun's other daughter, Florence Sin, married Ho Fook's other son, Ho Shai-cheuk. In other words, the Ho Tung family also cemented a relationship with the Sin Tak-fun family.

Another daughter of Ho Fook, Priscilla, was arranged to marry Andrew Tse, son of Francisco Tse. The Tse family was another famous comprador family, with roots originally planted in Macau. Francisco Tse married Elizabeth Ho, daughter of Ho Kom-tong. Francisco Tse's and his son's marriages in fact were cousin-marriages. Ho Kom-tong's son, Ho Shai-kit, married Winnie Choa, daughter of Choa Lap-chee, while Elsie, another daughter of Ho Kom-tong, was arranged to marry Choa Lap-chee's son, Choa Po-yew. Choa Lap-chee was a Malaccan Chinese who later migrated to Hong Kong and also served as a comprador in Jardines.

Another son of Ho Kom-tong, Ho Shai-wah, married May She (also known as May Zimmern). May She was from the She Ping-kwong (also known as

Andrew Zimmern) family, another well-known Eurasian family. She Ping-kwong was a sworn brother of Clara Cheung's father. She Ping-kwong's nephew, She Sheung-hin, married Lo Cheung-shiu, father of Lo Man-kam and Lo Man-ho.

Ho Fook's granddaughter, Susie, the younger sister of Stanley Ho Hung-sun (chairman of Macao Entertainment and Shun Tak Groups), married Teddy Yip. Teddy was one of the major partners and co-founder of Macau Entertainment. Through such intricate linkages, Stanley Ho and Teddy Yip could firmly control the casino business in Macau.

Stanley Ho's daughter, Pansy Ho, married Julian Hui, grandson of Hui Oi-chow. Hui Oi-chow was a famous shipping tycoon who became a billionaire in the 1930s. He was the founder of Central Holdings, a listed company in Hong Kong. Unfortunately, Pansy and Julian divorced in 1999. Although the couple separated, Stanley Ho still kept a good relationship with the Hui family (*Oriental Daily* 17 November 2000). Stanley Ho's other daughter, Jane, married Siu Pak-shing, son of Siu Ming. Siu Ming was the founder of the Hong Kong Funeral Home. He was the pioneer as well as the market leader of the funeral business in Hong Kong. Stanley Ho's other daughter, Daisy, married Ho Chi-kin, son of Ho Sau-hong. Ho Sau-hong was a famous camera dealer and property developer. Lawrence Ho, son of Stanley Ho, married Sharon Lo, granddaughter of Lo Kwai-cheung, founder of the Vitasoy Group (*Sing Tao Daily* 17 November 2000). Through these kinds of marriages, Ho's family connections extended laterally to the Lo Cheung-siu, Hui Oi-chow, Siu Ming, Ho Sau-hong, Cheung Chuk-shan and Lo Kwai-cheung families (Figure 5.1). In Figure 5.1, we can clearly see that their social relations are intermeshed like a 'bamboo web' as suggested by Evers (2000) which not only helped them to enhance their economic influence but also their social status.

Another influential 'marriage alliance' concerns the Li Shek-pang family. Through interconnected marriages, Li Shek-pang, Fung Ping-shan, Kan Tung-po, Chow Shauson, Kwok Wing On and some other prominent families firmly linked together. Li Shek-pang's daughter, Sylvia Li married Kwok Lam-po, the eldest son of Kwok Chun, who was the founder of the Wing On Department Stores in Hong Kong and Shanghai. Sylvia and Lam-po's son, Philip Kwok, who had a PhD from Harvard University, married Maxine Li, the eldest daughter of Li Shu-pui. Li Shu-pui and his elder brother Li Shu-fun were the founders of the Hong Kong Sanatorium Hospital, a first-class private hospital in Hong Kong. Li Shu-fun's family was famous for specializing in medicine. Li Shu-pui's wife was Ellen Li, whose story has been briefly discussed in the previous section. Li Shu-fun's daughter, Li Fu-yun, married Lambert Kwok, younger brother of Kwok Lam-po. This connection further cemented the Li and the Kwok families together.

Kwok Lam-po's other brother, Lamson Kwok, married Marri Chang, the youngest daughter of Chang Mou-tze. Chang Mou-tze was a dignitary of Jiangxi Province. Lamson's son, Kwok Chi-leung, married Loh Kung-yat, eldest

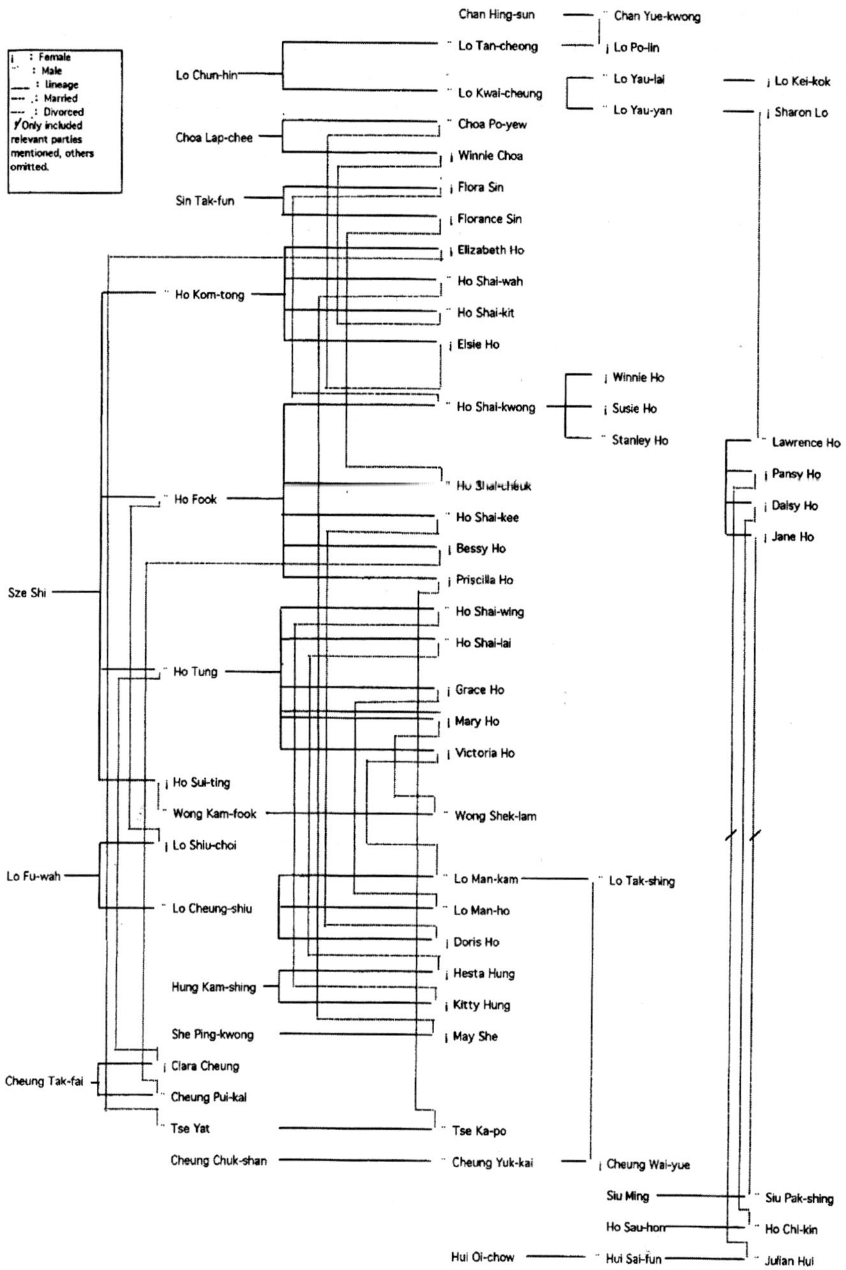

Figure 5.1 Marriage alliances of the Ho Tung family.

daughter of Loh Hau-pui. Loh Hau-pui was a leading construction tycoon who played a dominant role in the construction industry in Hong Kong. Loh Kung-yat's cousin was Christine Loh, an elected legislative councillor in 1998–2000. Christine's mother was from another prominent comprador family, the Mok Hing-yeung family, which served as the comprador of Butterfield and Swire for several decades.

Kwok Lam-po's sister, Kwok Wai-chun, married Chan Shu-kai. Chan Shu-kai's father, Chan Wai-chow was a former salt commissioner of Guangdong and Guangxi Provinces in the Qing dynasty. Shu-kai's brother, Chan Shu-kwai, was a famous businessman in Hong Kong. Kwok Lam-po's niece, Joyce Kwok, married Walter Ma. Walter's grandfather, Ma Wing-chung, was one of the founders of the Sincere Department Store. Ma Wing-chung and another founder, Ma Ying-biu, were townsmen and brothers-in-law. He and Ying-biu married two sisters from a large and well-known family in Xinhu, Guangdong.

Li Shek-pang's grandson, Li Fook-shu, married Woo Hey-tung's daughter, Daisy Woo. Woo Hei-tung's youngest son, Woo Pak-chun, was a senior solicitor and former legislative councillor. Li Koon-chun's other son, Ronald Li, married Low Hiu-wah, daughter of Low Min-nong, the sole distributor of British and American Tobacco (Far East) Limited. Sir Shauson Chow, the first Chinese executive councillor in Hong Kong, also linked with the Li Shek-pang family through marriage. Li Yue-chu, daughter of Li Koon-chun, married Chow Hau-leung, grandson of Chow Chi-nam. Chow Chi-nam is the nephew of Sir Shauson Chow.

> Another wedding that linked two of the bank's [Bank of East Asia] main family was arranged by Koon-chun for his eldest daughter, Yue-chu, a shy teenage girl who graduated from St. Paul's Girls College in 1924. She was affianced to Chow Hau-leung, a young man of an athletic bent who loved to swim and played soccer. He was the grandson of Chow Chi-nam, the bank's chief cashier.… The marriage between Yue-chu and Hau-leung linked the Li and Chow families.
>
> (Ching 1999: 71–2)

Clearly, Li Koon-chun tried to cultivate family connections with the Woo, Low and Chow families.

Li Fook-shu's son, David Li, married Penny Poon, daughter of Poon Kam-kai. Poon Kam-kai was a meticulous businessman who specialized in retailing and department stores. Kam-kai's son, Dickson Poon, is a glamorous and energetic young entrepreneur in Hong Kong who headed the distribution and department store businesses. David Li served as the chairman of the Bank of East Asia. Li Man-kiu, son of Penny and David, married Katie Lo (*Sing Tao Daily* 25 February 2001) but divorced later. Katie was the granddaughter of Lo Ying-shek. Lo Ying-shek was from an influential Chaozhou family in Hong Kong, who himself was the founder of the Great Eagle Group, and his second son, Lo Yuk-shui founded the Regal Hotel, Century Group and Poliburg Holdings. His third son,

Lo Hong-shui, founded the Shui On Group, while his eldest son, Lo Hung-shui, and third son, Lo Ka-shui, helped him to manage the Great Eagle Group. Ka-shui was the founding chairman of Hong Kong Growth Enterprises Market and had been appointed the chief executive officer of the Hong Kong Hospital Authority.

Li Shek-pang's other son, Li Tse-fong, married Tang Sau-ching, whose father once served as comprador of the Mercantile Bank. Tse-fong gained most of his banking knowledge and experience from his father-in-law (Ching 1999). Li Chok-chung, another son of Shek-pang, married the daughter of Mok Ching-kong. Mok Ching-kong was one of the co-founders of Bank of East Asia. The marriage between Chok-chung and Mok Ching-kong's daughter forged an invaluable connection between the Lis and the Moks.

Li Fook-tai, son of Li Tse-fong, married Cindy Yu. Cindy Yu's father was Yu Hung-kwan, a former premier of Taiwan, Republic of China. That was the reason why the Li family maintained close connections in Taiwan in the early days. Li Fook-kow, another son of Tse-fong, initiated a marriage with Woo Siu-che. Woo Siu-che was a benefactor and teacher of the so-called 'Three Musketeers' of property development, Kwok Tak-seng, Lee Shau-kee and Fung King-hei. Woo Siu-che's daughter, Judy Woo, married Li Fook-kow's son, Andrew Li. Andrew Li was the first chief justice of the Court of Final Appeal of the HKSAR. Judy's sister, Woo Mo-fong, married Chow Wing-kin. Chow Wing-kin was a prominent lawyer who was elected chairman of the Law Society while Mo-fong was an executive director of Li Ka-shing's flagship, Cheung Kong Holdings. Judy's brother, Sir Po-sing Woo, was the co-founder of a famous local legal firm, Woo-Kwan-Lee-Law Solicitors and Notaries. Li Fook-kow himself was a former secretary of home affairs and official member of the legislative and executive councils.

Li Wai-yin, daughter of Tse-fong, married Fung Ping-wah, the eldest son of Fung Ping-shan. Fung Ping-fun, the twin brother of Ping-wah, married Ivy Kan. Ivy's father was Kan Tung-po, the first general manager and key founder of the Bank of East Asia. Kan Tung-po, Fung Ping-shan, Li Koon-chun, Li Tse-fong, Mok Ching-kong, and Sir Shauson Chow were all co-founders of the Bank of East Asia.

> The marriage between Yue-chu and Hau-leung linked the Li and the Chow families. But the wedding that really cemented three of the bank's leading families occurred a few years later, in 1933, when the twin sons of Fung Ping-shan were married in a double wedding. One son, Kenneth Fung Ping-fan married Ivy, the eldest daughter of Kan Tung-po, while the other son, Fung Ping-wah married Wai-yin, the eldest daughter of Li Tse-fong. According to old Chinese beliefs, twins should be married on the same day, and these two were. Both were alumni of the University of Hong Kong.... The wedding was the social event of the season. It was accompanied by a lavish reception, attended by 1000 guests, many of whom were prominent bankers or businessmen. The head of the University of Hong Kong, in

> promising a toast, said, '[t]his afternoon we are doubly cementing an alliance between the great trading house of Fung and the Bank of East Asia, an arrangement full of happy augury. A double cord is not easily broken.' In 1933, and indeed for a long time afterwards, the Lis, the Kans and the Fungs were indeed inseparable. These lifelong friends, and their families, had been linked unto the next generation. Events in later decades would test the firmness of these bonds.
>
> (ibid.: 72–3)

Fung Ping-fun's son, Cyril Fung, married Kwok Chi-yee. Chi-yee's grandfather was Kwok Shun. Although they later divorced, the two families still maintained good relations.

Didier Li, great grandson of Li Shek-pang, married Michelle Huthart. Michelle's father was Robert Huthart, whose grandfather was one of the key directors of Lane Crawford. Didier and Michelle's marriage marked an intricate connection with the Li family. Didier himself founded the Pink Club and was known as the 'Godfather of the Rave Party' (Liu 2000; Howe 2000).

In addition, Kan Yuet-hing, son of Kan Tung-po, married Lee Shun-yin. Lee Shun-yin was from the Lee Hysan family. Lee Hysan emerged in the 1920s in the opium trade and was assassinated in 1928. Shun-yin's brother, R.C. Lee, a former legislative and executive councillor, took up the family business and brought it to another stage of growth. Kan Yuet-hing's brother, Kan Yuet-keung, was also a former legislative and executive councillor. Through their marriages, these two powerful families were also tightly linked together (Figure 5.2).

The powerful effect of marriage alliances can be illustrated by using these two major families as examples. In 1914 Lau Chu-pak, Ho Fook, Ho Kam-tong, Lo Cheung-siu and Chan Kai-ming founded the Tai Yau Bank. Lau Chu-pak and Ho Tung were close friends and both of them were Queen's College old boys and compradors in their day. Ho Fook married Lo Cheung-siu's sister, while two of Ho Tung's daughters married Lo Cheung-siu's two sons. Such marriages bonded the families together and explained why their cooperation and relationship always remained intimate. However, due to some undisclosed reasons, the bank didn't try to expand its business through absorbing public deposits, but just focused on syndicated loans in the Chinese mainland. As the Chinese Communist Party came to power in the late 1940s in the mainland, the bank suffered seriously and had to close down in the 1960s.

Another Chinese-funded bank, the Bank of East Asia, was also jointly founded by a group of intermarriages. As discussed above, all of the co-founders' families – the Lis, Kans, Fungs, Moks and Chows – were linked tightly by the inter-marriage relationship. Key positions such as chairman or general manager were served by these families alternately from the 1930s to the 1980s. From the 1980s onwards, since some of the families showed little confidence in Hong Kong's future and sold their shares, the Li family became the major shareholders and therefore held all the key positions (Bank of East Asia Limited 1989, 1994; Ching 1999).

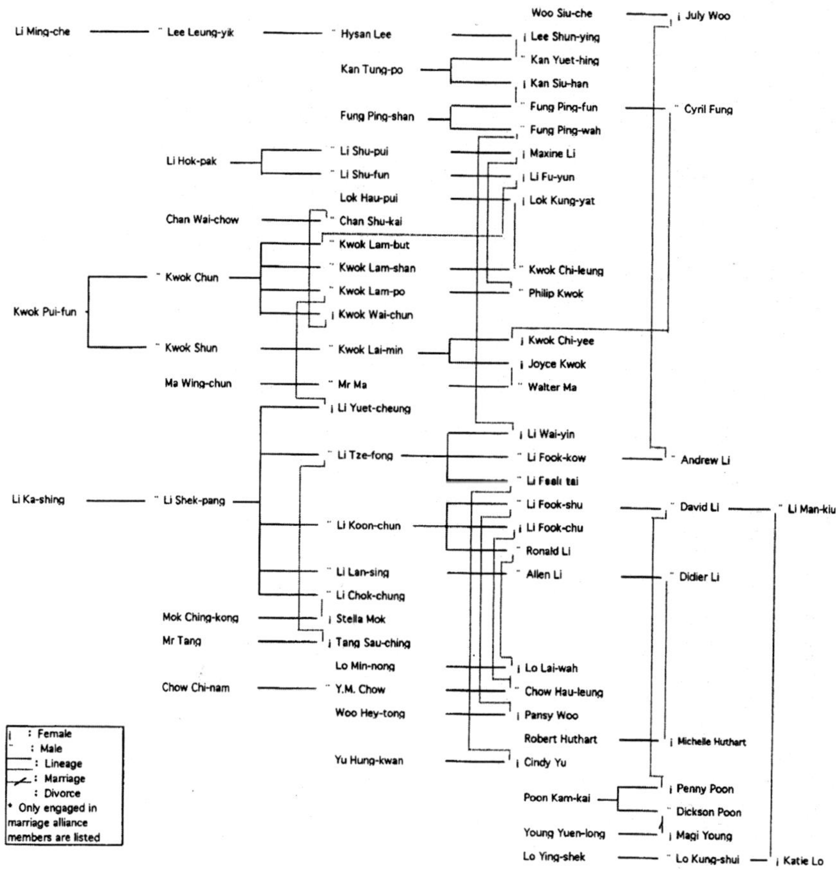

Figure 5.2 Marriage alliances of the Li Shek-pang family.

In fact, marriage alliances are not something unique in Hong Kong. In other Chinese communities, such as Singapore, Malaysia, Thailand and the Philippines, marriage alliances are also very common (*Apple Daily* 20 May 1999a).

> There is considerable intermarriage among members of this elite business community. The Tan Cheng Lock family is related by marriage to the Lee Choon Guan family. Other marriage links include S.Q. Wong's daughter being married to Lee Kong Chian's nephew and Tan Chin Tuan being married to the daughter of Wee Theam Seng, a former General Manager of OCBC [Overseas Chinese Banking Corporation]. Lee Kong Chian married the daughter of Tan Kah Kee, the leading business tycoon in Singapore in the early twentieth century.
>
> (Lim 1983: 288)

As a concluding remark, let me quote one social scientist's finding on the powerful effect of marriage. After finishing his research in the Philippines, Omohundro (1983: 69) found that marriage alliances serve as a mechanism for reinforcing business and social relations. He writes,

> When a Chinese man begins formal courtship of a Chinese woman, their families conduct intensive investigations into each other's background. When engagement occurs, the marrying families are well informed as to one another's characters, bank accounts and debts. This information, coupled with the enthusiasm generated by new recruits of successful merchants to the 'inner circle' of kinsmen, encourages immediate and hard-rocked mutual commercial proposals. The consequence of this endogamy and residential stability is a thick web of kin and business interconnections that serve to reinforce partnerships, import–wholesale–retail distributor chains, credit arrangements, commercial apprenticeships and other business deals.

Participation in charity and politics

If marriage alliances can be used to illustrate the formation of social networks, then participating in social services and charitable work can be used to illustrate the reinforcement of family interests and social connections. In order to cultivate and pass on their social connections, many parents may encourage their children to join charitable organizations or become involved in certain social activities. In fact, *facai lipin*, literally meaning earning money and erecting social status; or *fuce jiangshan tianxia*, which means when one becomes rich, one shall do charitable work to help other people in the world, are popular sayings of many Chinese people. The following reflects the mentality of many Chinese people.

> A wealthy person had to be charitable and public spirited so that he might be more readily accepted by the Chinese community which treasured such virtue.... Publicity and fame could be achieved through an act of charity. Here, Chinese leaders of the nineteenth century did often, consciously or unconsciously, make use of charity for the uplifting of their prestige and status in society. In fact, early Chinese leaders had set a good and admirable tradition in initiating or contributing funds for charitable works. Some hospitals and schools today in Singapore still bear the names of these generous community leaders.
>
> (Yong 1991: 8)

In fact, joining charitable and voluntary institutions, like the Tung Wah Group of Hospitals (TWGH), Po Leung Kuk (PLK), Community Chest, and Yan Chai Hospital (YCH) as a member or as a director of the board is generally regarded as respectful and prestigious within the community.

In her book, *Power and Charity*, Elizabeth Sinn (1989) tells us that in early Hong Kong, most of the influential local business elites were elected as members of the board of directors of the TWGHs, one of the longest and well-established charitable organizations in Hong Kong. She also goes a step further to point out that through such charitable works, directors could make peace with the emperor of China (Qing dynasty) and also improve their social status in the community. 'By providing welfare, the board of directors acquired moral authority' (Sinn 1997: 241), which could bring them fame and power in the community. Their progeny could also gain advantages.

In order to have a better understanding about this type of capital, we can turn our attention to the studied families' participation. Before we go further, let me divide their charitable participation into two major categories: (1) holding key positions in voluntary institutions; and (2) direct donations. These voluntary organizations can be further subdivided into: welfare providing organizations, like the TWGH, PLK and YCH; and non-service providing agencies, such as guilds, clubs or associations. Generally speaking, guilds and associations are referring to townsmen, clansmen and commercial associations. Donations can be classified as educational, social services, religious and cultural donations.

In this research, a clear correlation is found showing that the greater their donation and participation in charitable work, the better the family's name is in society. For instance, among the 26 interviewed families, nearly 34.6 per cent of them have their members sitting on the boards of TWGH/PLK/YCH. Sometimes, both father and sons are members of a certain association. F4 and his two sons, F7 and his father and brother, and F14 and his father, are some well-known examples. A large proportion of them has donated money or has become involved in education (73.1 per cent), social services (30.8 per cent), religious and cultural activities (34.6 per cent) (Table 5.2).

From the data, one can see that all of the ten wealthy long-established families have generously donated sums of money to charitable organizations. They have also held key positions, such as honorary chairman, advisor or director, in various voluntary agencies. Sometimes, more than one family member holds a key position in these organizations. For instance, Ho Tung, Ho Fook, Ho Kom-tong and Ho Shai-kwong held long-term chairmanships in the TWGH. These families also donated huge amounts of money to the association.

There is also strong evidence that social fame, donation and participation in social services go in parallel. A good indicator is the awarding of medals or titles from the government. Such awards usually refer to Justice of Peace (JP), Member of the British Empire (MBE), Order of the British Empire (OBE) and Knight Commander of the Order of the British Empire (KBE). Many of the studied long-established families and some of the Chaozhou families have received such rewards long ago as recognition of their contribution to the community.

As we know, charity and philanthropy are big and complex subjects. Sinn comments,

> People give for many reasons: Some give in order to gain fame and status, others give to earn good karma for this life and the next, or accumulate blessings for their descendants. Some give to flaunt their wealth, others give

Table 5.2 Charitable and philanthropic work of some studied families

Family	*Posts in TWGH, PLK or YCH*	*Posts in other clubs or associations*	*Donations to or participation in education*	*Donations to or participation in social services*	*Donations to or participation in religious activities*
Ho Tung family	C/D	C/D	$/P	$/P	$/P
Li Shek-pang family	D	D	$/P	$/P	$/P
Chau Wing-tai family	C/D	C/D	$/P	$/P	$/P
Fung Ping-shan family	C/D	C/D	$/P	$/P	$/P
Cheung Chuk-shan family	C/D	C/D	$/P	$/P	$/P
Hui Oi-chow family	C/D	C/D	$/P	$/P	$/P
Lee Leung-yick family	D	D	$/P	$/P	$/P
Wing On Kwok's family	C/D	C/D	$/P	$/P	$/P
Fung Pak-liu family	C/D	D	$/P	$/P	$/P
Tang Chi-ngong family	C/D	C/D	$/P	$/P	$/P
F1's family		C/D	$		
F2's family		C/D			
F3's family		D			
F4's family		C/D	P	P	P
F5's family		C/D	$/P		P
F6's family	C/D	D	P		
F7's family	C/D	C/D	$/P	$/P	$/P
F8's family	D	D	P		

F9's family	C/D	C/D	$/P	P	
F10's family	D	C/D	P	$/P	$/P
F11's family		D	P		
F12's family					
F13's family			P		
F14's family		D	P		
F15's family	C/D	C/D	$/P	P	$/P
F16's family	C/D	C/D	$/P	P	P
F17's family		D			
F18's family		D			
F19's family	D	C/D	$/P		
F20's family		D			
F21's family		D		P	P
F22's family		D			
F23's family		D			
F24's family		D	$/P		P
F25's family		D	P	P	
F26's family	D	D	P		P

Source: Interviews 1997–2000.

Notes
C: chairman/vice-chairman; D: director; $: monetary donation; P: post(s) held in particular organization(s); TWGH: Tung Wah Group of Hospitals; PLK: Po Leung Kuk; YCH: Yan Chai Hospital.
Honorary chairman or advisor is grouped as chairman for simplicity.
Multiple members are categorized as one individual.

> to build business connection, or to curry favor with this or that government. But let us not forget to include love, compassion and humanitarianism, for surely these too are behind much of the giving.
>
> (ibid.: 250)

However, the aim of this research is not to find out the motivation behind philanthropic and charitable work, nor does it intend to analyse their contribution to society. Attention will only be given to examining how charitable works upgrade people's social status, and ultimately how it is transmitted to their children, and then to sustaining the family welfare. The finding in this research confirmed research undertaken by Young (1977, 1991). In his study of the Singaporean Chinese, Young found that many famous Chinese leaders there had donated huge sums of money to charity, and their social status and leadership went up in parallel. Their good reputations were also carried over to their children after they died. He writes:

> Wealth was the main criterion for a man's status in society.... The criterion can be applied to descendants of early community leaders, such as Tan Tock-seng, Tan Kim-seng and Seah Eu-chin, who succeeded in not only preserving, consolidating but also extending the wealth so laboriously amassed by their forefathers. Besides, these descendants had an edge over other competitors for leaderships as they would rely upon the fame and popularity of their fathers who had earlier been accepted as community leaders by the Chinese in Singapore.
>
> (Yong 1991: 118–19)

When discussing family business development, the sensitive topic of political participation is rarely touched upon. In fact, similarly to participation in charitable work, participation in politics can also extend one's family influence and reinforce one's status in society.

> In the past, many businessmen had a meteoric rise when they were promoted to certain political position. For instance, when they were appointed as legislative or executive councillors, they would be invited to become honourable partners in other people's companies. Thus, both their business networks and wealth could expand. For those who came from wealthy families, the appointment as councillors, would bring further glory to the whole family.
>
> (*Capital* 1988d: 145)

As some scholars point out, 'Wealth itself might not be an ultimate source of power' (Ho 1976: 43). In the past, if any businessmen wanted to gain political influence, they had to buy an official title from the imperial court. Recently, many businessmen have tried to exercise their influence either by direct participation or through coalitions with political parties.

To a certain extent, political participation requires an extensive social network, personal reputation and economic backup. Although most of the studied Chaozhou families' political participation remained only at the lower levels, the tendency was clear. When their economic strength accumulated, their ambitions in politics also rose in parallel. For instance, among the 26 Chaozhou families, two of them with a longer family history and large businesses have already reached the top of the political echelon. F7's uncle was appointed as a legislative councillor in 1992 and elected as a representative to the National People's Congress (NPC). Unfortunately, he died from a heart attack during a vacation in Phuket, Thailand in 1998. F4 was a former president of the Chinese Chamber of Commerce. He was also an elected representative of the NPC. His second son was an elected legislative councillor.

Another group of respondents joined politics by other means. Having served the community for some years and accumulated a certain amount of wealth, they could first participate within the lower-level of politics, for instance, the urban council. F16, F14 and F15 are good examples. F16 and F15 served as council chairmen of their district councils. F1's son, F10, F6 and F21 were another category of respondents who had become involved in political matters. The Beijing government appointed them as members of the Chinese People's Political Consultative Conference (CPPCC) (Table 5.3).

From the above data, we can roughly see that most of the long-established families have deliberately cultivated their influence in politics. This pattern clearly contradicts the conventional thinking that Chinese businessmen tend to keep politics at arm's length: 'Politics is politics and business is business. Industrialists should not get involved in political affairs' (Wong 1994: 221).

Political apathy does not apply in many large wealthy families. Although Ho Tung himself did not join the government, his political interests were fully represented by his descendants. For instance, his younger brother, Ho Fook, was a

Table 5.3 Important political posts held by members of the studied Chaozhou families

Person	*Government/political post held in Hong Kong or China*
F7's uncle	Legislative councillor
F7's father	Representative (NPC)
F4's son	Legislative councillor
F4	Representative (NPC) President of the Hong Kong General Chamber of Commerce
F16	Regional councillor, chairman of regional council
F15	Urban councillor, chairman of urban council
F14	Urban councillor
F10	Member (CPPCC)
F10's son	Director of building and construction department
F21	Member (CPPCC)
F1's son	Member (CPPCC)
F6	Member (CPPCC)

Source: Interviews 1997–2000.

legislative councillor in the early 1920s. His sons-in-law, Lo Man-kam and Lo Man-wai, were both executive and legislative councillors from the 1940s to the 1950s. His other son-in-law, Young Kwok-cheung, was the first director of the Sanitary and Hygiene Department from the 1940s to the 1960s. His grandson-in-law, Lo Tak-sing, played a dominant role in Hong Kong politics from the 1970s to the late 1990s, and once served as an executive and legislative councillor, and was also appointed as vice secretary of the Basic Law Consultative Committee, an organization that was responsible for formulating the constitution for the HKSAR. His grandnephews, such as Henry Litton and Eric Ho, also played key roles in the government (Table 5.4). In other words, Ho Tung's family interests were overwhelmingly represented in the government.

The Li Shek-pang family's profound influence in politics is also without precedent. Many of Shek-pang's sons and grandsons were former legislative or executive councillors. Some still hold these posts. They also play a vital role in the judiciary system (Table 5.5). In politics, Li Tse-fong, Li Fook-kow, Li Fook-wo and David Li were former legislative councillors at different times. Among them, Fook-shu, Fook-kow and Andrew were members of the executive council, the most powerful government body in the colony of Hong Kong. In the judiciary, many of the descendants of Li Shek-pang were lawyers. Li Fook-sean was a former justice of the High Court and vice secretary of the Basic Law Consultative Committee. Gladys Li is a senior council (SC, formerly known as the Queen's Council, QC), who was also elected as the first woman to chair the Hong Kong's Barrister Association in 1996. Andrew Li was appointed as the first chief justice of the HKSAR in 1997, while Arthur Li was appointed as the Secretary for Education and Manpower in 2002. Up to now, no other families can match the Lis in power and influence in the judicial and political spheres of Hong Kong.

Like the Ho Tung and Li Shek-pang families, Chau Wing-tai's descendants also played an influential role in Hong Kong politics. Wing-tai's son, Siu-kay,

Table 5.4 Important government posts held by Ho Tung family members

Name	*Government post held*	*Relation with Ho Tung*
Ho Fook	Legislative councillor	Brother
Ho Shai-lai	General of the Republic of China	Son
Lo Man-wai	Urban, executive and legislative councillor	Son-in-law's brother
Lo Tak-sing	Urban, executive and legislative councillor	Grandson-in-law
Henry Litton	Justice of the Court of Final Appeal of HKSAR	Grand nephew-in-law
Ho Eric Peter	Secretary of Home Affairs Secretary of Industry and Commerce Executive and legislative councillor	Grand nephew-in-law
Young, K.C.	Director of Sanitary and Hygiene Department	Son-in-law

Sources: I. Cheng 1976, 1997; Zheng and Wong 2007, 2008.

Table 5.5 Important government posts held by Li Shek-pang family members

Name	*Government post held*	*Relation with Li Shek-pang*
Li Tse-fong	Legislative councillor	Son
Li Fook-shu	Executive and legislative councillor	Grandson
Li Fook-sean	Justice of the High Court	Grandson
Li Fook-wo	Legislative councillor	Grandson
Li Fook-kow	Secretary of Home Affairs, executive and legislative councillor	Grandson
Li Fook-siu	Chairman of the Stock Exchange of Hong Kong	Grandson
Li David	Legislative councillor	Great grandson
Li Andrew	Executive councillor, chief justice (Court of Final Appeal)	Great grandson
Li Chi-hei	Chairman of the Barristers' Association	Great granddaughter
Chow Shauson	Executive and legislative councillor	Grandson-in-law's grandfather
Woo Pak-chuen	Legislative councillor	Grandson-in-law's brother
Li Ellen	Legislative councillor	Son-in-law's mother-in-law
Fung Ping-fun	Executive and legislative councillor	Granddaughter's husband

Sources: Ching 1999; *Capital* 1988c.

was the first family member appointed as a legislative councillor in the early twentieth century. The Chau family business expanded rapidly after the appointment. Siu-kay further spread his businesses to shipping, insurance, money shops and property. Almost every business he touched turned to gold. Chau Tsun-nin and Chau Shek-nin were two key members of the Chau family. Both of them were appointed as urban councillors, then legislative councillors and finally executive councillors. They were eminent people in their time.

Compared with their fathers or grandfathers, the third generation's participation were less active. Only a few of them were willing to get involved in politics. For instance, Chau Cham-chiu was appointed chief commander of the Hong Kong Auxiliary Force and Chau Cham-sun was director of the Housing and Land Department (Table 5.6). Due to their pro-Taiwan political stance, the

Table 5.6 Important government posts held by Chau Wing-tai family members

Name	*Government post held*	*Relation with Chau Wing-tai*
Chau Siu-kay	Legislative councillor	Son
Chau Tsun-nin	Urban, executive and legislative councillor	Grandson
Chau Shek-nin	Urban, executive and legislative councillor	Grandson
Chau Cham-chiu	Chief commander of HKA police force	Great grandson
Chau Cham-sun	Director of Housing and Land Department	Great grandson

Sources: *Capital* 1988a; Yuet 1992; M.C. Ho 1991b.

Chaus, similar to the Ho Tung family, kept a low profile and were less enthusiastic in politics after the promulgation of the Sino-British Joint Declaration in 1984.

The Lee Leung-yick family, Fung Ping-shan family and the Fung Pak-liu family also played an influential role in politics. Both R.C. Lee and his brother, Sir Quo-wei, were former legislative and executive councillors. In addition, Sir Quo-wei also served as the second chairman of the Stock Exchange of Hong Kong. Lee Hong-chiu, nephew of R.C. Lee, who succeeded his uncle, was the third chairman of the Stock Exchange of Hong Kong (Table 5.7). Clearly, the Lees' influence in the Hong Kong stock market was remarkable.

Fung Hong-chu, son of Fung Pak-liu, also served the colonial government as an urban and legislative councillor from the 1960s to 1970s. Victor Fung was appointed as the chairman of the Trade Development Council and was elected to the chairman of Hong Kong Airport Authority in 2000 (Table 5.8). There was a rumour that Victor Fung would be the next chief executive of the HKSAR. In an interview, Victor Fung ruled out this possibility and claimed that he had no interest in politics (Chung 2000).

From all these of big families, we can see that their economic emergence and social reputation actually paved the groundwork for their political influence, while their political influence further ensured their business domination in society. Such a phenomenon is common in other regions. Lim (1983: 288)

Table 5.7 Important government posts held by Lee Leung-yick family members

Name	*Government post held*	*Relation with Lee Hysan*
Lee R.C.	Urban, executive and legislative councillor	Son
Lee Quo-wei	Executive and legislative councillor Chairman of Stock Exchange of Hong Kong	Nephew
Lee Hong-Chiu	Chairman of Stock Exchange of Hong Kong	Grandson
Kan Yuet-keung	Legislative and executive councillor	Son-in-law's brother

Sources: *Capital* 1989a; M.C. Ho 1991b; Poy 1998.

Table 5.8 Important government posts held by Fung Pak-liu family members

Name	*Government post held*	*Relation with Fung Pak-liu*
Fung Hong-chu	Urban and legislative councillor	Son
Fung Victor	Chairman of Trade Development Council Chairman of the HK Airport Authority	Grandson
Fung William	Member of the Basic Law Consultative Committee	Grandson

Sources: *Capital* 1995; C.W. Lui 2000a, 2000b; Li & Fung 1982.

writes, 'Some of the former directors of OCBC were prominent politicians. For example, Lim Boon Keng, Lim Peng Siang, Lee Choon Guan and Tan Cheng Lock, all served in the colonial Legislative Council in Singapore and Malaya.'

A general rule is that when one's socio-economic status is upgraded, one's political domination is also activated. When economic achievement integrates with social and political domination, one's family interests can be embedded tightly into the social and political system. Under their father's influence, certain sons or daughters can follow in their father's footsteps and enter social services or politics. Thus, they can extend their socio-political influence to the next generation. Yong (1991: 18) makes the following observation:

> By 1900, heredity seems to have emerged as an element in the pattern of Chinese leadership. For among the 15 leaders, seven of them came from three families. Tan Tock-seng and Tan Kim-ching, father and son, provided leadership between 1840–1890. Seah Eu-chin and son, Seah Liang-seah, held leadership in various periods extending from 1840 to 1920. Tan Kim-seng, Tan Beng-swee and Tan Jian-kim contributed in succession to the Chinese community their leadership, prolonging over a period of three generations, such a phenomenon could not have been a coincidence. This may be explained in terms more of wealth, upbringing and timing than of education and talent.

It is said that politics and business are symbiotic and they usually go hand-in-hand. When wealth is accumulated, social influence and social status also increase. Taking part in politics can further perpetuate their dominance in society. Bringing the successor generation to attend important events or to meet influential figures is generally regarded as a common method for cultivating the their personal connections. In conclusion, let me quote the following:

> Hong Kong's tycoons are expected to meet President Hu Jintao today [27th September] as an unprecedented autumn delegation season reaches its climax. The tycoons, including Li Ka-shing and Henry Fok Ying-tung, are making their first formal call on the new leadership ... many tycoons, including Mr. Fok and Lim Por-yen [also known as Lam Pak-yan], the former boss of Asia Television, are being accompanied by their children, prompting reports they are grooming a new generation with close ties to the leadership. Matthew Lim Kin-hong [also known as Lam Kin-hong], son [sic, nephew, refer to Chapter 3] of Mr. Lim, said he had come to learn to be a patriot. Chiang Chen, chairman of the Chen Hsiong Group, said, 'We mainly come here to talk about business. There is no other political motive.' His daughter, Chiang Lai-yuen, and his son, Chiang Chi-kin, are also in the delegation.... President Hu Jintao told the group of more than 80 of Hong Kong's richest business leaders, including Li Ka-shing, Henry Fok Ying-tung and Sir Gordon Wu Ying-sheung, that they 'must give all-out support' to Mr. Tung [the first Chief Executive of HKSAR] and his government....

> Mr. Hu remarked on the fact that many of the tycoons were accompanied by their 'next generations'. 'I am particularly happy to see that not only have we the first generation here, we are also joined by your second and third generations today.... This is truly a star-studded delegation.'
>
> (*South China Morning Post* 27 September 2003)

As the Chinese saying goes, *yichao tianzi yichao chen* (literally meaning a new chief brings in new aides), many of the patriarchs know that political connections need to be updated and renewed from time to time, or from generation to generation. Thus, they are fully aware of the importance of passing such connections to their offspring for safeguarding their family interests.

The essence of social capital

The main theme of this chapter has been exploration of how family business is aggrandized through the building of personal ties, the interconnection of marriage, and participation in politics and charity. As a conclusion, a cross-examination of the interconnection of these factors is provided. First, marriage alliances can ensure mutual cooperation among different families. After conducting an intensive study on British family businesses and their networks from 1904 to 1976, Scott and Griff (1984: 114) found that inter-marriage among large and wealthy families was quite common. Such marriage unions served as an important mechanism in cementing inter-family relationships and business cooperation. In their report, they write:

> Through intermarriage over generations with families such as Channon, Lennox-Boyd, and Hamilton-Temple-Blackwood, as well as with other branches of the Guinness family, Lord Iveagh's descendants built up an extensive kinecon group which in 1976 held 18.98 per cent of the brewery company and made up about half its board. A similar pattern of intermarriage was found in the kinecon group which participated in the controlling constellation of Marks and Spencer. From early in its history the Marks and Sieff families were closely intermarried, and their members also married into Sacher, Blond, Lerner, Susman, and Goodman families. Majority ownership was maintained until 1964 through the issue of non-voting shares, but by 1976 the kinecon group had just 1.6 per cent – though they filled almost half the board positions. Clearly, the survival of family influence depends upon many factors, but the ability to retain a significant block of shares through appropriate marriage strategies is a key element in that survival.

Their finding is consistent with this study. Many large families in Hong Kong also tried to build up their social capital by using marriage alliances. Berkowitz (1976: 176) echoes Scott and Griff's argument that marriage and business reinforce one another in such a way that 'large amounts of capital can be mobilized from within the cousinhood'. Similarly, Zeitlin and Ratcliff (1975: 33) argue that extensive intermarriage among propertied families is not only a consequence of close mutual interaction, but also serves to create reciprocal obligations, loyalties and to buttress the economic foundations. They point out,

> The complex pattern of extensive intermarriage among propertied families both results from, and in turn, reinforces and extends, a web of social interaction, mutual obligations and loyalties. Already sharing common interests, based on their common location in the productive process and propertied system, they are, thereby, unified into a social, rather than merely economic class.

Since marriage alliance emphasizes semi-blood relations and is more effective in transmission, it is generally regarded as one of the key modes of social capital that can sustain the next generation's control over their business.

In fact, semi-blood-ties marriage arrangements can also facilitate business cooperation. Kann (1973) argues that a marriage arrangement is part of a broader network of interaction in which each family aims to cement alliances and maximize its advantages. Tepperman (1972) suggests that large and wealthy families in Europe are maintained through cousin marriage and through cooperative business enterprises. In fact, such a phenomenon can also be found in this research. I find that many upper-class families directly or indirectly 'arranged' their children's marriages. In the minds of many patriarchs, a reliable marriage alliance can, on the one hand, promote mutual trust while, on the other hand, reducing friction among two families.

Like education, marital selection has an intermediate role in transmitting the force of family background and acts as a perpetuator of inequality (Brittain 1977: 27). In the modern world, romantic love and free marriage are frequently stressed in mate selection. However, some research indicates that 'free marriage' is not 'absolutely free'. Parental influence is still strong. Kaye (1999) points out that even in modern society, parents have considerable influence on mate selection. For the young men and women themselves, their criteria for choosing a wife or husband are also bounded by their socio-economic background. As Brittain (1977: 124) argues, people prefer to choose their life mate from among those of similar economic background: '[D]aughters tend to select husbands whose economic status is almost as closely related to that of their parents-in-law as is the relationship between sons and their own parents.... Marital selection thus tends to perpetuate inequality.' In other words, marriage can be used to transmit social capital in sustaining social status.

In discussing how family wealth is maintained, Hughes (1997) posits that financial capital alone cannot provide long-term wealth preservation. She suggests that successful long-term wealth preservation lies in the growth of a family human and intellectual capital that also determines its success, and that the growth of its financial capital provides a powerful tool to achieve this success. In this research, I found that many patriarchs also shared Hughes' viewpoint. In order to enhance their economic success, many of the studied families have tried their best to transform their economic capital into human, social and cultural capitals. They have also tried to pass all of these various kinds of capital to the next generation by enhancing their children's education, leadership, social status and political influence.

The mechanism of wealthy families becoming a part of charitable institutions allows them to translate their economic achievement into social domination. Such domination can be extended to the political arena. In other words, through marriage alliances, philanthropic work and direct political participation, long-established and wealthy families have already embedded their connections in society, and many of the studied Chaozhou families have also tried to use the same method to transmit their capitals. In other words, when talking about inheritance, we should not simply refer to the transmission of physical capital, but also human and social capital.

In conclusion, we can clearly see that because of the imperfection of market conditions, personal connections and social networks are used to cut transaction costs or to reduce uncertainty. In fact, the function of social capital goes beyond this. A well-connected social network not only can extend one family business interest to many other families' businesses by forming a 'bamboo web', but can also extend their influence from the economic arena to the circles of politics and community as a whole. Yong (1991: 123) comprehensively sums up these points: 'Wealth was invariably the single and the most indispensable factor for socio-political mobility.' However, we must admit that since social capital cannot be transmitted fully and not many of the family patriarchs pay due attention to the succession issue, problems may sometimes come out during transmission. In short, I argue that if the heir cannot inherit social capital from the patriarch, the possibility of keeping their business from one generation to the next will be weakened.

Notes

1 It is difficult to obtain information about sworn relationships. One of the possible methods is to look at newspaper obituaries. Quite a large number of families are willing to list their sworn relationships in their obituaries. For some more examples, please refer to the obituary section of *Ming Pao Daily* on 30 January 2001, 27 January 2001, 12 December 2000, 25 October 2000, 19 September 2000, 4 August 2000, 2 June 2000, 19 January 2000, 18 November 1999, 9 October 1999 and 10 June 1998.

6 Equal inheritance and economic development

Having thoroughly examined the mechanism of transferring ownership, leadership and personal connections, we understand that in order to reduce internal conflict, many families may choose to divide their estate before the parents die. Other evidence also shows that most parents try to establish their heirs' leadership before passing the baton on to them officially. Social networks and personal ties are also inculcated to ensure a smooth succession.

In this chapter I will first summarize some of the key findings to examine the inheritance system and the dynamism of Chinese family business with a brief comparison between the studied Chaozhou families and the long-established families. Then, I will synthesize all the aforemetioned arguments by re-examining the intertwined relationship between inheritance, competition and business adaptation. After that, I will go a step further and explore the origin of the self-employment mentality and the unconventional developmental process of large Chinese family enterprises. Finally, I will also try to discuss the myth of the equal inheritance system and its implication in economic development.

Equal inheritance and the dynamism of family business

In this study, it is discovered that many regional or dialect groups have been nearly assimilated into the mainstream culture, and the concept of a 'dialect minority' has gradually faded out in Hong Kong. However, different from other dialect groups like the Shanghainese, the Cantonese, the Fujianese and the Hakka, Chaozhou people are still generally perceived as being cohesive, united, frugal, hardworking, meticulous, superstitious and male-dominated.

When compared with other minority groups, Chaozhou people show certain special features. A strong sense of ethnic identity is still emphasized. In the interviews, many respondents stressed their regional origin and were proud of their own culture. In fact, it is a common observation that when Chaozhou people meet in a public area, even though all of them can speak fluent Cantonese, they would switch to Chaozhou dialect, or to a mixed code of Cantonese and Chaozhou dialect. They set up townsmen associations, townsmen schools and culture clubs. In order to keep their culture alive, the CCC organizes a series of social activities for Hong Kong-born Chaozhou people. These include

Chaozhou dialect classes, a *kungfu* tea-brewing course, Chaozhou music and opera appreciation class, and seminars on Chaozhou culture and history. If Chaozhou people win important awards or recognition, the CCC will usually offer their congratulations in the mass media, mainly via newspapers.

Chaozhou merchants show a strong ethnic identity and working style. Diligence and frugality are two key terms that are especially applicable to them. Many Chaozhou respondents claim that they work from five until nine everyday. This feature is not just limited to first-generation migrants – even some second- and third-generation local-born Chaozhou people also keep their habit of working long hours. Living a frugal life is another feature common to people in this study. Many Chaozhou merchants still insist on living a simple life, even when they have great wealth. For instance, extremely rich Chaozhou people like Li Ka-shing and Lam Pak-yan always claim that they prefer eating small fish to large deep-sea fish at lunch or dinnertime.

Strong business networks and social connections are another feature. Many Chaozhou merchants are inclined to help each other in order to compete with other regional groups. As a result, they form a mutual support system. Very often, when one Chaozhou person initially engaged in a certain trade, they would invite other Chaozhou people to follow. Following this they would form a coterie and erect certain restrictions to outsiders. The rice business is a typical example. Other businesses, like plastic flowers, canned and dry food, and textiles and garments, are also dominated by Chaozhou businessmen. In this research, many respondents told how they have cultivated their children's networks by taking them along to business meetings or social gatherings. Unlike Shanghainese and Fujian merchants, who emphasize capital backup and company image, Chaozhou merchants generally stress pragmatism and flexibility. Therefore, they are usually perceived as being more cost-sensitive.

The perception of male superiority is still prevalent in the Chaozhou community. It is a typical patrimonial community. Family estate and company shares are mainly passed on to sons. Daughters are normally excluded from the line of inheritance. It is rare to find female members having the same access to the family property and company shares. Although some female members are assigned to high-ranking management posts, the proportion is far from equitable. Many parents still prefer to give birth to sons rather than daughters. For the wealthy families, girls have more or less an equal chance for an education, but this is often at risk during a time of family crisis or financial difficulty. The inequality between males and females in the Chaozhou community is still obvious.

Strong semi-religious belief is another key area that makes them distinct. Ancestor worship and *fengshui* (geomancy) are two main kinds of semi-religious belief. Many respondents revealed that they have remitted money to their home towns to build their ancestors' grave. When the first batch of Chaozhou people settled in Hong Kong, the Hungry Ghost (*Yulan*) Festival, a folk festival in Chaozhou that was held on the seventh lunar month in the Chinese calendar for all the ghosts from the netherworld, was transplanted to their new home. This festival is still held annually in Hong Kong, and because of this, Chaozhou people are viewed by others as 'highly superstitious and organized'.

However, Chaozhou people also share common cultural values – such as respect for seniority, emphasis on family values, filial piety, honesty and sincerity – with other regional groups. In other words, the Chaozhou families solidly reflect certain core features of inheritance, business adaptation and economic development characteristics of the Chinese culture. Although the arrangement of family real estate and company shares are generally confined to the sons, the inculcation of human and social capital mainly cover both sons and daughters. In short, the case of Chaozhou people supports the argument that Chinese culture itself is highly adaptive and flexible in coping with the changing environment.

Through the study of the Chaozhou and the long-established families, I can roughly generalize that, during the start-up and expansion period, most of the founding patriarchs rely heavily on family economic and human capital support, such as personal savings or labour. When family businesses reach the mature stage and diversification is required, Western management concepts and outside professionals will be absorbed. In addition, it is also found that inheritance and transmission of family business is not simply confined to economic capital. Other capital, such as human and social capital, are equally emphasized. Some important findings can be summarized as below.

First, the principle of equal inheritance. In a highly modern and Westernized metropolis like Hong Kong, the transmission of family real estate and company shares are still confined to blood (birth) male heirs. Daughters are generally excluded from the line of inheritance. Traditional patrimonial practice regarding passing on the property to sons rather than daughters (*chuannan bu chuannu*) is still upheld.

Second, the transmission of invisible capital. Conventionally, inheritance only refers to the transmission of economic capital. In fact, it is observed that human capital and social capital are equally important. For those who have experienced smooth transmission of their family businesses, transmission of human capital (such as education and leadership) and social capital (such as personal ties and business connections) are equally stressed. For those less successful successions, the opposite was the case.

Third, the continuity of family business. Although family division is common, it doesn't necessarily lead to the disintegration of the family business. In order to maintain their family's reputation, integrity and benefit to all members, some families may choose to keep the family business intact as they see such an arrangement can retain their competitiveness in the market.

In this research, it is found that equal inheritance among sons is not only maintained in the Chaozhou ethnic group, but Chinese society as a whole. In principle, each son (even illegitimate ones) generally obtains a more or less equal share of the family property and company shares. However, there are some minor variations. For instance, if some sons have committed more towards the family business, more shares will be given to them. In other circumstances, to compensate sons who have not finished their education or have not yet married, more shares will be assigned to them. However, according to one respondent, such an arrangement reflects the actual 'equality' among sons.

Although daughters are generally excluded from the line of inheritance, there are some exceptions. In the study, it is found that daughters rarely have equity in the family firm. Instead, parents prefer giving them dowries when they marry. Most of the respondents still hold the view that daughters are 'temporary members' of the family. A daughter will eventually marry and bear their husband's surname. Then, they will become an 'outsider'. Giving them company shares will complicate the management of the family businesses. However, two pairs of daughters who left school early to help their parents in establishing the businesses were given a certain proportion of the family estate and a certain amount of company shares. Such an arrangement, as told by one of the interviewees, is to signify the great contribution they have made in building up the family enterprises. In other words, although family estate passes mainly along the male line, it does not imply that it is a completely rigid system.

As discussed earlier, when talking about inheritance, conventional arguments only dwell on such concepts as economic capital, simply being money or real estate. Little attention is given to the transmission or inculcation of human capital and social capital. In fact, these two types of capital are also very crucial for family and business development. In this research, it is found that many respondents are fully aware of such elements and pay great attention to upgrading their children's education, leadership, personal ties and business connections.

Education is regarded as one of the most important elements that can increase a person's stock of human capital. Many respondents agreed that they would give their children as much education as possible if they could afford it. In fact, there is much evidence showing that many of the studied families have invested heavily in their children's education. When the family financial condition improves, both sons and daughters would have equal opportunities for education. A common feature is that at least one of the studied families has obtained a university degree. Some even obtained a higher degree such as a Master's or doctorate – a much higher and more remarkable attainment when compared to the general public.

Developing leadership skills in the children is treated as another key element in maintaining their human capital. Leadership is a driving force for business growth. Losing this spirit implies the business cannot sustain the momentum to grow. In this study, it is found that many respondents had tried to foster their children's leadership abilities when the heirs were very young. For instance, one of the respondents said that he would play a 'buy and sell' game with his son when he was a little baby. He suggested that such a game could inspire his son's interest in business. When his son got older, he even let him attend company meetings or join him on business trips. He argued that given more chance of involvement, his son would develop a sense of responsibility, commitment and leadership.

There are other stories about establishing leadership for the new generation. Like many of the long-established families, many Chaozhou respondents also encourage their children to participate in social activities. For instance, some of them recommend their children join charitable organizations such as the CCC, TWGHs PLK, Rotary Club or the Lion's Club. Some even encourage their children to take an active role in serving the community or in organizing social activities. In their mindset, organizing or participating in social activities is just like taking part in extracurricular activities when their children were still in school. The experience and skill it offers can supplement pure theory learned from books.

Personal ties and business networks are the key elements of social capital. As we know, social capital can enhance business opportunities, on the one hand, while reducing transaction costs, on the other. In my earlier study of Chaozhou rice entrepreneurs in Hong Kong, I found that many of these Chaozhou entrepreneurs liked to establish their sons' social connections by taking them to social or business gatherings. I further found that the transmission of social connections and personal ties would not be affected even when the father had passed away. Of course, the transmission would be easier if the parents were still alive. However, even when the parents have died, their previous good connections could still have some far-reaching effect on their children.

Compared with economic capital, human and social capital are 'non-exclusive', and both sons and daughters have equal access to them. Successful transmission of family businesses should therefore not only focus on the transfer of economic capital, but should also pay due attention to human and social capital. However, since the transfer of such types of capital is more complicated and less predictable, these make the succession and inheritance process highly controversial and critical.

It seems clear that there is a strong conflicting force within the Chinese families. And it seems clear that such force originates from the equal inheritance system. In the research, it is found that improvements in a family member's education, leadership and business networks may further accelerate the splitting up of a family. When the father finds that he can no longer keep his sons united, or when he foresees that internal conflicts will plague the family, he will choose to divide the estate and shares, and thus different family members will inevitably go their separate ways. *Niaoda lichoa, jiada bifen* (a baby bird will fly away when it grows up, while a large family will split up) is a frequently quoted idiom. In other words, division of families is perceived as normal, natural and inevitable.

Although a family will divide eventually, as a legal entity, business division does not always follow. Wong (1988: 155) argues that 'Equality in legal claims to the *jia* (family) estate does not mean physical division of industrial property.' In this research, there is clear evidence that even if the family estate has been divided and company shares allocated among heirs, the family enterprise will not dissipate in a similar fashion. One of the young respondents said: 'This enterprise was founded by my grandfather. Its expansion or decline reflects our family's reputation and status in the community or *xianqi fulao* [townsmen and elders]. We must try our best to keep the business growing.' In other words, a divisive force plaguing the family does not always appear in the business.

In addition, the stability of a business can be maintained after the restructuring of the organization. As more educated people join the management, reformation and modernization commonly occur. The introduction of Western-style management ideology, which emphasizes transparency, accountability, monitoring and delegation, can reduce the over-reliance on family members and also enhance the confidence of those family members who aren't involved in the family business. This explains why most of these reformations are initiated by family members themselves. After that, non-family professionals can also be attracted to the business and absorbed into the management, and thus further improve the business' vitality and efficiency. This process is common if the family business finally goes public and is listed in the stock market. Clearly, although family estates divide from generation to generation, family businesses do not necessary follow the same path.

In this research, it is also found that although envy, jealousy, emotion, passion and sentiment are frequently quoted in family relations, rational calculation, formalization and depersonalization are equally stressed in business, particularly in wealthy families. Even when there are family disputes, they may choose to settle rationally, so that their major businesses would not be affected. Throughout this book, I argue that only on very special occasions do a tiny number of family members choose to settle their family dispute in a sensational way. In fact, most of my respondents deliberately adopted a rational approach in managing their family businesses. Thus, they have mechanisms to overcome the inherent weaknesses of family businesses, that is, inefficiencies, conflicts and dissention.

In a nutshell, it is found that the equal inheritance system in fact is the origin of the economic dynamism of Chinese family businesses. My simple explanation of this assertion is that equal inheritance breeds sibling comparison. Sibling comparison then generates competition at different levels, and motivates each son to work hard, which then lays the groundwork for economic development. In Chinese societies, such as the Chinese mainland (after the 1980s), Taiwan, Hong Kong and Macau, and other regions with a large Chinese population, such as Singapore, Thailand and Indonesia, where equal inheritance applies, the strong entrepreneurial drive and remarkable economic development provides solid evidence to support the above arguments.

Equal inheritance and internal competition

Apart from making the argument that a complete succession process should equally address economic capital, human capital and social capital, I go a step further to suggest that the equal inheritance system in fact can assist economic development. In the past, equal inheritance was criticized as the source of internal family conflict. This study finds that not all family conflict is destructive or malicious. In fact, constructive and positive conflict can stimulate sibling competition and cooperation. Equal inheritance can, on the one hand, create a fair base for internal comparison, and on the other, offer initial capital for career development. In other words, the equal inheritance system can serve two major functions: competition and initial capital.

First, equal inheritance not only implies that each son can get an equal share of the family property, but an equal starting point for the comparison of each sibling's level of ability and hardwork. If one can excel over other siblings after division, one will be designated 'capable and hardworking'. For those who do not make clear advancement – but rather decline – after division, they will be labelled 'incapable' or 'dependent on their parents' fortune'. Psychological stress and anxiety will thus be generated. In order to prove one's ability, each son will try his best to compete with his siblings. Such anxiety in fact is the source of competition. In Weber's opinion, competition is the main force that leads to economic expansion. In fact, sibling competition is not confined to business; some try to engage in a professional job and some start their own businesses, while some stay in family management. As a result, it is common to discover that in those large families, different family members are generally diversified intentionally or unintentionally into different fields.

Second, equal inheritance can offer start-up capital to those sons who have an interest in founding their own businesses. This capital includes money, leadership, personal ties and business networks. With this initial capital support, some siblings can seek independence when they find their autonomy or freedom is compromised. This psychological motivation is the origin of the self-employment mentality, or in Schumpeterian terms, entrepreneurship. This spirit, in fact, is also the essence of charismatic leadership.

Therefore, equal inheritance breeds comparison. Comparison generates competition. Competition is the breeding ground for leadership and entrepreneurship, which are the major forces for economic development. In fact, in Chinese societies such as Taiwan, Hong Kong, Singapore and even Macau, where equal inheritance applies, the strong entrepreneurial drive and remarkable economic development offers solid evidence in supporting the above arguments. In the subsequent paragraphs, let me elaborate these arguments one by one.

When talking about inheritance and business patterns, many people will quickly make a simple comparison between the Japanese primogeniture system and the Chinese equal inheritance system. Then, they will grossly jump to the conclusion that the Japanese inheritance system can assist capital accumulation, increase corporate longevity and aid economic development, while the Chinese inheritance system shows the opposite. Clearly, the equal inheritance system among heirs becomes the principal target for attack. Ho (1976) argues that a downward trend of social mobility of most Mandarin officials in the Qing dynasty was mainly due to the dividing force of the equal inheritance system.

Other scholars come from a similar perspective. After making a comparison between the Meiji Reformation and the Self-Strengthening Movement, Levy (1955) concludes that the Chinese family system, implicitly including the inheritance system, is the stumbling block that led to the failure of the movement. Chau (1991) goes a step further to argue that the equal inheritance system does not favour capital accumulation and corporate longevity. In other words, nearly all of the scholars conclude that the Chinese equal inheritance system is dysfunctional towards economic development.

In this research, I find it is quite true that there is centrifugal force inside the family and this force can lead to division of the family estate. However, as I mentioned earlier, from a Weberian perspective we can see an equally true picture that since most of the studied families have undergone a process of rationalization, this dividing force does not always appear in business. As a legal entity, it can more effectively accommodate family conflict. Generally speaking, after careful design and rational calculation, family members can come to a mutual agreement that keeping a united business offers more advantages to family members. Thus, they may choose to maintain their businesses intact, rather than break them up.

In addition, I even find that the mechanism of capital levelling from generation to generation only narrowly reflects the situation in the family estate. It does not deal with human and social capital. Evidence also shows that the inheritance system can initiate competition, which further generates momentum to push the family business forward. F20 shared with me his views on family division:

> I remember that my second son has urged me to divide the estate and give him most of the company shares. He feels he is smarter and has worked harder than others have. He even accuses my third son, who shows little enthusiasm for work, as being lazy. If I insist on keeping the family property undivided, it will hurt his incentive and creates direct confrontation between these two sons. Therefore, I divided the family property and assigned each of them to manage a subsidiary. As a result, each son can have his own area of development. To my surprise, after the partition, not only my second son works harder. They know that their effort will finally reflect on the balance sheet. My third and fourth sons also work harder. I am really happy to see such change.

Equal inheritance explicitly hoists up the flag of 'equality'. Since each son can more or less get an equal share of his father's wealth, division creates a criterion for sibling comparison. If, after estate division, son A's wealth decreases while son B's wealth increases, son A will be labelled as inferior while son B is superior. There is a saying that *fenjia sannian xian gaodi*, which means that one can see who is more capable after estate division after three years (Yue 1989). In other words, psychological stress and anxiety are generated naturally after estate division, and this psychological stress will motivate siblings to compete with each other on different levels.

As discussed in previous chapters, when talking about capital, economic capital is only a part of it. Human capital (education, experience and leadership) and social capital (personal ties, social reputation and business networks) shall be equally emphasized. Unlike economic capital, human capital and social capital are less tangible. As pointed out earlier, many of the respondents prefer giving their offspring as much in terms of education and social connections as possible. Very often, good educational qualifications and a strong leadership personality can lead to sibling competition. This competition will motivate them to decide their own career: whether to join the family enterprise, to leave for a professional career, or to start their own business is a very complex decision. It involves family members' rational calculation, discussion, cooperation, accommodation and the patriarch's strategic deployment.

Lots of in-depth studies show that successful personal ties and business networks can reduce transaction costs and increase business opportunities (Landa 1983). The transmission of social capital from father to sons can enhance their business competitiveness. F6's story can be used to illustrate this point. When his father died, F6 was only a small child. Although his father had left him some property, it was less significant when compared with a well-established network. When F6 decided to start his own business, his father's social capital came on to the stage. F6 got his initial bank loan on the recommendation and personal guarantee of one of his father's well-trusted friends. He said:

> When I was introduced to the senior people [both in the local or Chaozhou community], they usually added an elaboration: 'He is the son of XX [F6's father's name].' And they would reply, 'Good boy! You look like your father and equally outstanding.' You see, my father has still kept his good reputation in the circle.

Another similar case concerns George Ho, an illegitimate son of Sir Robert Ho Tung. When his father died, he was given $50,000 as a gift. It was a tiny sum of money when compared with his father's multi-million dollar estate. George Ho, however, was not restricted from using his father's reputation and social capital. In fact, when he later started up his own business, his father's well-connected networks helped him greatly. To cite an example, when George Ho wanted to apply for a radio broadcasting licence in the early 1970s, his father's close friends, such as Sir Shiu-kin Tang and Sir Tsun-lin Chau, and his brother-in-law, Lo Man-ho, helped him (Zheng and Wong 2007).

Chau Cham-wang, son of Sir Tsun-nin Chau, had a similar story. Cham-wang did not want to join the family enterprise, but showed keen interest in setting up his own business at an early age. In 1983 he founded Peace Mark Limited, which produced clocks and watches. In an interview, sharing with the reporter his experience in starting up the business, he admitted that his success was mainly due to his father's influence: 'When some of my uncles learned that I was son of Sir Tsun-nin, they showed enthusiasm, offered help and pointed me in the right direction.... Such assistance was critical, especially during the start-up period' (Mak 1992: 21–2).

From the above cases, we can infer two things: (1) equal inheritance sets a base for comparison, which is the prerequisite for competition; and (2) inheritance cannot narrowly refer to the passing on of economic capital – social capital and human capital are also essential. Because of the non-exclusive nature of social capital, sons can have equal right to access it. In order to compete for this resource, each son will do his best to maximize their usage. As a result, there is sibling competition for leadership and social achievement.

Family adaptation and business diversification

In the past we felt that Chinese family businesses were very conservative and against change. In fact, I find quite the opposite – that the Chinese family is a highly flexible unit and can adapt to the competitive environment easily in restructuring the organization or way of doing business in order to spread the business risk. In the following paragraphs, light will be shed on this mechanism of adaptation, diversification and reformation.

Literally, adaptation means 'a process of adapting, fitting, or modifying; (or) a process of adjustment to environmental conditions.... It is a continuing process through which the organization of groups is modified to meet the requirements of their social and physical environment' (*The Webster's Third New International Dictionary* 1986). Under the principle of 'survival of the fittest', any species that wants to survive must adapt to the environment. Likewise, if the Chinese family system wants to maintain its vitality and agility, it must adapt to the natural as well as the sociopolitical environment.

Political instability and social unrest were frequent occurrences in Chinese history. Within the last century, there were nationwide wars, large-scale population migrations, revolutionary movements, colonization and semi-colonization. It was very difficult for the family system to remain unshaken after all these serious events. Maintaining diversity and having a more flexible structure, it seems, can offer advantages. Equal inheritance among heirs can more effectively reduce risk and enhance diversity.

After initiating a systematic comparison between the Japanese family businesses and the Chinese family businesses, Chen and Qiu (1984: 17) make the following succinct comment:

> If we say that the growth and development of Japanese business is like a bamboo, it is straight and can grow in great height. Then, we can say that their businesses are only hard on the outer surface but empty inside. There isn't any blood connection [in the family business].

In fact, not only Chen and Qiu argue that Japanese family and business do not have any blood connection. Other scholars have also come to a similar conclusion after their in-depth research or observation. Chamberlain (1971: 17) comments as follows:

> It is strange but true, that you may often go into [a Japanese] family and find half-a-dozen persons calling each other parent and child, brother and sister, uncle and nephew, and yet being really either no blood-relations at all, or else relations in quite different degrees from those conventionally assumed.

Because the Japanese family turned 'blood family into artificial corporation', its family or inheritance system lost much of its natural character. That is why Macfarlane (1998: 121) states that 'the lineage or *ie*, was not based on birth [blood – original note] but on choice [contract – original note]'.

Because of the practice of the primogeniture inheritance system, we can see that when they do not have a natural heir, an adopted son or son-in-law can be crowned as the unquestionable successor. This practice clearly differs from the Chinese equal inheritance system. In Chinese culture, only blood-tied male heirs (even illegitimate sons) have the unchallengeable right of access to their parents' property. Adopted sons or sons-in-law do not have equal rights. In other words, blood connections are the single most important criterion for a descendant's legitimacy (Wang 1977, 1985).

If bamboo is used to represent Japanese family business, then the banyan tree is a reasonable analogue that I propose represents Chinese family business. What does the banyan tree look like? The description in the *Compact Oxford English Dictionary* (1993: 104) is:

> Banyan tree is a remarkable East Indian tree. The branches of which drop shoots to the ground that take root and support their parent branches. Extending in this way, one tree will often cover a large expanse of ground.... Sir T. Herbert describes the banyan as a tree, or rather twenty trees, the boughs rooting and springing up a whole acre together.... Named by us the Banyan Tree from their adorning and adoring it with ribbons and streamers of varicolored Taffata.

Clearly, the impression that 'the branches of which drop shoots to the ground that take root and support their parent branches' is very similar to many sons (branches) with a strong desire for starting up their different types of stores or businesses (shoots) to further support their 'parent' business or family. More interestingly, as the banyan tree 'symbolizes strength, stability, sturdy health, longevity, and perseverance despite the odds' (Jim 1995: 289), it also fits very well with the typical nature (or image) that Chinese family and business are (ideally) organized and developed this way. In fact, in order to survive harsh conditions and turbulent times, Chinese family and business have evolved from time to time to become highly adaptable and flexible units. Li (1982: 90) comments:

> In different environments, due to certain special requirements, some principle will be emphasized while another principle will become hidden. As a result, it [the family system] may be incorrectly interpreted as deviating from the traditional principle. In fact, this phenomenon can be simply corrected by looking into the interaction of the underlying principle. It is not difficult to understand that the basic principle does not change. Chinese family tries to adapt to different circumstances. The highly adaptable and flexible nature of the family system cannot be observed from the structure of family but from its growth and development.

When Cohen (1976: viii) first arrived in Yen-liao, a county in central Taiwan, in the 1960s, he observed a similarly striking phenomenon: 'I soon discovered that the so-called "large", "extended", or "joint" form of family was commonplace, to the extent that more than half of the village population were members of such units.' Why were there so many 'large, extended and joint' families? Cohen went further, to argue that it was due to the special conditions in Yen-liao. Yen-liao had fertile land that was excellent for tobacco growing. Tobacco growing is the major cash crop for the local economy, and very labour-intensive. During the planting, ploughing and harvesting seasons, the need for labour was exceptionally strong. Because of such special labour requirement, if the families still insisted on dividing up, they would be driven to a less favourable situation and it would be very difficult to adapt to the 'atypical environment'. Therefore, Cohen (ibid.: 236) further comments:

> With short-lived families unable to bring tobacco to their farms or combine farming with other enterprises.... Given the limitations of farming, the heightened interdependence characteristics of the Yen-liao joint families could not so commonly emerge in the traditional environment, because it would have to be in the form of diversification.

Why does the pattern of family structure become different there? Cohen (ibid.: 114) gives us his conclusion in his book: 'A deep interest in the joint holdings, for it is important to all of them that the maintenance of the common body of holdings be compatible with their own interest.' In other words, 'own interest' is the real factor. Maintaining 'joint holdings' can bring better benefits to all family members. Thus, they prefer to keep this type of family structure together.

Since the inheritance systems in Japanese and Chinese families are completely different, adaptation mechanisms also vary. The variation clearly leads to the contrasting features in their organizational structure, management style, business practice and family pattern. However, I will argue that such differences do not imply that the Japanese family business is more efficient and can facilitate economic growth, while the Chinese family business is inefficient and therefore suffocates economic development.

Adaptation implies diversification and spread of risk. Because of persistent and dramatic social unrest and political instability in the Chinese mainland, dividing up the family estate among sons, it seems, can avoid the problem of 'putting all the eggs in a single basket'. Viewed from this perspective, the division of the family estate is similar to encouraging each son to seek independence or to start their own business, and therefore accelerates the process of diversification. F2's family is a typical example. F2 said:

> Our main business was dry food import and export trading. In the 1950s, due to the imposition of a trade embargo against mainland China, my business was hit badly. I learnt from that experience and later diversified my

> business. In the 1970s, I found all my sons were mature. If all of them joined the same business, it would be too risky and conflict would be inevitable. I therefore diversified our business to different areas. For instance, since my eldest son was a trained electronic engineer and had good connections in semi-conductor production, I went into that field and he was responsible for it. My second son had an interest in button production and he was assigned to take charge of that area. My third and fourth sons head the property investment firm. Each son has his own autonomy.

In the survey, other respondents, like F3 and F8, had also reported to me that they had diversified their businesses to different fields in quite similar patterns and rationales.

The Lo Kwai-cheung family is another typical case. As mentioned in Chapter 2, although some of the Lo family's members joined the Vitasoy Group, many of them left the flagship company to start their own businesses. For instance, Lo Tang-cheung and Lo Kai-muk started Café de Coral, while Lo Fong-cheung founded the Fairwood Fast Food and Sun Generation Restaurant. Lo Kai-fook, one of the third generation, started the East-East Noodle and Fook Do-Do Restaurant. Clearly, the Lo Kwai-cheung family nearly monopolizes the restaurant market in Hong Kong. Although the Lo cousins and nephews are competitors in the fast-food market, most of them still keep their shares in the Vitasoy Group (see Chapter 2).

Another example is the Li Shek-pang family. After the second generation took over the family business, Li Koon-chun, the eldest son, was directed to manage the family businesses, which were mainly shipping and rice. Li Tse-fong, the second son, was told to start a bank business (Bank of East Asia Limited) with other merchants, while Li Lan-sang, another son, was to found Kowloon Dairy Products Limited. A special pattern of 'brotherhood division of labour' was clearly formed. As the family expanded continuously to the third, fourth and fifth generations, specialization of cousins/nephews became more common. Some become professionals, government officials, started their own businesses or were delegated to manage their family businesses. For example, Ronald Li, youngest son of Koon-chun, left the family business and started his own business and founded the Far East Exchange (later incorporated into the Stock Exchange of Hong Kong) and became its first chairman. Didier Li, the fourth generation of the family, set up Pink Entertainment. Although the Lis may criticize each other in public and give the outsiders a false impression that they are not that 'harmonious', most of them, however, have maintained strong linkages with each other. Each branch still keeps a controlling share in the Bank of East Asia (see Chapter 2).

To sum up, I find Chinese family business relies much more on 'horizontal growth' rather than 'vertical expansion'. Like the banyan tree, '[The tree would] send down roots from the boughs and form another tree that can support the parent tree.' The aerial root, like the spirit of seeking self-autonomy or independence, symbolizes a strong desire to create one's own base for growth and expansion. When such roots touch the ground and are given favourable conditions, they will finally grow and expand into 'another tree', that is, another enterprise. As a result, 'one tree will often cover a large expanse of ground'. Traditionally, a Chinese family does not stop sons from creating their own businesses, but encourages them to do so. Different sons are asked to diversify to different businesses. Some are directly related to the family main business, some are less related. In all cases, they not only maintain a strong level of interconnectedness, but also form an 'atypical' business structure.

Unconventional path of growth

After a detailed account of the adaptation and diversification mechanism, let me now turn my attention to examining how Chinese family businesses adjust their structure to fit the Hong Kong environment. When discussing Hong Kong's success, the highly entrepreneurial, flexible and efficient feature of Chinese family business there is always commented upon. A striking fact is that quite a large number of them have operated in Hong Kong for over three generations. Such a phenomenon deviates from what people traditionally perceived, which was that Chinese family business is small, less efficient and short-lived. How do they differ now?

I can draw out some common features about the path of Chinese family business succession and growth. The first feature is that most of the founders were refugees from the Chinese mainland who also came from a poor family background. They were forced to earn money to support their family when they were very young and a great proportion of them only had obtained informal or primary education. Nearly all of them were indirectly forced to start their own business instead of engaging in a formal job or entering the government bureaucracy. Some of them were forced to leave their home towns by war, such as the Japanese invasion in the 1930s, civil wars or other repeated political turmoil such as the Communist takeover and the Cultural Revolution. Some left to be reunited with their parents or brothers in Hong Kong. In other words, they would more or less be categorized as 'refugees'. They earned their fortunes from scratch, and their stories were usually labelled as 'Horatio Alger-style success stories'.

General trading was the basic form of business that they commonly engaged in at the very beginning. This type of business required a small amount of initial capital and simple organizational structure, but had high flexibility. They provided services mainly to the Chinese community and worked long hours all year long, without days off on Sundays, Saturdays or public holidays. Although they worked restlessly and industriously, their net profits were small and scant. In order to save their meagre earnings, they had to live a frugal and simple life. They put their savings into their children's education or re-invested them in their businesses.

In this research, I find that Li Shek-pang, Fung Ping-shan, Hui Oi-chow, Fung Pak-liu and the Wing On Kwok families are all examples of people who started their businesses with very little. Of the 26 Chaozhou families, only four claimed that they were from affluent families. The other 22 said they were from poor backgrounds. Even for these four affluent respondents, their families had also suffered during wars or conflicts in the Chinese mainland. They had to start all over again from nothing in Hong Kong (see Chapter 2 and the Appendix).

After years of ceaseless work, some entrepreneurs gradually accumulated economic capital. Years at the grindstone also gave them solid experience as well as extensive business networks. They expanded their businesses by seizing every opportunity. Manufacturing and wholesaling businesses were some of the major areas that offered them promising returns. Most of the Chaozhou respondents earned their 'first bucket of gold' from the middle of the 1950s to the 1970s, when Hong Kong's economy was taking off.

Years later, they turned into 'millionaires'. Seeing that the property and financial markets were highly profitable, they wanted to get a slice of the cake. Since they had already established well-connected business networks and personal ties at this stage, some of them plunged successfully into the financial and property markets. The prosperity and promising growth of these markets from the 1980s to the 1990s also served as the impetus for their businesses' further expansion.

When their businesses grew larger, their organization became less flexible and less efficient. To avoid excessive bureaucracy and also to gain new market outlets, diversification and internationalization became a reasonable step that a family business could take. Many family leaders diversified their businesses to other market segments or explored new products. For instance, some family businesses expanded their market outlets to Taiwan, Southeast Asia or the West. Some tried to upgrade the quality of their products and services in order to enhance their competitiveness. If their financial backing was strong enough, some would even try to explore new areas, such as high-technology products, the internet, entertainment or public utilities. At this stage, family undertakings have become fully fledged business concerns. They had also evolved from traditional, paternal and personalistic to a modern, formalized and highly sophisticated organization.

In his paper, *Chinese Family Firm: A Model*, Wong (1985) constructs a simple model to explain the growth of the Chinese family business. He suggests that the development of Chinese family business usually follows a pattern of establishment, centralization, segmentation and disintegration. He also argues that these phases tend to coincide with generation shifts inside the family. Generally speaking, the founding entrepreneurs come from poor family backgrounds. After unremitting toil and effort, they created a platform for the family to expand and grow. Since the founding entrepreneur has centralized all power, he can mobilize all the family capital when he sees it is right for expansion. As a result, family business can effectively respond to the market. The joint efforts of his siblings also accelerates business expansion.

Both the family and the firm will experience fundamental change when the founding entrepreneur dies. Each son has a more or less equal share of the family assets, and some of them prefer to keep their share in the family business while some like to withdraw from it. This is where there is room for conflict. In other words, the process of fragmentation occurs in the second generation. However, as Wong explains, since the relationship between the siblings is still close, conflict is kept below the surface. Thus, the family business can still loosely stand under the same family banner and will not disintegrate immediately.

When the third-generation leaders are promoted to the management team, internal conflict is intensified and galvanized. The relationship between members of the third generation is comparatively less close than the previous generation. Therefore, when conflict emerges, it is less easy for them to reconcile and make compromises. They may choose to wind-up the family business and make their own fortunes. As a result, the family business will come to its disintegrative stage. Wong (ibid.: 61) implicitly draws the conclusion that Chinese family business can seldom last beyond three generations: 'Family enterprises in their Chinese guise are apparently short-lived. As common wisdom has it, they seldom last beyond three generations.' Although Wong has suggested that Chinese family firms can be highly adaptable, he does not show the concrete mechanism to show which type of firm survives, or in what manner they do so.

It is true that Wong's model is generally valid in analysing the rise and fall of small-to-medium firms. However, I find it far from satisfactory in explaining the phenomenon of wealthy long-established families. For the large family firms, although family property is divided between each son (or branch) in the second or third generation, it does not necessarily lead to business disintegration. In other words, I think Wong's model does not take the following three points into consideration: first, it underestimates the propensity of rational calculation, cooperation and collaboration among family members; second, it also underestimates the impact of education, networks and socio-political factors; and third, it does not take the evolution of the firm and family structure into account.

Throughout my research I observe that improved education in a large family can automatically 'prune the family tree' and reduce family disputes. A well-connected network and socio-political background can link different families together. Division of the family estate can be a rational plan or a tactic of adaptation. The restructuring of firm and family can reduce internal family conflict while also increasing family members' cooperation and business efficiency. All of these can enhance family consolidation and business competitiveness.

In addition, I also find that the developmental process of large family businesses only partially follows what Wong has suggested. In other words, I would argue that if any family business pays attention to the transfer of economic capital, human capital and social capital in their succession, the possibility of keeping its business from one generation to the next will increase in parallel. If my speculation is correct, we may reasonably ask the following questions: What will be the new developmental path of the Chinese family firm? What are the factors that make these families excel in maintaining their business vitality, efficiency and solidarity from generation to generation?

As mentioned earlier, I find most of the Chinese family businesses generally go through the initial two stages as Wong has suggested. In the first stage, the founding entrepreneur works ceaselessly and lives an extremely simple life. Due to the lack of capital and business connections, the founding entrepreneur can only afford to set up a small business at the beginning. Long hours of work and a frugal life style pave the foundation for growth of the family business. Some of the second generation, usually including the eldest son, start to help their father in running the business at this stage. Their early participation in the family business gives them very good down-to-earth business training. Their personal networks and leadership style gradually develop. That is why they can understand more thoroughly about business operation and the company's culture. Having served as key assistants to the founders, they are trained with better product knowledge (Figure 6.1).

The family business expands step by step in a gradual way. After earning the 'first bucket of gold', the founding entrepreneur expands the business to other areas, such as manufacturing and wholesaling. Some may even dabble in the property market. This marks the second level, the expansion stage. This stage is also similar to the model that Wong has constructed. During this stage, the second generation is further promoted to a high level of management. Since some second-generation members have achieved a comparatively better education, for example, college or university, they will bring in new ideas and inspiration. This 'new blood' may introduce reform and modification.

Due to the high concentration of power in the founder's hands, decision-making is still prompt and therefore can effectively respond to market competition. If they can seize opportunities as they arise, the family business can expand quickly. Another feature is that the better-off the family becomes, the greater the

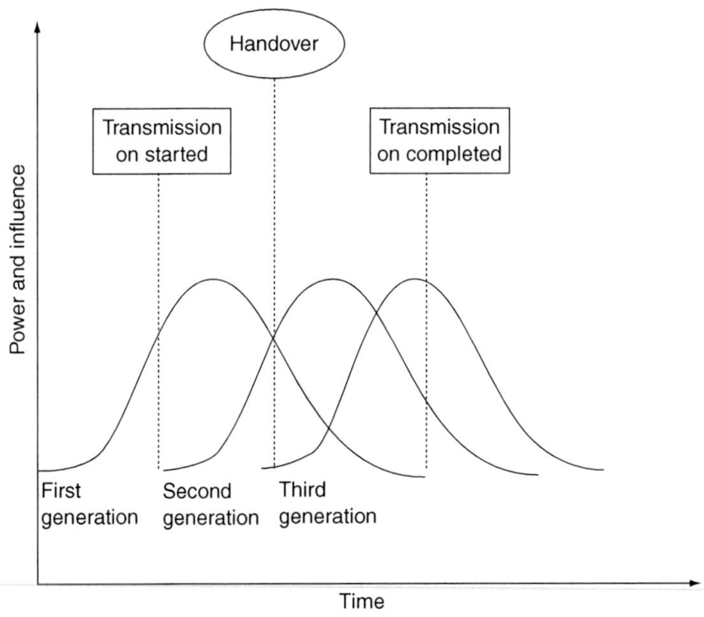

Figure 6.1 Succession and transmission of Chinese family business.

investment in their children's education. Some third-generation members may begin to participate in the business. Such participation lays the groundwork for the future transmission of leadership and personal ties to the third generation.

The maturity of the second generation also means the ageing of the first. Illness and old age are symbiotic. The founder has to pass the baton to his heirs – this is the moment of handover. To some extent, although the founder has declared his retirement, he may still retain a certain amount of control in the company. The predecessor still treats himself as mentor or advisor. Taken in a positive light, such a practice can serve as a stabilizing force on the family business. For instance, when Fung Hong-chu announced his retirement, his sons Victor Fung and William Fung took over the leadership. Fung Hong-chu stepped off the stage and only served as advisor. He only gave his opinion on critical issues.

Another example is F1. When F1's son left an international petroleum company and joined the family business, F1 planed to retire. Several years later, when F1 found his son could independently manage the company, he passed the leadership on and only remained as honorary chairman. The management was fully taken up by his son and his partner's son. Although F1 was regarded as being retired, he still wielded influence. He visited the company very frequently. F2, F10 and F11 are similar examples. One of the special features is that their family property was divided according to the details of their will. Although most of their sons or daughters have married and moved away, they still maintained good relations and strong connections. Their businesses also remained unaffected.

The death of the founder implies the complete taking up of leadership of the second generation (transmission completed). If the terms of the will are written clearly enough, very few disagreements or conflicts will occur. When the second generation gets a completely free hand to run the company, they may experience teething problems, such as management struggles or insufficient support of regular clients and old employees. Such short-term setbacks can quickly be overcome when the new leadership successfully manage crises. Then, their businesses can continue to grow. But, if initial teething problems cannot be tackled effectively and turned around, the new leadership may be challenged and the stability of the business may be affected. The problem may become more critical if there is disagreement among family members. Whether a family business can survive such difficulties depends very much on the amount of human capital and social capital that the new generation has already acquired and can exercise.

If the new leadership has obtained sufficient human and social capital for commanding, the probability of solving the transmission problems will be high. Thus, their businesses have a better chance to keep on expanding. The continual growth of business triggers off diversification. A greater involvement of the third generation implies a gradual transmission of leadership to another generation.

Later, when the second generation hands over the helm to the third generation, different problems may arise. By then, these problems are the increasing expansion of the family business and the over-accumulation of capital in a single field. Such over-concentration means rising business risk and uncertainty. In addition, increased family size also puts pressure on the family enterprise. If the new leadership cannot solve the problems properly, the stability of the business may once again come under threat. In order to divert conflict and attract well-educated family members to contribute to the family business, diversification is the only option. Through spreading the business, family members can be deployed to different areas.

In this research, it is found that there are four categories of diversification. The first one is diversification of products. F1 developed other products like pig feed and cow feed beside his main product line of poultry feed. Lee Kam Kee and Eu Yan Sang are other examples. Market diversification is another category that they frequently used. For instance, Li & Fung, Bank of East Asia and Wing On Holdings set up different selling outlets or offices around the globe (see Chapter 2). Allocating sons or daughters to different businesses or departments is the third method for accommodating family members' interests. For example, F2 assigned his eldest son to the semi-conductor business, the second son to zipper and button production, and the third and fourth sons to the property sector. Through such a division of labour, his four sons can, on the one hand, enjoy their own sphere of autonomy, while on the other, retain their veto in the main family business. F3 gives his first brother a free hand in managing the rice wholesaling business; his second brother and he were responsible for rice importation while his youngest brother operates a travel agency.

Apart from diversification into different fields, in order to 'prune the family tree' and avoid too many members getting involved in a single family business, some members may even be encouraged to develop their own professional careers. For example, many of Li Shek-pang's descendants have become lawyers, government bureaucrats, physicians, university professors, musicians and engineers. It is the fourth category of diversification – the diversification of family members into different professions and careers.

In fact, diversification can be interpreted as a careful and strategic deployment of family human capital. Wolf (1968) argues that division of labour can enable the family to support itself more effectively than if they are divided into small nuclear family units. Willmott (1960) stresses that diversification can give each member enough freedom to develop individual operations and exercise responsibility. Moench (1963) supports this argument by citing many examples to prove that diversification prevails in larger families. Cohen (1976: 236) also echoes this point and writes that 'diversification was more characteristic of the wealthy families, whichever larger and able to invest in many directions'.

In other words, after careful design and rational calculation, many families prefer to maintain their businesses intact, even though they have to separate or divide their family estate. They are aware that if they divide their family business, they may lose their competitive edge, and therefore can no longer enjoy the so-called 'economy of scale'. From the diversification of family members, we can clearly see a careful and rational arrangement of family personnel and investment. Since family business has been diversified, it may be less risky or less dangerous when some members face financial problems or even collapse. The business is no longer solely dependent on a single family member or *fang* (branch).

The transfer of leadership and social networks from the third generation to the fourth generation marks the fourth stage of family business development (Figure 6.2). After several decades of development, the conventional organization, as well as its management mechanism, may become ineffective and unresponsive when meeting with the ever-changing and competitive business environment. Although repeated organizational modifications have been conducted by previous generations, such adjustments are far from adequate.

Reformation, both structurally and philosophically, is the important topic at this stage. Equipped with excellent qualifications and education, the fourth generation may introduce Western-style management philosophy and theory into the Chinese family business system. If the reformation can be carried out effectively and successfully, the traditional and paternalistic business will evolve into a modern and sophisticated organization. This critical stage is the turning point. If the family can overcome any possible friction involved in the leadership transmission, its business can evolve into a self-perpetuating organization, and therefore can be maintained in this 'plateau' for generations if there is no dramatic environmental change. Otherwise, it will fail and gradually decline.

There are some clear features at this stage. First, the organization places more emphasis on rules and regulations than previously. Delegation of power is more frequent, communication and promotion becomes more formalized. Not all

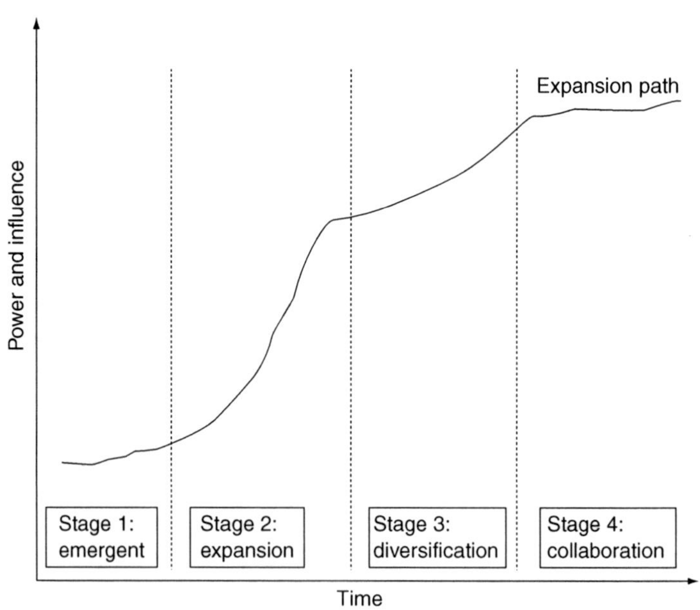

Figure 6.2 Large Chinese family business: an unconventional development path.

important management posts are held by family members. Some well-qualified professionals are appointed to the board of directors. On the other hand, more and more family members become professionals. The new family leader needs to collaborate and cooperate with his other family members and professional outsiders. Each of them also performs their own work without interference from others. In other words, if family members can manage the inheritance issue properly, and can transfer their human and social capital effectively, their businesses can live from generation to generation without disintegration.

Equal inheritance and *jiazu jituan*

From the above-discussed developmental path, we can easily identify that there is a mechanism to prevent a family business from declining even though lots of obstacles or crises arise from time to time. If the family business can overcome all these stumbling blocks and pass from generation to generation, its business structure will become quite different when compared to their Japanese or the Korean counterparts.

As mentioned earlier, since the Chinese family businesses rely equally on horizontal and vertical expansion, their businesses grow and become structured like the banyan tree. Instead, the Japanese businesses put strong emphasis on 'vertical expansion' and therefore grow into a bamboo-style structure. In order to have a better understanding on this concept, I propose the special structure of *jiazu jituan*, which literally means 'family-based consortium', to describe the Chinese family business group for differentiating itself from the Japanese zaibu (or kietartu) or the Korean chaebol.

Conventionally, when talking about family-controlled businesses, we simply called them *jiating qiye* or 'family enterprises', without too much differentiation. In order to describe this type of business structure more appropriately and specifically, some scholars try to 'invent' their own terms. Freedman (1971) suggests that since all descendants are from the same ancestor, this type of structure can be described as a 'lineage corporate'. Hamilton, *et al.* 1987) seem dissatisfied with this term. They coined another term, 'patrilineal network' in reference to business groups or firms that are integrated under the rule of the patriarch. Although the revised term explains better the real nature of interconnections among family members, there is something still missing. It cannot explain other kinds of relationship, such as those who have left the family enterprise to join a professional field or others who have created their own business that may directly compete with their parents' business.

I think *jiazu jituan* is more appropriate, as it implies sons or nephews can either run their own enterprises independently or jointly (like a banyan tree), some maintain very close business relations, while some may compete with each other – but also hold a certain amount of shares in the parent company and share common social capital – while they also maintain an unbreakable social relationship. On the whole, they are held under the banner of the same ancestor (*zu*), grandfather or father. Therefore, this type of structure cannot be simply regarded solely as a 'family enterprise' or treated as totally unrelated business units. In fact, this type of distinctive family business structure is a reflection of the impact of the equal inheritance system.

Diversification of the family businesses inevitably leads to organizational restructuring. Conventionally, Chinese family businesses are regarded as conservative, unresponsive and resistant to change. In fact, many family firms adapt to the external environment by implementing organizational restructuring. In this research, it is clearly found that many respondents' families have introduced reforms to their businesses. F4 and F7's banking businesses are typical examples. F4's son told me his experience in reforming the company:

> When I joined the company, I suggested reforming the bank structure. I remembered that my father took it seriously but asked me to be patient and to observe more. Four years later, I put the same proposal forward again. That time my father had a long discussion with me. He asked me many questions – from the colour of the new uniform, staff attitude, delegation to monitoring, in great detail. The proposal was finally accepted and reformation began. Although there was resistance and friction, most of it could be tackled. Father's firm and supportive attitude was crucial, especially when there was opposition from high-level management.

F7's family bank also carried out reformation in the late 1980s. After successfully reforming the bank, their traditional family bank was transformed into a modern organization. As a result, Standard & Poor's, an international credit assessment company, upgraded their credit rating. At the beginning of the new millennium, the family bank even took a drastic step to rename the bank by taking out the first word that indicated their surname in order to 'de-familiarize' its image.

Professionalization is one of the key areas of reformation. It requires not only upgrading family members' human capital (more education and more professional training), but also absorbing non-family professionals into the management team. Commenting on Robert Kuok's vast business empire in Asia, one fund manager notes that 'many of the people who actually run Robert Kuok's businesses are not linked to the family empire. Obviously he has to trust these lieutenants, but he is prepared to delegate' (Gilley 1998).

A recent *Harvard Business Review* reports that Victor Fung, the third-generation leader of a leading global trading firm based in Hong Kong, has also confirmed the trend towards professionalism in his family firm, Li & Fung Group (Magretta 1998). Other examples, like Eu Yan Sang, Wing On Group, Bank of East Asia, Lee Kam Kee and Lee Chung Shing Tong, have also conducted various levels of organizational restructuring.

Although many respondents show a positive attitude to absorbing professionals into their firms, we still need to bear in mind that the level of delegation to non-family members is kept to a certain level. During the interview, many respondents voiced a cautious view. They have an ambiguous stance, especially those from small- and medium-sized enterprises. F5 comments: 'I have reservations about it. I agreed to absorb professionals (into the management). But I think there is no need for separating the ownership and management.' Although he refuses to give concrete reasons, his concerns are obvious. He still perceives professionals as outsiders. If they are given a free hand to manage the company, he fears the family will lose control over the business. There are other reasons behind this ambiguous stance. One of them is the self-employment mentality.

In their survey on Chinese entrepreneurship in Hong Kong, Zheng and Wong (1999: 204) identified that there is a strong desire for self-employment among their respondents. Over 73 per cent of them said that after years of work, they would start their own businesses if they had the opportunity. Employees do not wholeheartedly commit to their work, but are thinking about creating their own enterprise someday. This cautious attitude also reflects F5's worry about potential competition from his employees. He mentioned clearly that if his employees are given too much delegation and if they finally leave the company to start their own businesses in a similar field, they will become their direct competitors.

To sum up, adaptation, diversification, reformation and equal inheritance are all interrelated and function with each other. The equal inheritance system acts as the catalyst for adaptation. Adaptation leads to diversification and organizational restructuring. Diversification and reformation has forced the Chinese family business to develop its own type of business structure. Therefore, *jiazu jituan*, a distinctive type of structure that looks like a banyan tree, can be more or less understood as a reflection of business evolution and development.

Equal inheritance and economic development

As an overall conclusion, we can now go back to the theoretical issue that was raised at the beginning. In Chapter 1, I presented the conventional view on the equal inheritance system and business operation (Figure 1.1). After this in-depth study, it is found that the negative side of the equal inheritance system is clearly over-exaggerated. In fact, although there are certain weaknesses in particular areas, there are also strengths in others. To be more specific, this system not only poses little threat to business expansion, but can also reduce destructive internal conflict by motivating family members to work harder. In other words, it can indirectly facilitate economic development.

First, although the equal inheritance system may weaken economic capital formation in certain aspects, it does not affect human capital and social capital transmission and accumulation. Instead, it creates a base for sibling comparison. Comparison generates psychological stress and anxiety. Such stress and anxiety will turn to competition. According to Weber (1947, 1978), competition is a driving force for the development of modern capitalism. In this study, it is found that sibling competition is a key element that motivates each member to work harder and to excel over others. This driving force is generally called the 'self-employment mentality'. It is the drive to free oneself from subjugation, to found one's own kingdom, and to prove that one is superior to other siblings. This kind of entrepreneurial spirit can ensure family members earn more capital in the next generation (Figure 6.3).

Second, paternalism and internal family conflict can generate the force for self-autonomy and independence. Improved education can invite sibling competition for leadership and self-determination. Because of the equal inheritance principle, every son is not excluded from the line of heredity leadership, as suggested by Weber. Not all members can be absorbed into management. Some members may choose to set up their own business while others may prefer to engage in professional careers. As a result, strong dynamism may be generated inside the family, while diversification of family personnel may become a common feature. The stability and prosperity of the family (*jiazu*) as a whole can further be enforced or sustained.

Third, mistrust of outsiders and little delegation imply that family members will be appointed to key management positions. Business networks and personal connections are also held by these members. This phenomenon usually appears in the first generation. When the business grows larger and larger, the educated second or later generation will join. Then, reformation and organizational restructuring also follow. A certain proportion of professional outsiders may be

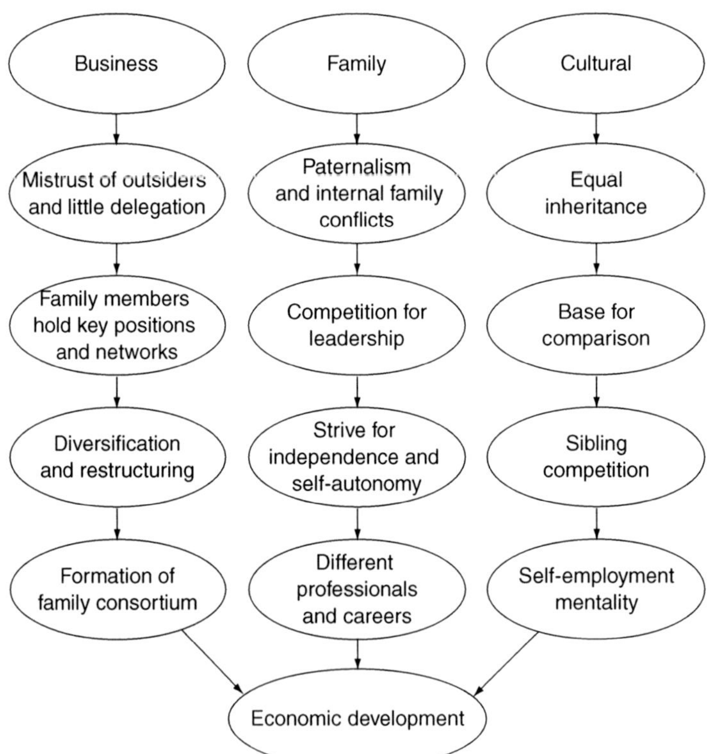

Figure 6.3 Chinese family business and economic development.

absorbed into the upper-middle levels of management. In order to reduce the risk of over-concentration of investment and the practical need to accommodate different family members' interests, family businesses will diversify. Some members may leave the family businesses and start their own careers. Although they work in different fields, they may maintain connections with the core family business at some critical level. As a result, they form a special type of structure, *jiazu jituan*, as suggested.

Looking from this perspective, we can gain a better understanding of many interconnected concepts, like family division, blood-tie connections and organizational restructuring, as well the mechanism of adaptation of Chinese family business. In addition, it also reasonably explains why the Chinese culture puts strong emphasis on equal right, self-employment, child education, business connections and social networks. Whatever the criteria is, the equal inheritance system cannot be simply regarded as a stumbling block for business operation.

In his book, *Emigrant Entrepreneurs*, Wong (1988) suggests an insightful concept called 'entrepreneurial familism' in reference to the special management style of Chinese family enterprise. He argues that the family itself can be regarded as a unit of economic competition. It provides the source of capital and network support, and acts as an agent for innovation and risk taking. This concept in fact is derived from the self-employment mentality. To be specific, the self-employment mentality reflects the entrepreneurial spirit of each individual, while 'entrepreneurial familism' reflects the spirit of the family as a whole. In other words, the meaning of both concepts is similar.

However, what is the origin of 'entrepreneurial familism'? Wong does not provide a concrete response. If we look closer at the equal inheritance system, we can get a reasonable answer. In short, it is clear that the equal inheritance system can stimulate 'entrepreneurial familism' in two ways. First, it creates a criterion for sibling comparison. Comparison generates stress and anxiety, as each son will try to excel over the others. Self-autonomy is the ultimate goal.

Second, it offers initial economic capital, while the family social capital can bring valuable business opportunities. All of these types of capital can help those sons who want to be free from subjugation to start their own business. Others may prefer to work in large corporations. Some become professionals or government officials while others are delegated to manage the family enterprise. Whatever career they chose, their family social capital can give them a certain level of assistance.

So, my main argument is clear. In order to advance their family or themselves and also to reduce risk of uncertainty or over-concentration in a single family business, many Chinese families implicitly motivate their members to compete with each other or intentionally try to diversify their members to different fields. As a result, their family members may compete with each other or they may cooperate or accommodate each other. This driving force, in fact, is the origin of the self-employment mentality.

As an overall conclusion, I would like to use Pan's (1947) research finding to summarize the main argument of this book. In the early 1930s, Pan conducted intensive research in Jiaxin, Jiangsu Province to study family mobility, adaptability and continuity in the Ming and Qing dynasties. In his 91 clan (family) samples, he found that most of these large families or clans had lasted over five generations. For instance, he discovered the shortest family line had only lasted for four generations, while the longest had lasted for over 21 generations. On average, each family would last for 8.3 generations. Although there are various criticisms about Pan's research methodology and criteria in obtaining data, the finding is obvious: given a stable environment, Chinese family can be maintained for over three generations.

In this study, a similar result is found. Chinese family business is definitely not short-lived or unstable in Hong Kong. In fact, my research findings go beyond this, and further discover that the equal inheritance system not only can reduce internal family disagreement, but can create a base for sibling competition. Competition is the cornerstone of capitalist society, as it can fuel economic development and technological advancement. In other words, the equal inheritance system per se may not definitely lead to short-lived Chinese family businesses if there is no dramatic change in the environment. The equal inheritance system may even have the opposite effect of helping the business to expand.

Appendix

Background of the studied Chaozhou families

F1's family

F1 was born in Chaozhou and graduated from a teachers' college. Although he had a stable teaching job in his home town, he gave it up when he decided to leave for Hong Kong, where he worked in his brother in law's trading firm. He was praised for his hard work and good management of the company. Due to the sudden death of his mother during the Japanese invasion, he returned to his home town to handle funeral matters. Some years later, he again came to Hong Kong since he still considered Hong Kong an ideal place for career development. With experience and connections, he started a trading company in partnership with his brother-in-law. At first, the company only focused on general trading. Some years later, his company was chosen by an internationally well-known poultry feed giant as its sole agent in Asia.

F1 tried very hard to promote poultry feed, and the business grew rapidly. Five years later, he had nearly monopolized the market. In the 1970s, he moved a step forward by setting up his own poultry feed production factory in Yuen Long, New Territories. He became a leading figure in this business and was known as the 'King of Poultry Feed'. In the 1980s, he expanded his business to the Chinese mainland by setting up another production plant in Guangdong Province. Today, the company is still a leading poultry feed giant in South China.

F1 and his partner, both aged over 80, still have a close relationship. Both of their sons joined the company in the late 1980s. Each of them was delegated to head different businesses and, like their fathers, the sons also maintained very good relations. F1's only son, who held a doctoral degree, had already taken over all of the business, and F1 admitted to me that he had retired. Like his father, F1's son was active in the CCC's activities. When he first joined the association, he was elected as a key member of the Youth Committee. Later, he was promoted to become a vice chairman of the CCC. It is generally believed that he will soon become chairman.

F2's family

F2 was the second son. His grandfather was an educated person in Chaozhou. When he was six years old, his father went abroad to Thailand to seek his fortune. Since the family had an uncle in Thailand, his father worked with him. Later, his father set up his own business and moved his company's office to Hong Kong. Some years later, his elder brother came to Hong Kong to help his father. Their business grew gradually.

Unfortunately, his elder brother died at the early age of 21. At that time, F2 had just graduated from secondary school and was planning to study at university. Because of his brother's sudden death, he was forced to give up studying and instead went to Hong Kong. Struck by his brother's sudden death and also worried about the company's financial situation, his father's health also deteriorated. He died one year later. F2 understood that it was his responsibility to prevent the family business from collapsing. He worked very hard and after many years of effort, he became successful. He expanded the business to zipper production, semiconductor production and property investment.

F2 has four sons. All of them are university graduates. Each is responsible for a type of business. For instance, the eldest son is responsible for zipper production; the second son is in charge of semiconductor production; and the third and fourth sons are delegated to manage investment and property. All of them are shareholders in the family company and have equal shares. F2 claimed that he only visited his company once or twice a month as he had retired. Although F2 is one of the directors of the CCC, he is not as active as other directors.

F3's family

F3's father came to Hong Kong after the end of the Second World War. He started a rice firm with his relatives' help. At the beginning, F3's father only had a very minor role in the business. Later, as the company further expanded, his involvement increased and he even took over as leader. Being the eldest son, F3 was called to Hong Kong to help. Some years later, F3's other brothers also came to join them.

With the joint effort of father and sons, they become a registered rice importer in the early 1950s. Since rice was a profitable business, they earned their 'first bucket of gold' at that time. Later, they spread their business to rice wholesaling, while F3's second brother was asked to manage it.

In the late 1980s, since the rice wholesaling business started to contract, they shifted their business to other areas. One of them was the 'mobile ice-cream' business. It was an innovative idea and the business grew quite well. In the 1990s, they even transplanted the concept to Shanghai and Guangzhou. In addition, they also expanded their investment to the travel and property markets. F3's youngest brother was responsible for the tourist business and the third brother was in charge of property and investment. Some of the third generation have joined the family firms. F3's son and nephews have been groomed to take over leadership in the business.

F4's family

F4's father was an outstanding businessman and was a millionaire in Thailand. He was a founder of a famous bank in Thailand. F4's father was born in Thailand but educated in Chaozhou. Due to political reasons, his father later shifted part of his business to Hong Kong. F4's father married and had two wives. One lived in Chaozhou and one in Thailand. F4 was the eldest son. He and his second younger brother were born to their 'big mother' while F4's third through to seventh younger brothers were born to their 'small mother'. At the age of 15, F4 came to Hong Kong while his second younger brother migrated to Thailand to join his 'small mother' and other brothers. F4's father thought that F4 should stay in Hong Kong to manage the family business here.

F4 was sent to the USA for banking training in his early 20s. He recalled that during those years in the USA, he start at the bottom, as an office boy and clerk. Upon graduation, he came back to Hong Kong and hoped that he would join the management team. However, he was disappointed when his father still wanted him to work at a relatively low level. He was also instructed to work in each department, such as personnel, loan and mortgage, remittance, and customer services. Some years later, he was finally promoted to the post of general manager. Now he is the president of the family bank.

In addition to banking, F4's family also specializes in insurance, rice, warehousing and the property business. F4 has two sons and two daughters. All of them are university graduates and have married. His eldest son is mainly responsible for the banking business while his younger son, an elected legislative councillor and appointed executive councillor, is in charge of their insurance business. All of the family businesses in Thailand are managed by F4's other brothers. Each person is clearly assigned to a specific area. The family is now preparing to handover the management to the third generation.

F5's family

F5 and his elder brother came to Hong Kong to join their grandfather after their father passed away in Chaozhou. His grandfather ran a goldsmith shop and employed four to six workers. F5 worked as an apprentice, or to be specific, an 'office boy', whose duties included cleaning the shop, boiling water and assisting other workers in the shop. Later, he was promoted to salesman. His grandfather taught him many skills for doing business, and frequently discussed the philosophy of business with F5.

When F5's grandfather passed away, F5's uncles preferred to divide the family estate (*fengjia*). By principle, F5 and his brother, representing one branch, was given around HK$50,000 and some fixed assets. He then started his own business – an imitation jewellery firm. In the 1970s, imitation jewellery was fashionable and popular. His business grew rapidly and F5 earned the title of 'King of Imitation Jewellery'.

Later, F5 expanded his business to other major cities, such as Shanghai, Guangzhou, Beijing and Chongqing. He also diversified his investment to taxis, property and financial markets. F5 has two sons and three daughters. All of them studied overseas. One of them came back to Hong Kong when he obtained his MBA degree and is now working in the family firm, preparing for a role in management. F5 preferred his children to work outside to gain experience before helping him.

F6's family

F6 was a young and energetic businessman. His father was a rice wholesaler in the 1950s. Unfortunately, his father passed away when he was just a child. Since no suitable family member was mature enough to manage the business at that time, his mother sold it. F6 was brought up by his mother singlehandedly. He understood that he had the responsibility to regain the family reputation and thus he studied very hard. After graduating from secondary school, he went to the USA to further his studies.

Having obtained his university degree, F6 came back to Hong Kong and worked in an integrated circuit (IC) manufacturing firm. Three years later, he left and started up his own IC manufacturing factory. F6 worked industriously and his business grew steadily. Now F6's company is one of the leading companies specializing in high-tech IC manufacturing. F6 has a son who has just been promoted to Form Six. He often takes him on business trips or to meet foreign counterparts when there is the opportunity. F6 wants to train his son to take over the family business when he is old enough.

F7's family

F7's grandfather was one of the most well-known businessmen in early Hong Kong. He migrated at the turn of the twentieth century. After years of unremitting toil, he opened a bank in Western District, which mainly served the working class, especially Chaozhou people. His marketing strategy was successful and the bank prospered. In the middle of the 1960s, the bank faced a serious crisis. Rumour spread that due to heavy losses in investment, the bank would soon go bankrupt. F7's grandfather was shocked. He tried to seek help from other banks. At that time, the leading bank, HSBC, promised to offer assistance. However, this message later was misinterpreted as 'The Hong Kong and Shanghai Bank had taken over [the] family bank'. Struck by this incorrect translation or interpretation, F7's grandfather fell seriously ill and died some days later. F7's father and uncles, who were studying in England at that time, were called back to take over the bank and manage the crisis.

F7's father, being the eldest son, took the leading role and made every effort to solve the problems that had emerged. His father united all his uncles together and negotiated with the HSBC and other related companies. Finally, the bank-run rumour subsided. Although the family bank needed many years to recover, his father's shrewdness in tackling the crisis and keeping all the family together was praised not only in the Chaozhou community, but society as a whole.

The family tried to reconsolidate after the incident and gradually regained its vitality in the late 1970s. F7's father assigned each of the family members to manage one part of the business. For instance, F7's second uncle was the bank's chief executive director. His third uncle was in charge of the investment business. His fourth uncle was the general manager of the group's personnel department. Later, the bank also diversified to financial investment and the property market, and went public in the early 1980s. One of F7's uncles was appointed a legislative councillor in the 1980s. In 1997, his second uncle was elected a representative of the People's Congress of the PRC. However, this uncle passed away in his mid-50s in 1998, the day after my interview with F7.

F7 and his eldest brother joined the management team after finishing their studies in the UK. Recently, F7 has become active in the CCC and has been elected as one of the association's vice chairmen. Clearly, the family is now preparing to pass the baton to the third generation, and that explains why both F7 and his brothers hold key director posts on the management board.

F8's family

F8's father was a well-known Chaozhou merchant who migrated to Hong Kong in the early 1930s. At first, F8's father engaged in general trading. Then he shifted to garment and plastic flower manufacturing. Some years later, he further switched to manufacturing of watchbands. Seeing that clocks and watches were a promising business, F8's father opened his own retail shops in Western District and Mong Kok, and successfully captured the market, to emerge later as the market leader. This rapid emergence clearly marked the turning point of their family business.

In the 1980s, F8's father retired and F8 took over the business. He expanded their family business to property, hotel and supermarket concerns. F8 is the eldest son and has two younger brothers. All of them have degrees from the USA or Canada. F8 and his second brother even have Master's degrees. His sister married a famous Chaozhou tycoon in Hong Kong, while his third brother also married a Chaozhou tycoon's daughter. F8 himself was an active member in the CCC and served as the first chairman of the Youth Committee, and later the chairman of the CCC. Their family business is now managed by the third and fourth generation.

F9's family

F9's family is another famous family in Hong Kong. His father and uncles came to Hong Kong in the 1920s. At the beginning, his family engaged in 'gold-trading'. It was a highly profitable but risky business. They earned their 'first bucket of gold' in the early 1940s as the Chinese mainland was invaded by the Japanese. After the war, their investment expanded naturally to banking. Since they focused on serving businessmen (as a commercial bank), their business grew quickly as Hong Kong's economy took off. Later, they further diversified to other areas such as finance, insurance, hotels, property and fashion businesses.

Although all of F9's uncles passed away some years ago, and their shares for each branch (*fang*) had been allocated, they still kept the main business intact. They appointed some family members to run the business while others were involved in other businesses or professional careers. For instance, some of his brothers are doctors, engineers, or architects. F9 himself is a lawyer.

One of F9's brothers married a Chinese banker's daughter, while one of his sisters married a famous Hong Kong tycoon. According to F9, all of his sisters and brothers were university graduates. He even pointed out that his nephews' and cousins' education level is far higher than F9's generation.

F10's family

F10's family was well-known in Chaozhou before Liberation occurred on the Chinese mainland. After the Communists took over, F10's father was killed and all of their businesses, properties and land were confiscated by the government. With the help of his relatives, F10 fled to Hong Kong in the early 1950s.

Since F10 had brought some jewellery and money when he fled to Hong Kong, he had some initial capital to set up business there. At first, he only engaged in small trading. In 1966, on the recommendation of a trusted friend, he bought a denim manufacturing factory from an industrialist who planned to leave Hong Kong for the USA. This marked the turning point. F10 emerged as a 'denim king'. In the 1980s, F10 gained great orders of garments and expanded his business to the property market. He auctioned several plots of land in Yau Tong and Sai Kung, and then built two seven-storey blocks of warehouses there. By the end of the 1980s, F10 moved his denim dying and spinning plant back to the Chinese mainland.

Now, F10 is nearly retired and the business is run by his youngest son. His eldest son is a high-ranking government official who shows little interest in business, while his second son prefers to run his own business. According to F10, he has divided most of the property to each son (and grandsons) in equal proportions. However, the family's main business – denim manufacturing – is still in operation. F10 plans to hand over this business in a few years.

F11's family

F11's family was also famous in Shantou, Chaozhou. His grandfather set up a textile factory in Shanghai in the 1910s. His father also worked there. His father married a local Shanghai girl. F11 was born in Shanghai and studied there. During the Japanese invasion in 1937, F11 moved to Chaozhou and later fled to Hong Kong. However, when Hong Kong was occupied in 1941, F11 moved back to Chaozhou, but returned to Hong Kong prior to the Communist takeover.

Some of F11's brothers and uncles fled to Taiwan, Australia, Europe and the USA.

At first, F11 engaged in kerosene and coal trading. Having found that the profit margin was small, he shifted to sugar trading. After some years, and with the assistance of his elder brother in Taiwan, F11 switched to cement trading and imported cement from Taiwan. From the 1950s, Hong Kong's population increased tremendously, so the demand for cement for building houses, roads and other infrastructure also increased greatly. Although the business was highly profitable, high transportation costs and unstable shipping schedules levelled off a great proportion of profit. Since F11 predicted that Hong Kong's economy would take-off and thus the demand for cement would grow even higher, he partnered with some other businessmen to set up a cement extraction and refinery factory in Hong Kong. The business was extremely profitable, so he started up another, larger scale cement company later in a joint venture with the Japanese, and emerged as one of the cement market leaders in Hong Kong.

In addition to the cement business, F11 also expanded his investment to shipping, property, automobile trading and button manufacturing. Some of F11's sons helped him and held key positions, while some of his son became professionals. Although F11 retired several years ago, he still keeps visiting his business everyday. According to F11, his frequent visits to the company are to make sure that the business is proceeding on the right track.

F12's family

F12's father was a businessman who opened a trading firm in Guangzhou in the 1930s. F12 helped his father after finishing secondary school. F12's aunt married one of his father's trading partners. Later, F12 left Guangzhou for Hong Kong and set up his own trading firm in Nam Pak Hong, Western District, in the early 1950s. Since F12 had good networks throughout Southeast Asia, Chaozhou and Guangzhou, his business was quite successful. One of his major businesses was rice trading. He registered himself as a rice importer when the colonial government implemented the rice importation registration policy in the 1950s. In those days, rice business was profitable. Seeing that there were good prospects, F12 also set up wholesaling and retailing firms, a so-called 'one-dragon' service.

In the 1980s, F12 expanded his business to warehousing and property investment. F12 has three sons. All of them graduated from overseas universities. After finishing their studies, all of them joined the family business. Now, each son is responsible for each company. Although F12 mentioned that he has retired, he still firmly controls the rice importation business. Some people claimed that the rice business was a 'sunset' business, but F12 seemed to disagree. He told me that he had reservation over this assertion and suggested that rice was the main staple of the Chinese. So, he thought that rice trade could still be prosperous if it was run properly, and could generate stable and reasonable returns.

F13's family

F13's father was a businessman who opened a trading firm in Shanghai in the 1930s. F13 helped his father when he had just graduated from junior secondary school. He had two younger brothers. Although he would have liked to continue his studies, he had to sacrifice his education when his father asked him for help. He accepted his father's suggestion that he was the eldest son and therefore had greater responsibility for the family business. Their business in Shanghai was quite successful and they also became a wealthy family. One of his brothers was an alumnus of the Fudan University of the class of the early 1940s.

Before the Communist Party took over the Chinese mainland, the whole family moved to Hong Kong. Since F13's father had connections with rice merchants in Hong Kong, they took over a wholesaling firm from a local rice businessman and started another avenue of business.

Some years later, F13 saw that the textile industry could offer good prospects, so he set up a textile factory in Tsuen Wan, New Territories. F13's second brother was admitted as a solicitor and set up his own law firm in Central. His other brother, who later graduated from Hong Kong University, helped him manage the factory. In the 1970s and the 1980s, since foreign orders for textile products, especially from the USA, were extremely regular, their textile assembly lines needed to run nearly 24 hours a day, without Sundays or public holidays off.

In the late 1980s, when Central government announced plans to deepen its economic reform, F13 decided to shift his major production line to Dongguang, where he employed over 400 workers at the beginning. Beside the rice and textile businesses, F13 also diversified their family investment to property, restaurant and household appliance trading businesses. All of F13's sons and nephews graduated from overseas institutions. Some of them have joined the management team. At the age of nearly 80, F13 still holds the principle of 'retire but not rest' and keeps his monitoring role in the businesses.

F14's family

F14 went from being a factory worker to a business tycoon without a good educational background. He came to Hong Kong during the Japanese invasion. On his relatives' recommendation, he worked in a trading firm. After 15 years of hard work, he had accumulated some money, and started his own business in the 1960s. As an experienced textile technician, he understood that garment and textile manufacturing generated a vast number of by-products. With inspiration from a Japanese friend, he collected all of these by-products and recycled them to produce an 'artificial fabric'. This kind of fabric was a good insulator for industrial purposes. F14 became the pioneer in this market and his business brought him his 'first bucket of gold'.

In the interview, F14 reiterated that he has an outgoing personality and was fond of connecting and building relations with others. Thus he had many friends.

In the 1980s, with recommendations from his townsmen, he joined other Chaozhou merchants to take over the Carrinna Restaurant and later the Chaozhou City Restaurant. In the late 1980s, he even expanded his investments to the property market and the entertainment business, which further aggrandized the family-controlled conglomerates.

F14 has three sons and three daughters, who are all university graduates. Three of them hold doctoral degrees and one holds a Master's degree. His eldest son lives in the USA and is a famous cardiologist. His second daughter is a professor at Harvard University. His third son, who worked with him, is also a PhD holder. He is now planning to pass the baton to this son.

F15's family

F15's grandfather was a poor villager who converted to Christianity when Western religions first penetrated the treaty ports of Shantou, after the First Opium War. Because of this completely different religious faith, F15's family was expelled from his village to Shantou, where they would get protection from the Christian Church. With the assistance of various clergymen, F15's grandfather set up a goldsmith shop in Shantou, and the business became prosperous. F15's father was born in Shantou and studied there. After finishing secondary school, his father chose to work in the shop.

In the late 1920s, their whole family left Shantou to go to Hong Kong. F15's father therefore restarted their goldsmith shop there. After many years of operation, their business expanded. Later, they even opened a 'money shop' (*qianzhuang*). At that time, the currency was backed with gold or silver, the so-called 'gold or silver standard system', so the demand for gold and silver was huge. Because of this, his father earned a lot of money and became a famous tycoon. In 1956, F15's father passed away and F15 took over leadership of the business.

In the mid-1960s, since the colonial government wanted to tighten the control of the banking system, all old-style money shops were asked to register as 'banks' under the then banking ordinance. They, however, preferred not to register since they didn't regard Hong Kong as a place of permanent residence. In this sense, they missed a golden opportunity to turn their 'money shop' into a bank.

With good connections with some prominent legislative councillors in Hong Kong, F15's company was registered as one of the major rice importers as early as 1953, even though they had no previous experience in the field. Their investment in rice importation gave them promising returns. In the 1980s, when 'five kilogram bag rice' became popular, they also copied the formula by packaging their own brand-named 'bag-rice'. Backed up with a good network, they became one of the market leaders in the field. Later, they expanded their business to property and warehouses.

At the age of nearly 85, F15 has semi-retired. His elder brother is a retired professor at Stanford University. His other brother was a senior and well-known solicitor in Hong Kong, while one of his brothers helped him to manage the family business. The youngest brother was a chartered public accountant who ran his own accountancy and audit firm. F15's sons and nephews have prepared to take over the family business. The new generation members still show little confidence in Hong Kong's future – they all hold passports from Western countries.

F16's family

F16's father came to Hong Kong in the late 1920s. His father first worked in their relative's rice shop in Western District when he was very young. Later, when two of F16's uncles came to join his father in Hong Kong, the three brothers decided to set up their own rice retail firm. The first shop they opened was in Tsuen Wan, since they considered it was a newly developed residential area with market potential not yet captured. As expected, their businesses went quite well. With the increasing development of Tsuen Wan, their business also expanded. They invested all they had earned by opening other retail shops in adjacent districts such as Kwai Chung, Sham Shui Po, and then spread to Wong Tai Sin, Sun Po Kong and Kwun Tong.

F16's father estimated that as the population grew, Tsuen Wan would become a prosperous town and thus land prices would be pushed up. To put his speculation into practice, his father bought a large amount of farmland at an attractively low price, and his speculation was finally proved correct. So, their family emerged as one of the biggest landlords in Tsuen Wan. In the 1980s, they sold some of their land for an extremely high price. Three plots of land were reserved for building their family's landmark building in the centre of the town: the '[F16] Brothers' Commercial Building', a well-furnished 30-storey commercial complex.

In the early 1980s, F16's family shifted the family business from rice to financial investment. His family owned a registered non-deposit-taking financial company. Later, they further expanded to their business to mortgage, real estate development and textile and garment manufacturing. At this stage, their family business had successfully diversified.

Approaching 60, F16 plans to train the new generation to take over. All of F16's sons and nephews are university graduates. Some of them have joined the management board. According to F16, the mission of the new generation is to make their family business a publicly listed company.

F17's family

F17 left Chaozhou in his early 20s after he had graduated from secondary school. He came to Hong Kong in 1950, a year after the Communist Party takeover of the Chinese mainland. At first, he worked in a British trading firm as a salesman. In order to upgrade his education qualifications, he went to evening school to study English and accounting. After years of unremitting work and study, he gained experience and connections in addition to professional qualifications.

Then, F17 came to calculate that if he would become a boss, the prospects would be better than being just an employee. He then left the trading firm and set up his own small plastic flower factory in San Po Kong. At the beginning he only employed two or three workers. Much of the work was done by his wife and children. Since he had good experience in soliciting buyers in Western countries, he successfully won regular orders, and thus his business grew steadily.

By the late 1970s, he bought a piece of land with 5,000 square feet to build his own 12-storey factory. He also expanded his business to Christmas decoration products. Since these kinds of products were popular in Western countries, he earned an attractive profit from it. In order to upgrade product quality and the company's image, he set up a design team to develop new products to meet the ever-changing market demand, and gradually became one of the market leaders in the field. Some of his company's products also won awards in Hong Kong and overseas.

F17 has three daughters and one son. All of his daughters have married and only his youngest son is still a bachelor. Only one daughter worked in the family business. Another daughter migrated to Canada with her husband's family in 1985. His son, a recent Toronto University graduate, has worked in the company for one year. F17 confirmed that he planned to hand over the leadership to this son when he had the ability to handle all matters in the business independently. He further ruled out that he would give some part of his property to his daughters except for dowries, since his daughters would eventually marry into another family.

F18's family

F18's father was a trader in Chaozhou. He died when F18 was only 19 years old. As he found it difficult to earn a living in Shantou, F18 left for Hong Kong when he was 22. When he first arrived at Hong Kong, he lived in his father's sworn-brother's shop in Nam Pak Hong, a busy and pulsating business centre in Hong Kong. He observed business there for nearly three months. Finally, he set up a dry food trading company with two other partners. Since one of F18's partners had good connections in Thailand, Burma and Singapore, their business grew satisfactorily. However, the harmonious relations did not last long. Since one of his partners perceived that it was his personal connections that brought profit to the company, he suggested that they split up the business. Although F18 and another partner did not want to do so, they had no other alternative but to accept.

Considering that they had good experience and business skills, F18 and his partner set up their own company. They tried very hard to solicit suppliers, as well as customers. Since F18 was a hardworking and well-trusted person, many suppliers preferred to ask him to be an agent for their products. F18's reputation spread around Nam Pak Hong and his company also emerged as one of the leading companies in the field. Later, F18 further expanded his market outlets to Japan and Western countries. In the late 1980s, in order to diversify the business risk, he even invested in the property and financial markets, and canned food production in the Chinese mainland. Today, his company is the market leader in the canned food exporter business.

F18 has three sons and two daughters. One of his sons set up his own shoe factory in Guangdong Province. His second son worked as a general manager in an investment bank – most of the financial advice is given by this son. His youngest son worked in another bank as a management trainee. F18 tried to persuade him to join the family business but failed. At present, no one wants to do so, and therefore F18 still plays an active role in running the business.

F19's family

F19's father was an influential business figure in the Chaozhou community in Hong Kong who arrived in the 1920s. His father opened a rice firm in Nam Pak Hong at first and later became one of the leading registered rice importers. F19 was born in Hong Kong and joined the family business immediately after he had completed his secondary school. He helped his father to consolidate the rice business after the end of the war in 1945. When their rice business had developed fully, they expanded to wholesaling, restaurants and the property market.

F19's elder brother passed away at a young age. His younger brother is a legal practitioner who showed little interest in the family business. One of his younger brothers even chose to settle in Australia after finishing his university education there. Although each branch still has its share in the family business, it is managed solely by F19. In recent years, F19 has asked some of his nephews to join the management team of the business.

F19 has four daughters and one son. All of them have married. His eldest daughter and his son have worked with him for a period of time. His eldest daughter worked as his personal secretary while his son was appointed as general manager. His second daughter was a chartered public accountant and was a partner of a well-established accounting firm, Deloitte Touche Tohmatsu (Hong Kong). Two of his other daughters migrated to the USA after marrying. At the moment, the leadership of the family business has been passed to his son and nephews.

F20's family

F20's father came to Hong Kong in 1950 and then worked in a textile factory. F20 joined his father in 1956 at the age of 18, and also worked in the factory. In order to improve his educational level, F20 attended evening school to learn English. Since he had quite good English, he later got a salesman's job in a British firm in Central. After some years of work, he had accumulated some money and also some business connections. Added to some savings from his father, F20 set up a small garment subcontracting firm in Mong Kok.

At the very beginning, he considered the subcontracting work as a sideline business and still worked at the British firm. Thus, he admitted that he had burnt the candle at both ends at that time. By day, he worked in the office, by night, he managed his small business. After a lengthy period of unremitting toil, he got bigger and regular orders from large trading firms. In order to pay greater concentration to his business, he resigned from his job and moved into a bigger office. He worked even harder and tried his best to upgrade his service and product quality. His efforts paid off and he could get orders directly from the US buyers. Thus, his business expanded gradually. Now he owns an 11-storey industrial building in Mong Kok, a multi-complex factory in Changping, Guangdong Province, and lots of other property in Hong Kong.

F20 has three sons and one daughter. All of them are university graduates. The second son has also obtained an MBA degree in the local university. All of them, including his daughter, work in the family business. F20 himself is the chairman of the company. His eldest son is the general manager, while his second son is in charge of the accounting department. His third son is responsible for the production department and his daughter is manager of the design and fashion department. She graduated with a Bachelor's degree in art and design in Australia. F20 hopes that all his children can work harmoniously together and contribute their talent to make the family business more prosperous.

F21's family

F21 and his parents came to Hong Kong after the surrender of Japan in 1945, when he was only two years old. At first, his father worked as a coolie while his mother took some contract-out (or piece work) jobs to earn some extra money for the family budget. Around 1950, one of their relatives recommended his father to a well-known Chaozhou plastic flower manufacturer. That meeting completely changed their life, and then F21's father set up a small cottage firm to do some processing work for that manufacturer. At first his parents employed no other workers and everything was done by their own hands. Their business expanded little by little.

F21 has two brothers and two sisters and he was the eldest son. In the interview, F21 admitted that he didn't like school, so after finishing Form Five, he didn't ask for further education but chose to work in a bank as a junior accounting clerk. He spent nearly 15 years at the bank and was promoted to assistant branch manager. During that time, his father's business was flourishing and later shifted to focus on ornament production. In 1986, his father contracted severe pneumonia and asked him to take over the business. All his brothers and sisters also tried to persuade him to join, so he left the bank to accept his father's offer.

One year, his father died. Since his father had already divided the business before he died and all of them had reached the consensus that their business should remain intact rather than being divided up, the family business kept on expanding under F21's leadership. In order to improve the company image and production process, F21 even initiated restructuring. After that, the company's efficiency and profitability was further enhanced.

After the June Fourth Incident in 1989, many Hong Kong people decided to leave, and F21's brothers and sisters also joined the queue and migrated to

Western countries. F21, who considered Hong Kong an ideal place for a career, decided to stay. In fact, he even bought several flats and a number of car parks in Kwai Chung, as property prices were quite attractive at that time. In the early 1990s, he even took a step further to move the company's production process to Guangdong, where land prices, wages and material costs were cheaper as very few Hong Kong people would like to live there. All the property he bought appreciated greatly after the Incident and he made a huge profit when he realized some of the property in 1996. His investment in China also paid off, and this provided further momentum for the family business expansion.

In 1996, his two brothers flew back to Hong Kong and rejoined the family business. His second brother was assigned to head the accounting department, while his youngest brother was asked to be head of the production department. Later, F21's eldest son also joined the company and was asked to manage the factory in Guangdong. Although there are some arguments sometimes among them over business strategy, F21 thinks is natural thing in a big family. Thus, all of them still prefer to keep their family business united rather than divided.

F22's family

F22 came to Hong Kong to join with his elder brother in 1951. At that time, his brother was a waiter in a café shop. Since he was young at that time, his brother sent him to secondary school. Later, since his brother could no longer afford it, F22 was forced to leave school to work. At a result, F22 joined his brother in the café as a waiter. However, he still insisted on attending evening class to learn English and accounting. After he obtained an intermediate level of accounting, he left the café and joined an accounting firm. Later, he was awarded a higher diploma certificate and a job at the Inland Revenue Department (IRD). Then, he rose gradually to become a chartered public accountant and auditor.

In 1978 he left the IRD and started up his own taxation and secretarial firm in Central. His connections with a high-ranking official in the IRD provided him with certain advantages. F22 was an active member of the CCC and served as an honorary accountant to the association. He had good connections with other Chaozhou merchants and this brought him regular Chaozhou clients. His accounting firm grew steadily.

F22 has two daughters and two sons. All of them are university graduates from English universities. His two daughters joined the company after graduation. His eldest son went to Australia to study for an MBA degree and later found a job in Sydney. He chose not to return to Hong Kong. His youngest son is a chartered public accountant and he chose to work in a multinational corporation and therefore didn't join the family business. Although all his sons show little interest in taking over his business, F22 does not feel disappointed. He confidently believes that when he reaches retirement age, his sons will finally join the company.

F23's family

F23's father was a vice captain of a British-registered vessel. He came to Hong Kong in 1950. F23, his mother and his brother joined him in 1953. At the age of 11, F23 attended Primary Five in Hong Kong. Then he went to secondary school. After matriculation, F23 was recommended by his father's Western friend to join a famous and well-established legal firm in Hong Kong – Johnson, Stokes and Master – as a solicitor trainee. After several years of training and practice, he was admitted as a qualified solicitor.

F23 worked in Johnson, Stokes and Master for a couple of years, and then left to set up his own solicitor and notary firm. F23's uncle was a famous Chaozhou merchant in Hong Kong who recommended F23 to serve as legal advisor to the CCC and his own clansmen's association. He was also appointed by a Chaozhou-funded bank as its legal representative.

F23 has one daughter and one son. His son is still studying medicine at the University of Hong Kong, while his youngest daughter is studying law at a Hawaiian university. F23 hopes his two children can have their own careers.

F24's family

F24's father was a businessman in Vietnam. In the 1950s, the whole family fled to Hong Kong. F24 was 21 years old at the time. When they arrived in Hong Kong, he found it difficult to get a job. All the family members were worried and had to rely on their savings, which they had brought from Vietnam. Since F24 was a college graduate, he later got a part-time teaching job at an evening school. Having settled down in Hong Kong, F24 started to prepare for his future. With his relative's help, he started a fur and feather clothing manufacturing factory in Hung Hom. Since that market segment was not yet developed at that time, F24's products attracted customers' attention. He received regular orders from Europe and America. According to F24, his company's products occupy nearly 45 per cent of the German market and around 12 per cent of the whole European market. F24 was recognized as the leader of the fur and feather clothing market.

F24 has two younger brothers. All of them work in the company and are responsible for different departments. F24's only son joined the company after he obtained his MBA degree from the University of York, UK. Although F24 hoped to train his son for leadership, his son's performance did not match his expectations. He told me that his son is a timid and conservative person. However, one of his nephews has recently joined the company and appears capable and smart. F24 and his brothers are wondering who will be the future leader. In F24's mind, he still hopes his son will try harder to win the leadership post.

F25's family

F25 came to Hong Kong in 1961 at the age of 20. He worked in a medium-sized textile factory as an ordinary worker. Being a hardworking employee, he was praised well by his boss. Some years later, he married one of his boss' daughters. With his father-in-law's help, he set up his own textile factory in Cheung Sha Wan in the early 1980s. He worked very hard and his business grew steadily. In 1985, he employed over 150 workers. Later, since F25 thought that wages and rent had increased to an unaffordable level, and his confidence in Hong Kong's future was weak, he chose to sell the business and also his property. He then migrated to Canada.

In 1992 he regained his confidence in Hong Kong and returned. He even went a step further to set up a camera production line in Guangdong Province. He readjusted his business strategy and reconsidered Hong Kong as an ideal place for career development. His camera factory, which focused on producing digital cameras, faced difficulties at the beginning. Workers in the Chinese mainland were not skilful enough, and he had to spend a lot of time training technicians to operate the processing and assembly line more efficiently. Although the major market of his product was China, he also tried to sell cameras in Southeast Asia and Africa.

F25 has two sons and one daughter. All of them are still in Canada and work there. Even though F25 has tried to persuade them to come back, his children seem have adapted to foreign society and show no intention of returning. F25 told me that he was a liberal and respected his children's choice and therefore did not press them to follow in his footsteps.

F26's family

F26's father was a landlord in Chaozhou who fled to Hong Kong prior to Liberation in the Chinese mainland. F26 was categorized as a son of the 'black fives' (five types of people who were criticized by the Communist Party). He and his brother later managed to flee to Hong Kong and joined their father in the 1960s. F26's father opened a textile factory in San Po Kong, Kowloon. He helped his father and took an evening class to upgrade his English. In 1978 F26's father passed away and he took over the business accordingly. His wife and younger brother also worked in the firm.

Under the leadership of F26, the family business expanded rapidly and became one of the leading firms in manufacturing raw cloth. In the 1980s, F26 tried to diversify his investment and therefore set up a travel agency and a property development company. In the early 1990s he even moved his manufacturing plant to the Chinese mainland.

F26 has two sons and one daughter. All of them were sent to New Zealand after they had finished at their primary school in Hong Kong. His eldest son has been in the company for three years following his graduation. F26 hopes this son can learn more before his retirement.

Glossary

Personal names

Chan But-son	陳弼臣
Chan Chiu-ying	陳朝英
Chan Hoi-tai	陳海泰
Chan Kai-ming	陳啟明
Chan Ping-cheung	陳炳章
Chan Shu-kai	陳樹佳
Chan Shu-kwai	陳樹渠
Chan Shu-yuen	陳樹源
Chan Tai-ho	陳大河
Chan Wai-chow	陳維周
Chan Wun-wing	陳煥榮
Chang Fei	張飛
Chau Cham-chiu	周湛樵
Chau Cham-lam	周湛霖
Chau Cham-sun	周湛燊
Chau Cham-wang	周湛湟
Chau Cheuk-fan (Tai-fai)	周卓藩 (大輝)
Chau Hau-nin	周孝年
Chau Ka-ho	周嘉灝
Chau Kai-bong	周啟邦
Chau Kai-lim	周啟廉
Chau Kai-yin	周啟賢
Chau Ka-lai	周嘉禮
Chau Ka-wan	周嘉宏
Chau Shek-nin	周錫年
Chau Siu-kay (Man-fai)	周少岐 (文輝)
Chau Tsun-nin	周俊年
Chau Wing-tai	周永泰
Chau Yam-kiu (Yat-fai)	周蔭橋 (日輝)
Chau Yick-nin	周奕年
Chau Yiu-nin	周耀年

Chen Fu-qian	陳福謙
Cheng Ka-shing Henry	鄭家成
Cheng Yu-tong Uncle Tong	鄭裕彤-彤叔
Cheung Chao-chun	張楚贊
Cheung Che-tong	張織堂
Cheung Fai-tong	張輝堂
Cheung King-tong	張鏡堂
Cheung Kit-tong	張傑堂
Cheung Kwan-hong	張鈞康
Cheung Kwan-tong	張鈞堂
Cheung Miu-ching	張妙清
Cheung Miu-ping	張妙萍
Cheung Pui-tong	張沛堂
Cheung Shun-cheong Sloan	張詢昌
Cheung Wai-cheng	張惠貞
Cheung Wai-ming	張惠明
Cheung Wai-yin	張惠賢
Cheung Yuk-kai	張玉階
Cheung Yuk-kei	張玉麒
Cheung Yuk-leung	張玉良
Cheung Yuk-lun	張玉麟
Chiang Kai-shek (Jiang Jieshi)	蔣介石
Chim Pui-chung	詹培忠
Chiu Kam-hing Kathy	趙金卿
Chiu Sheung-chow	趙相秋
Choi Cheung-kok	蔡章閣
Chou Enlai	周恩來
Chow Chi-nam	周志南
Chow Hau-leung	周孝亮
Chow Sau-sung	周修祟
Chow Shauson	周壽臣
Chow Wing-kin	周永健
Chuang Ching-um	莊靜庵
Eu Kong	余廣
Eu Tong-sen	余東旋
Fung Fook-tin	馮福田
Fung Hing-biu Robert	馮慶彪
Fung Hing-cheung Kenneth	馮慶鏘
Fung Hing-chiu Cyril	馮慶炤
Fung Hing-lun Lawrence	馮慶麟
Fung Hon-chu	馮漢柱
Fung Hong-hin	馮漢興
Fung King-hei	馮景禧
Fung Kit-see	馮傑時
Fung Kwok-chor	馮國礎

Fung kwok-hon	馮國康
Fung Kwok-king Victor	馮國經
Fung Kwok-lun William	馮國麟
Fung Lai-wah	馮麗華
Fung Mo-ying	馮慕英
Fung Pak-liu	馮柏燎
Fung Ping-fun	馮秉芬
Fung Ping-kan	馮炳芹
Fung Ping-shan	馮平山
Fung Ping-wah	馮秉華
Gu Xian-rong	辜顯榮
Ho Chi-kin	何志堅
Ho Chiu-fong Daisy	何超鳳
Ho Chiu-king Pansy	何超瓊
Ho Eric Edward or Eric Ho-tung	何鴻章
Ho Eric Peter	何鴻鑾
Ho Florence or Florence Yeo	何孝姿
Ho Fook	何福
Ho Grace	何堯姿
Ho Hung-chim	何鴻潛
Ho Hung-ngai Rubbie	何鴻毅
Ho Hung-sun Stanley	何鴻燊
Ho Irene or Irene Cheng	何艾齡 (鄭艾齡)
Ho Kom-tong	何甘棠
Ho Shai-kee	何世傑
Ho Shai-kim Edward or Edward Ho-tung	何世儉
Ho Shai-kwong	何世光
Ho Shai-lai Robert	何世禮
Ho Shai-wing	何世榮
Ho Shai-yiu	何世耀
Ho Sze-man (Bosman)	何仕文
Ho Tung	何東
Ho Victoria Jubilee	何錦姿
Ho Yau-chung	何猶忠
Ho Yau-long Lawrence	何猶龍
Ho Yiu-tai Gallent	何耀棣
Ho Yuen-yuen Susie	何婉婉
Hui Chun-hang Julian	許晉亨
Hui Chun-kuen	許晉權
Hui Chun-lim	許晉廉
Hui Chun-ling	許晉齡
Hui Chun-wo	許晉和
Hui Chun-yee	許晉義
Hui Kin-koi	許建居
Hui Kin-kong	許建江

Hui Ki-pak	許岐伯
Hui Oi-chow	許愛周
Hui Sai-fun	許世勳
Hui Sze-fun	許仕芬
Kan Siu-han Ivy	簡笑嫻
Kan Tung-po	簡東浦
Kan Yuet-hing	簡悅慶
Kan Yuet-keung	簡悅強
Kan Yuet-wai	簡悅威
Ko Chor-yuen	高楚源
Kwan Yu	關羽
Kwok Chi-bun Benjamin	郭志彬
Kwok Chi-hang	郭志亨
Kwok Chi-ho	郭志浩
Kwok Chi-hong	郭志康
Kwok Chi-kuen Philip	郭志權
Kwok Chi-leung	郭志樑
Kwok Chi-piu	郭志標
Kwok Chi-shun	郭志純
Kwok Chi-yan	郭志仁
Kwok Chi-yat	郭志一
Kwok Chun [Gockchin] Philip	郭泉
Kwok Lam-but Lambert	郭琳弼
Kwok Lam-po	郭琳褒
Kwok Lam-shan Lamson	郭琳珊
Kwok Lam-shun	郭琳純
Kwok Lam-yeung	郭琳驤
Kwok Lock [Gocklock] James	郭樂
Kwok Ping-luen	郭炳聯
Kwok Pui-fun	郭佩勳
Kwok Shun [Gockson] William	郭順
Kwok Tak-seng	郭德勝
Kwok Wing-leung Andy	郭永亮
Lam But-chung	林拔中
Lam F.L.	林風林
Lam Kin-hong	林建康
Lam Kin-ming	林建名
Lam Kin-ngao Peter	林建岳
Lam Kuan-chuang	林炯燦
Lam Leung-kwong	林良廣
Lam Ming-chu Pearl	林明珠
Lam Pak-yan Uncle Lam	林百欣-林伯
Lau Chu-pak	劉鑄伯
Lau Luen-hung	劉鑾雄
Lee Chak-sun	李澤生

Lee Cha-ming	利策名
Lee Chi-kong	利志剛
Lee Ding-cheong Peter	利定昌
Lee Hau-wo	利孝和
Lee Hin-bun	利憲彬
Lee Hon-chiu	利漢釗
Lee Hysan	利希慎
Lee Kam-tong	李錦棠
Lee Leung-yick	利良奕
Lee Man-tat	李文達
Lee Man-yick	利文奕
Lee Quo-wai	利國偉
Lee Richard Charles (R.C.)	利銘澤
Lee Shau-kee	李兆基
Lee Shun-yin	利舜賢
Lee Siu-nam	陳兆南
Lee Siu-tan	陳兆旦
Lee Tak-yan	利德仁
Lee Tun-yan	利敦仁
Lee Wai-chung	李惠中
Lee Wai-hung	李惠雄
Lee Wai-man	李惠民
Lee Wai-sum	李惠森
Lee Wing-hon	利榮康
Lee Wing-sum	利榮森
Lee Wing-tat	利榮達
Li Chi-hang Dora	李志行
Li Chi-hei Gladys	李志喜
Li Chok-chung	李作忠
Li Dao-ming	李道明
Li Fook-cheung	李福象
Li Fook-chiu	李福釗
Li Fook-hoi	李福海
Li Fook-kow	李福球
Li Fook-kuen	李福權
Li Fook-kwan Cornel	何福鋆
Li Fook-luen	李福聯
Li Fook-pui	李福培
Li Fook-sean	李福善
Li Fook-shu	李福樹
Li Fook-siu Ronald	李福兆
Li Fook-sum Alan	李福深
Li Fook-tai	李福泰
Li Fook-wo Aubry	李福和
Li Fu-yun	李芙蓉

Li Kar-seng (Li Shek-pang family)	李家成 (李石鵬家族)
Li Ka-shing	李嘉誠
Li Kin-choi	李建財
Li Koon-chun	李冠春
Li Kwok-cheong	李國祥
Li Kwok-cheung Arthur	李國章
Li Kwok-lun	李國麟
Li Kwok-nung Andrew	李國能
Li Kwok-po David	李國寶
Li Kwok-wai Didier	李國緯
Li Lan-sang	李蘭生
Li Man-bun Brian	李民斌
Li Man-chun Peter	李民俊
Li Man-kiu Adrian	李民橋
Li Man-ying Alexander	李民英
Li Shek-pang	李石朋
Li Shu-fun	李樹芬
Li Shu-ming	李世民
Li Shu-pui	李樹培
Li Siu-pang	李少彭
Li To-ming	李道明
Li Tse-fong	李子芳
Li Tza-kai Richard	李澤楷
Li Tza-kwai Victor	李澤鉅
Li Wai-yin Doris	李惠賢
Li Xian-nin	李先念
Li Yue-chu	李如珠
Li Yuen-kwan Maxine	李婉群
Li Yuet-sheung Sylvia	李月嫦
Lin Jia-yin	林甲寅
Lin Ping-hou	林平侯
Liu Bei	劉備
Lo Cheung-siu	羅長肇
Lo Chun-hin	羅進興
Lo Doris	羅巧貞
Lo Enid	羅德貞
Lo Fong-cheung	羅芳祥
Lo Fu-wah	羅富華
Lo Hong-shui	羅康瑞
Lo Hung-sui	羅孔瑞
Lo Kai-fook	羅開福
Lo Kei-lok Joy	羅其樂
Lo Kwai-cheung	羅桂祥
Lo Man-ho	羅文灝
Lo Man-kam	羅文錦

Lo Po-ying Katie	羅寶盈
Lo Sau-yan Sharon	羅秀茵
Lo Shui-choi	羅瑞彩
Lo Tak-shing	羅德丞
Lo Tang-cheung	羅騰祥
Lo Ying-shek	羅鷹石
Lo Yuk-shui	羅旭瑞
Loh Hau-pui	陸孝佩
Loh Kung-wai Christine	陸恭惠
Loh Kung-yat	陸恭一
Low Lai-wah Irene	勞麗華
Low Min-nong	勞冕農
Lui Chi-wah	呂志華
Lui Ming-choi	呂明財
Ma [Kwok] Chi-ching Joyce	馬(郭)志清
Ma Kai-cheung	馬介璋
Ma Kam-chuang	馬錦燦
Ma King-wah Walter	馬景華
Ma Pak-leung	馬百良
Ma Wick-yee	馬域宜
Ma Wing-chung	馬永燦
Ma Ying-biu	馬應彪
Ming Kar-fook	明嘉福
Ming Mei-lin	明美蓮
Mok Ching-kong	莫晴江
Ngan Shing-kwan	顏成坤
Poon Chi-kong	潘志剛
Poon Dee-dee	潘楚穎
Poon Dickson	潘迪生
Poon Kam-chui Penny	潘金翠
Poon Kam-kai	潘錦溪
Siu Ming	蕭明
Siu Pak-shing	蕭百成
Tam Oi-ling	譚愛玲
Tan Soon-gie George	陳松青
Tang Chi-ngong	鄧志昂
Tang Sau-ching	鄧秀清
Tang Shiu-kin	鄧肇堅
Tang Wing-cheung David	鄧永鏘
Tsai Lai-king	蔡麗瓊
Tso Man-kam	曹文錦
Wang Cha-pong alias Lo-kat or Uncle Kat	王澤邦, 又名老吉或吉叔
Wang Hang-chiu	王恆炤
Wang Hang-li	王恆利
Wang Hang-san	王恆新

Wang Hang-yu	王恆裕
Wang Kin-cheung	王健鏘
Wang Kin-san	王健燊
Wang Kin-yee	王健儀
Wang Kwai-cheung	王貴祥
Wang Kwai-fa	王貴發
Wang Kwai-shing	王貴成
Wang Sau-yip	王守業
Wang Yu-hon	王豫康
Wang Zhao-jun	王昭君
Wen-sheng (Tang dynasty princess)	文成
Woo Hey-tong	胡熙堂
Woo Mo-fong	胡慕芳
Woo Mo-ying	胡慕英
Woo Pak-chun	胡百全
Woo Po-king Daisy	胡寶瓊
Woo Po-sing	胡寶星
Woo Siu-che	胡兆熾
Wu Yan-sheung Gordon	胡應湘
Yan Dou-meng	顏斗猛
Yan Xi-shan	閻石山
Yeo Chee-hey	楊至希
Yeo Chee-wai	楊至偉
Yeo Chee-yeow	楊至耀
Yeo Keng-lian	楊景連
Yeo Thian-hwa	楊天華
Yeo Thian-in	楊天恩
Yeo Thian-kiew	楊天球
Yeo Thian-seng	楊天成
Yeo Way-cheung	楊為章
Yeo Way-din	楊為定
Yeo Way-hing	楊為興
Yeo Way-li	楊為理
Yeo Zhianying	葉劍英
Yip Tak-lee Teddy	葉德利
Young Kwok-cheung	楊國章
Young Shangkun	楊尚昆
Yu Hung-kwan	余鴻鈞
Zheng Xinxian	鄭湘先

Place names

Banchaio	板橋
Beijing	北京
Changping	常平

Chaoan	潮安
Chaoyang	潮陽
Chenghai	澄海
Cheung Sha Wan	長沙灣
Chongqing	重慶
Dongguang	東莞
Fengshun	豐順
Foshan	佛山
Fujian	福建
Gaoxiong	高雄
Guangdong	廣東
Guangxi	廣西
Guangzhou	廣州
Han River	韓河
Hangzhou	杭州
Huilai	惠來
Hung Hom	紅磡
Jiangsu	江蘇
Jiangxi (Kiangsi)	江西
Jiaxing	嘉興
Jiedong	揭東
Jiexi	揭西
Jieyang	揭陽
Keelung (Jilong)	基隆
Kwai Chung	葵涌
Kwun Tong	官塘
Lukang	鹿港
Meizhou	梅州
Mong Kok	旺角
Namhai	南海
Namsui	南水
Nanao	南澳
Nanjing	南京
Oi Kwan Building	愛群大厦
Puning	普寧
Raoping	饒平
Sai Kung	西貢
San Po Kong	新浦崗
Sham Shui Po	深水涉
Shandong	山東
Shanghai	上海
Shantou	汕頭
Sichuan	四川
Suzhou	蘇州
Tai Po	大埔

Tiananmen Square	天安門廣場
Tsuen Wan	荃灣
Waitun	圍屯
Wong Tai Sin	黃大仙
Wufeng	霧峰
Xinhui	新會
Yau Tong	油塘
Yuen Long	元朗
Zhangzhou	漳州
Zhejiang	浙江

Company names

Carrinna Restaurant Group	佳寧娜
Chekiang Commercial Bank	浙江商業銀行
Eu Yan Sang	余仁生
Great Eagle Holdings	鷹君集團
Hang Seng Bank	恆生銀行
Heng Tai	香泰
Jiaotong University	交通大學
Kam Hing Hong [Firm]	錦興行
Kam Yuen	金源
Key Lap Enterprise	基立企業
Kin Tai Long or Kin Tye Lung	乾泰隆
Kwong Sang Hong	廣生行
Lai Cheong Lung	禮昌隆
Lee Chung Shing Tong	李眾勝堂
Lee Kam Kee	李錦記
Li & Fung	利豐
Lui Hing Hop	呂興合
Ma Pak Leung	馬百良
Nam Pak Hong	南北行
Nam Wo Hong [Firm]	南和利
On Kee [Trading]	安記
Paliburg Holdings	百利寶集團
Peace Mark	宜進利
Po Leung Kuk	保良局
Qing Hua University	清華大學
Shun Cheong Shipping	順昌船務
Siu Fung [Trading]	兆豐
Sui On	瑞安
Sui Shing Hong [Firm]	瑞成行
Sun Hung Kai Groups	新鴻基集團
Tang Tin Fook Money Shop	鄧天福銀號
Tung Wah Group of Hospitals	東華三院

Wai Kat Money Shop	維吉銀號
Wang Lo Kat	王老吉
Wing Hang Bank	永亨銀行
Wing Long Bank	永隆銀行
Wing On	永安
Wo Fat Sing	和發成
Yan Chai Hospitals	仁濟醫院
Yee On Money Shop	宜安銀號
Yeo Hiap Seng	楊協成
Ying Kee	英記

Terms

Baijiazi	敗家子
Bo Ying Compound	保嬰丹
Chaozhou hua (Chaozhou dialect)	潮州話
Chuannan bu chuannu	傳男不傳女
Chut Lee Powder	七厘散
Dafu buguo sandai	大富不過三代
Dushu shizi	讀書識字
Facai lipin	發財立品
Fang	房
Fengshui	風水
Fenjia	分家
Fenjia sannian xian gaodi	分家三年顯高低
Fuce jiangshan tianxia	富則兼善天下
Gezhan suochang	各展所長
Guanghu hua or yueyu	廣府話或粵語
Guangzong yaozu	光宗耀祖
Hakka (kejia)	客家
Han dynasty	漢朝
Jiada bifen	家大必分
Jianghu diwei	江湖地位
Jiasheng	家聲
Jiating qiye	家庭企業
Jiazu jituan	家族集團
Jiazu	家族
Jieyi	結義
Junzi zhize sandai erzhan	君子之澤、三代而斬
Kaoqu gongming	考取功名
Kingdom of Jin	晉國
Kingdom of Qin	秦國
Kuangchung yauzhu	光宗耀祖
Kungfu tea	功夫茶
Kuomintang (Nationalist Party)	國民黨

Mahjong (a popular local game)	麻雀 (遊戲)
Ming dynasty	明朝
Niaoda lichoa	鳥大離巢
Pak Foong Pill	白鳳丸
Po Chai Pill	保濟丸
Qiangzhuang	錢莊
Qiaoxiang	僑鄉
Qing dynasty	清朝
Saarchi	沙紙
Tan dynasty	唐朝
Tongjie gongcai	同居公財
Tongxianhui	同鄉會
Tongzhi	同治
Tufan	吐番
Xian	縣
Xianqi fulao	鄉親父老
Yichao tianzi yichao chen	一朝天子一朝臣
Yulan Festival (Hungry Ghost Festival)	盂蘭節
Zhou dynasty	周朝
Zongqinhui	宗親會
Zuci	祖祠
Zufen	祖墳
Zuye	祖業

Bibliography

In English

Alcorn, P.B. (1982) *Success and Survival in the Family Owned Business*, New York: McGraw Hill.

Allen, M. (1987) *The Founding Fortunes: A New Anatomy of the Super-Richest Families in America*, New York: Trumen Talley.

American College Dictionary. (1956) (edited by Barnhart, C.L.), New York: Random House.

Argyle, M. (1994) *The Psychology of Social Class*, London: Routledge.

Auwers, L. (1978) 'Fathers, sons, and wealth in colonial Windsor, Connecticut', *Journal of Family History*, 3: 136–49.

Bank of East Asia. (1989) *Bank of East Asia 70th Anniversary*, Hong Kong: Bank of East Asia.

——. (1994) *Bank of East Asia 75th Anniversary: Commemorative Book*, Hong Kong: Bank of East Asia.

Barnes, L.B. and Kriger, M.P. (1986) 'The hidden side of organizational leadership', *Sloan Management Review*, Fall: 15–25.

Becker, G. (1964) *Human Capital*, New York: Columbia University Press.

Beckhard, R. and Dyer Jr., W. (1983) 'Managing change in the family firm: issues and strategies', *Sloan Management Review*, 24: 59–65.

Beckhard, R., Davis, P. and Hollander, B. (1987) 'A note to the reader', in J. Ward, *Keeping the Family Business Healthy: How to Plan for Continuing Growth, Profitability, and Family Leadership*, San Francisco: Jossey-Bass, pp. 1–2.

Bendix, R. (1971) 'Charismatic leadership', in R. Bendix and G. Roth (eds), *Scholarship and Partnership: Essays on Max Weber*, Berkeley: University of California Press, pp. 212–20.

Berkowitz, S.D. (1976) 'The dynamics of elite structure', unpublished PhD thesis, Brandeis University.

Bottomore, T.B. and Rubel, M. (1963) *Karl Marx: Selected Writings in Sociology and Social Philosophy*, Harmondsworth: Penguin Books.

Boudon, R. (1974) *Education, Opportunity and Social Inequality*, New York: John Wiley and Son.

Bourdieu, P. (1986) 'The forms of capital', in J.G. Richardson (ed.), *Handbook of Theory and Research for the Sociology of Education*, New York: Greenwood Press, pp. 241–58.

Brittain, J.A. (1977) *The Inheritance of Economic Status*, Washington: The Brookings Institution.

Brown, F.H. (1993) 'Loss and continuity in the family firm: the effect on leadership succession', *Family Business Review*, 6: 263–81.

Calder, G.H. (1961) 'The peculiar problems of family business', *Business Horizons*, 4(3): 93–102.

Census and Statistics Department. (1969) *Hong Kong Statistics: 1947–1967*, Hong Kong: The Government Printer.

——. (1972) *Hong Kong Population and Housing Census: 1971*, Hong Kong: The Government Printer.

——. (1982) *Hong Kong 1981 Census: Main Reports*, Hong Kong: The Government Printer.

——. (1992) *Hong Kong 1991 Population Census: Main* Reports, Hong Kong: The Government Printer.

Chamberlain, B.H. (1971) *Japanese Things: Being Notes on Various Subjects Connected with Japan, for the Use of Travelers and Others*, Rutland, VT: Tuttle.

Chan, K.B. and Chiang, C. (1994) *Stepping Out: The Making of Chinese Entrepreneurs*, Singapore: Prentice Hall.

Chau, T.T. (1991) 'Approaches to succession in East Asia business organizations', *Family Business Review*, 6: 161–80.

Cheng, I. (1976) *Clara Ho Tung: A Hong Kong Lady, Her Family and Her Times*, Hong Kong: Chinese University Press.

——. (1997) *Intercultural Reminiscences*, Hong Kong: David C. Lam Institute for East–West Studies, Hong Kong Baptist University.

China Mail. (1928) 'Macao Opium', 17 April.

——. (1928) 'Lee Hyson Killed', 30 April.

Ching, F. (1999) *The Li Dynasty: Hong Kong Aristocrats*, Hong Kong: Oxford University Press.

Chung, S.P.Y. (1999) 'Surviving economic crises in Southeast Asia and southern China – Eu Yan Sang business conglomerates 1876–1941', in *An International Conference on Chinese Traditional Enterprises and Entrepreneurship in Prosperity and Adversity: South China and Southeast Asia During the Twentieth Century*, Hong Kong: Centre of Asian Studies.

Cohen, M.L. (1970) 'Developmental process in the Chinese domestic group', in M. Freedman (ed.), *Family and Kinship in Chinese Society*, Stanford: Stanford University Press, pp. 21–36.

——. (1976) *House United, House Divided: The Chinese Family in Taiwan*, New York: Columbia University Press.

Coleman, J.S. (1990) *Foundations of Social Theory*, Cambridge: Harvard University Press.

Commerce and Industry Department. (1967–1969) *Statement by the Honorable T.D. Sorby in the Legislative Council and Background Information on the Rice Trade*, Hong Kong: The Government Printer.

Compact Oxford English Dictionary. (1993) London: Oxford University Press.

Conger, J.A. (1989) *The Charismatic Leader: Behind the Mystique of Exceptional Leadership*, San Francisco: Jossey-Bass.

Conger, J.A. and Kanungo, R.N. (1998) *Charismatic Leadership in Organizations*, Thousand Oaks: Sage Publications.

Cosier, R.A. and Harvey, M. (1998) 'The hidden strengths in family business: functional conflict', *Family Business Review*, 11: 75–9.

Cunningham, J.B. and Ho, J. (1994) 'The dynamics of growth and succession in entrepreneurial organizations', *Journal of Enterprising Culture*, 2(1): 571–600.

Danco, L.A. (1987) 'Forword', in J. Ward, *Keeping the Family Business Healthy: How to Plan for Continuing Growth, Profitability, and Family Leadership*, San Francisco: Jossey-Bass, pp. 1–3.

Davis, P. and Stern, P. (1980) 'Adoption, survival and growth of the family business: an integrated systems perspective', *Human Relations*, 34(4): 207–24.

Deen Jr., J.W. (1972) 'Patterns of testation: four tidewater counties in colonial Virginia', *American Journal of Legal History*, 16: 154–76.

DeGlopper, D. (1972) 'Doing business in Lukang', in W.W. Willmott (ed.) *Economic Organization in Chinese Society*, Stanford: Stanford University Press, pp. 297–326.

Diamond, D.N. (1969) *Kun Shen: A Taiwan Village*, New York: Holt, Rinehart, and Winston.

Donelley, R. (1964) 'The family business', *Harvard Business Review*, 42: 93–105.

Evers, R. (2000) 'Rethink urged for traditional Asian business model', *Hong Kong iMail*, 30 August 2000, p. B3.

Freedman, M. (1957) *Chinese Family and Marriage in Singapore*, London: Her Majesty's Stationery Office.

——. (1971) *Chinese Lineage and Society: Fukien and Kwangtung*, London: The Athlone Press.

——. (1979) *The Study of Chinese Society: Essays by M. Freedman*, Stanford: Stanford University Press.

Freedman, S.D. (1991) 'Sibling relationships and intergenerational succession in family firms', *Family Business Review*, 4: 3–20.

Fukuyama, F. (1995) *Trust: The Social Virtues and the Creation of Prosperity*, London: Hamish Hamilton.

Fung, K.K.V. (1997) 'Evolution in the management of family enterprises in Asia', in G.W. Wang and S.L. Wong (eds), *Dynamic Hong Kong: Business and Culture*, Hong Kong: University of Hong Kong Press, pp. 216–29.

Gallo, M.A. (1988) 'The family business in the Spanish economy', Research Report, IESE, Universidad de Navaira, Barcelona, pp. 12–23.

Gibbon, A. and Hadekel, P. (1990) *Steinberg: The Break Up of a Family Empire*, Toronto: Macmillan.

Gilley, B. (1998) 'Over to you: tycoon Robert Kuok hands the reins to his successors', *Far East Economic Review*, 161: 10–14.

Goody, J. (1976) 'Inheritance, property and women: some comparative considerations', in J. Goody, J. Thirsk and E.P. Thompson (eds), *Family and Inheritance: Rural Society in Western Europe, 1200–1800*, London: Cambridge University Press, pp. 10–36.

——. (1987) 'Inheritance', in J. Eatwell, M. Milgate and P. Newman (eds), *The New Palgrave: A Dictionary of Economics*, New York: Stockton Press, pp. 851–5.

Granovetter, M. (1985) 'Economic action and social structure: the problem of embeddedness', *American Journal of Sociology*, 95: 481–510.

Guldin, G.E. (1977) 'Overseas at home: the Fujianese of Hong Kong', unpublished PhD thesis, University of Wisconsin, Madison.

Gundersen, J.R. (1998) 'Women and inheritance in America: Virginia and New York as a case study, 1700–1860', in R.K. Miller, Jr. and S.J. McNamee (eds), *Inheritance and Wealth in America*, New York: Plenum Press, pp. 193–214.

Hamilton, G.G., Orru, M. and Biggart, N.W. (1987) 'Enterprise groups in East Asia: an organizational analysis', *Financial Economic Review*, 161: 78–106.

Handler, W. (1990) 'Succession in family firms: a mutual role adjustment between entrepreneur and next-generation family member', *Entrepreneurship Theory and Practice*, 15(1): 37–51.

Harvey, M. and Evans, R. (1994) 'Family business and multiple levels of conflict', *Family Business Review*, 7: 331–48.

Ho, P.T. (1976) *The Ladder of Success in Imperial China: Aspects of Social Mobility: 1368–1911*, New York: Da Capo Press.

Howe, K. (2000) 'Pink power', *South China Morning Post: Features*, 1 September, p. 1.

Hughes, J. (1997) *Family Wealth: Keeping it in the Family*, New York: James E. Hughes, Jr. Co.

Jehn, K.A. (1997) 'A qualitative analysis of conflict types and dimensions in organizational groups', *Administrative Science Quarterly*, 42: 530–57.

Jensen, A.R. (1973) *Education Difference*, London: Methuen.

Jensen, M. (1989) 'The eclipse of the public corporation', *Harvard Business Review*, September–October.

Jim, C.Y. (1995) 'Transplanting two champion specimens of mature Chinese banyans', *Journal of Arboriculture*, 21(6): 289–95.

Johnston, R.F. (1910) *Lion & Dragon in Northern China*, New York: Dutton.

Kann, R.A. (1973) 'Dynastic relations and European power politics: 1848–1918', *Journal of Modern History*, 45: 127–40.

Kao, R.W.Y. (1995) *Entrepreneurship: A Wealth Creation and Value-Adding Process*, Singapore: Prentice Hall.

Kaye, K. (1999) 'Mate selection and family business success', *Family Business Review*, 12(2): 107–15.

Kaye, K. and McCarthy, C. (1996) 'Healthy disagreements', *Family Business*, 1: 71–2.

Kets de Vries, M.F.R. (1988) 'The dark side of CEO succession', *Harvard Business Review*, January–February.

Kirzner, I. (1973) *Competition and Entrepreneurship*, Chicago: University of Chicago Press.

——. (1979) *Perception, Opportunity, and Profit: Studies in the Theory of Entrepreneurship*, Chicago: University of Chicago Press.

Kotter, J.P. (1990) 'What do leaders really do?', in Harvard Business School (ed.), *Business Review on Leadership*, Massachusetts: Harvard Business Review, pp. 37–60.

Kwong, C.K.P. (1984) 'Family life cycle and family structure in East Asia, 1950–1980', in H. Schubnell *et al.* (eds) *Population Politics in Asian Countries*, Hong Kong: University of Hong Kong Press, pp. 567–617.

Kwong Sang Hong Limited. (1990) *Kwong Sang Hong Limited: 80th Anniversary*, Hong Kong: Kwong Sang Hong Limited.

Lan, L.L. (1999) 'The take-over saga of Yeo Hiap Seng Limited', *Asian Case Research Journal*, 3: 169–94.

Landa, J. (1983) 'The political economy of the ethnically heterogeneous Chinese middleman group in Southeast Asia: ethnicity and entrepreneurship in a plural society', in L. Lim and P. Gosling (eds), *The Chinese in Southeast Asia: Ethnicity and Economic Activity*, Singapore: Maruzen Asia, pp. 86–116.

Landon, K.P. (1941) *The Chinese in Thailand*, New York: Russell and Russell (reprinted in 1973).

Lansberg, I. (1988) 'The succession conspiracy', *Family Business Review*, 1: 119–43.

Lau, C.K. (1985) 'How Chiu Chow (Chaozhou) bred success', *South China Morning Post*, 25 February.

Lau, L.B.Y. and Wong, Y.H. (2000) 'Eu Yan Sang (Hong Kong) Limited', *Asian Case Research Journal*, 4: 121–34.

Leach, P. (1991) *The Family Business*, London: Kogan Page.

Leibenstein, H. (1978) *General X-Efficiency Theory and Economic* Development, New York: Oxford University Press.

Levine, J.H. and Roy, W.S. (1979) 'A study of interlocking directorates: vital concepts', in P.W. Holland and S. Leinhardt (eds), *Perspectives on Social Network Research*, New York: Academic Press, pp. 349–78.

Levinson, H. (1971) 'Conflicts that plague family business', *Harvard Business Review*, 49: 90–8.

Levy Jr., M. (1955) 'Contrasting factors in the modernization of China and Japan', in S. Kuznets, W.E. Moore and J.J. Spengler (eds), *Economic Growth: Brazil, India, Japan*, Durham, NC: Duke University Press, pp. 23–36.

Li, E.S.P. (1993) *My Life: Dr Ellen Li*, no publisher (bilingual).

——. (1998) *My Way: Dr Ellen Li: Her Life and Her Contribution*, no publisher (bilingual).

Li & Fung. (1982) *Li & Fung Limited: For 75 Years, a Mirror of Hong Kong's Success*, Hong Kong: Li & Fung.

Lim, M.H. (1981) *Ownership and Control of the One Hundred Largest Corporations in Malaysia, Kuala Lumpur*, Oxford: Oxford University Press.

——. (1983) 'The ownership and control of large corporations in Malaysia: the role of Chinese businessmen', in L. Lim and P. Gosling (eds), *The Chinese in Southeast Asia: Ethnicity and Economic Activity*, Singapore: Maruzen Asia, pp. 275–315.

Litz, R.A. (1995) 'The family business: toward definitional clarity', *Family Business Review*, 8: 71–81.

Liu [Wang], H.C. (1959) *The Traditional Chinese Clan Rules*, New York: Augustin.

Macfarlane, A. (1998) 'The mystery of property: inheritance and industrialization in England and Japan', in C.M. Hann (ed.) *Property Relations: Renewing the Anthropological Tradition*, London: Cambridge University Press, pp. 104–23.

Mackie, J.A. (1992) 'Overseas Chinese entrepreneurship', *Asian-Pacific Economic Literature*, 6(1): 41–64.

McNamee, S.J. and Miller Jr., R.K. (1998) 'Inheritance and stratification', in R.K. Miller Jr. and S.J. McNamee (eds), *Inheritance and Wealth in America*, New York: Plenum Press, pp. 193–214.

Magretta, J. (1998) 'Fast, global, and entrepreneurial: supply chain management, Hong Kong style: an interview with Victor Fung', *Harvard Business Review*, 65(5): 103–14.

Marcus, G. (1980) 'Law in the development of dynastic families among American business elite: the domestication of capital and capitalization of the family', *Law and Society Review*, 14: 859–903.

Menkhoff, T. (1990) 'Towards an understanding of Chinese entrepreneurship in Southeast Asia: small trading firms in Singapore', Working Papers 138, Department of Sociology, University of Bielefeld.

Menschik, P. and Jianakoplos, N.J. (1998) 'Economics of inheritance', in R.K. Miller Jr. and S.J. McNamee (eds), *Inheritance and Wealth in America*, New York: Plenum Press, pp. 45–60.

Miyamoto, M. (1984) *Family Business in the Era of Industrial* Growth, Japan: University of Tokyo Press.

Moench, R.U. (1963) 'Economic relations of the Chinese in the Society Islands', unpublished PhD thesis. Harvard University.

Mommsen, W.J. (1974) *The Age of Bureaucracy: Perspectives on the Political Sociology of Max Weber*, Oxford: Basil Blackwell.

Murphy, R. (1988) *Social Closure: The Theory of Monopolization and Exclusion*, London: Oxford University Press.

Navin, T.R. (1991) 'Passing on the mantle: management succession in industry', in C. Aronnof and J. Ward (eds), *Family Business Sourcebook*, Detroit: Omnigraphies Inc, pp. 80–93.

Numazaki, I. (1986) 'Networks of Taiwan big business: a preliminary analysis', *Modern China*, 12: 487–534.

——. (1991) 'The role of personal networks in the making of Taiwan's Guanxiqiye (related enterprises)', in G. Hamilton (ed.), *Business Networks and Economic Development in East and Southeast Asia*, Hong Kong: University of Hong Kong Press, pp. 77–93.

Omohundro, J.T. (1974) 'The Chinese merchant community of Iloilo City, Philippines', unpublished PhD thesis, University of Michigan.

——. (1983) 'Social network and business success for the Philippine Chinese', in L. Lim and P. Gosling (ed.), *The Chinese in South East Asia: Ethnicity and Economic Activity*, Singapore: Maruzen Asia, pp. 65–85.

Parkin, F. (1979) *Marxism and Class Theory: A Bourgeois Critique*, New York: Columbia University Press.

Postiglione, G. (1999a) 'Schools demonstrate capitalist qualities', *South China Morning Post*, 1 October.

——. (1999b) *China's National Minority Education: Culture, Schooling and Development, 1999*, Hong Kong: Oxford University Press.

Poy [Lee], T.W.V. (1995) *A River Named Lee*, Canada: Calyan Publishing Ltd.

——. (1998) *Building Bridges: The Life and Times of Richard Chares Lee*, Canada: Calyan Publishing Ltd.

Redding, S.G. (1988) 'The role of the entrepreneur in the new Asian capitalism', in P.L. Berger and M.H.H. Hsiao (eds), *In Search of an East Asian Development Model*, New Brunswick: Transaction Books, pp. 99–112.

——. (1990) *The Spirit of Chinese Capitalism*, New York: De Gruyter.

——. (1991) 'Weak organizations and strong linkages: managerial ideology and Chinese family business networks', in G. Hamilton (ed.), *Business Networks and Economic Development in East and Southeast Asia*, Hong Kong: University of Hong Kong Press, pp. 30–47.

Richardson, R.J. and Thayer, S.K. (1993) *The Charisma Factor: How to Develop Your Natural Leadership Ability*, New Jersey: Prentice Hall.

Rosenblatt, P.C. (1991) 'The interplay of family system and business system: family farms during economic recession, *Family Business Review*, 6: 45–57.

Rosenfeld, J.P. (1998) 'Will contests: legacies of aging and social change', in R.K. Miller Jr. and S.J. McNamee (eds), *Inheritance and Wealth in America*, New York: Plenum Press, pp. 173–92.

Sabean, D. (1976) 'Aspects of kinship behavior and property in rural western Europe before 1800', in J. Goody, J. Thirsk and E.P. Thompson (eds), *Family and Inheritance: Rural Society in Western Europe, 1200–1800*, London: Cambridge University Press, pp. 96–111.

Schultz, T.W. (1971) *Investment in Human* Capital, New York: Free Press.

Schumpeter, J.A. (1934) *The Theory of Economic Development: An Inquiry into Profits, Capital, Credit, Interest, and the Business Cycle*, Cambridge: Harvard University Press.

Scott, J. (1988) 'Trend report: social network analysis', *Sociology*, 22(1): 109–27.

Scott, J. and Griff, C. (1984) *Directors of Industry: The British Corporate Network: 1904–1976*, Cambridge: Polity Press.

Selvin, H.C. (1960) *The Effects of Leadership*, Illinois: The Free Press of Glencoe.

Seymour, K.C. (1993) 'Intergenerational relationships in the family firm: the effect on leadership succession', *Family Business Review*, 6: 263–81.

Sherrin, C.H. (1994) *Probate, Hong Kong: FT Law and Tax*, Asia Pacific Publisher.

Shils, E.A. (1965) 'Charisma, order and status', *American Sociological Review*, 30: 199–213.

Silin, R.H. (1976) *Leadership and Values: The Organization of Large Scale Taiwanese Enterprises*, Cambridge: Harvard University Press.

Sinn, E. (1989) *Power and Charity: The Early History of the Tung Wah Hospital, Hong Kong*, Hong Kong: Oxford University Press.

——. (1997) 'Philanthropy and the business world', in G.W. Wang and S.L. Wong (eds), *Dynamic Hong Kong: Business and Culture*, Hong Kong: University of Hong Kong Press, pp. 230–52.

Sito, P. (2000) 'Red ink swamps NWD (New World Development)', *South China Morning Post*, 26 October, B1.

Skinner, G.W. (1957) *Chinese in Thailand: An Analytical* History, Ithaca, NY: Cornell University Press.

——. (1958) *Leadership and Power in the Chinese Community of Thailand*, Ithaca, NY: Cornell University Press.

Smilor, R. and Sexton, D. (1996) *Leadership and Entrepreneurship*, Westport, CT: Quorum Books.

Smith, C.T. (1995) *A Sense of History*, Hong Kong: Hong Kong Educational Publishing Company.

Sparks, D.W. (1978) *Unity is Power: The Teochiu of Hong Kong*, PhD thesis, University Microfilms International.

Sung, L.S. (1982) 'Property and lineage of the Chinese in northern Taiwan', *Bulletin of the Institute of Ethnology, Academia Sinica*, 54: 25–45.

Sussman, M.B., Cates, J.N. and Smith, D.T. (1970) *The Family and Inheritance*, New York: Russell Sage Foundation.

Swinth, R. and Vinton, K.L. (1993) 'Do family-owned businesses have a strategic advantage in international joint ventures?', *Family Business Review*, 6: 19–30.

Tepperman, L. (1972) 'The natural disruption of dynasties', *Canadian Review of Sociology and Anthropology*, 9: 24–43.

Titus, S., Rosenblatt, P. and Andersen, R. (1978) 'Family conflict over inheritance of property', *Family Coordinator*, 28: 237–46.

Tong, C.K. (1991) 'Centripetal authority, differentiated networks: the social organization of Chinese firms in Singapore', in G. Hamilton (ed.), *Business Networks and Economic Development in East and Southeast Asia*, Hong Kong: University of Hong Kong Press, pp. 155–75.

Traver, J.D. (1952) 'Intra-family farm succession practices', *Rural Sociology*, 17: 266–71.

Useem, M. (1984) *The Inner Circle: Large Corporations and the Rise of Business Political Activity in the US and UK*, New York: Oxford University Press.

Wang, S.H. (1977) 'Family structure and economic development in Taiwan', *Bulletin of the Institute of Ethnology, Academic Sinica*, 44: 1–11.

Ward, J.L. (1987a) 'Siblings and the family business', *Loyala Business Forum*, 6: 1–3.

——. (1987b) *Keeping the Family Business Healthy: How to Plan for Continuing Growth, Profitability, and Family Leadership*, San Francisco: Jossey-Bass.

Warner, W.L. and Abegglen, J.C. (1955) *Occupational Mobility in American Business and Industry, 1928–1952*, Minnesota: University of Minnesota Press.

Weber, M. (1947) *The Theory of Social and Economic Organization*, translated by A.R. Henderson and T. Parsons, London: William Hodge and Co. Ltd.

——. (1978) *Economy and Society*. (edited by G. Roth and C.W. Wittich), Berkeley: University of California Press.

Webster's Third New International Dictionary: Unabridged. (1986), Massachusetts: Merriam Webster Inc.

Whitten N. and Whitten D. (1972) 'Social strategies and social relationships', *Annual Review of Anthropology*, 1: 247–70.

Williamson, O.E. (1975) *Markets and Hierarchies: Analysis and Implications*, New York: Free Press.

Willmott, D.E. (1960) *The Chinese of Semarang: A Changing Minority Community in Indonesia*, Ithaca, NY: Cornell University Press.

Wing On Holdings Limited. (1981) *Wing On Holdings Limited*, Hong Kong: no publisher.

Wing On Life Assurance. (1975) *Wing On Life Assurance, 1925–1975*, Hong Kong: Eurasia Publishing Corp.

Winter, M. and Fitzgerald, M. (1993) 'Continuing the family-owned home-based business: evidence from a panel study', *Family Business Review*, 6: 417–26.

Wolf, A.P. (1981) 'Domestic organization', in E.D. Ahern and H. Gates (eds), *The Anthropology of Taiwanese Society*, Stanford: Stanford University Press, pp. 134–49.

Wolf, M. (1968) *The House of Lim*, New York: Appleton Century Crafts.

——. (1972) *Women and the Family in Rural Taiwan*, Stanford, CA: Stanford University Press.

Wong, B., McReynolds, B.S. and Wong, W. (1992) 'The family firms in the San Francisco Bay area', *Family Business Review*, 5: 355–72.

Wong, G. (1991) 'Business groups in a dynamic environment: Hong Kong 1976–86', in G. Hamilton (ed.), *Business Networks and Economic Development in South East Asia*, Hong Kong: University of Hong Kong.

Wong, S.L. (1985) 'The Chinese family firm: a model', *The British Journal of Sociology*, 36(1): 58–72.

——. (1988) *Emigrant Entrepreneurs: Shanghai Industrialists in Hong Kong*, Hong Kong: Oxford University Press.

——. (1994) 'Business and politics in Hong Kong during the transition', in K.P.B. Leung and T.Y.C. Wong (eds), *25 Years of Social and Economic Development in Hong Kong*, Hong Kong: University of Hong Kong Press, pp. 217–35.

——. (1996) 'Chinese entrepreneurship and economic development', in B.L. McCormick and J. Unger (eds), *China After Socialism: In the Footsteps of East Europe or Eastern Asia*, New York and London: M.E. Sharpe Inc, pp. 138–43.

Works of Mencius, The. (1949) (translated by J. Legge) in *The Chinese Classics, Vol. II*, (reprinted in 1994), Taipei: SML Publishing Inc.

Yeung, H.W.C. (2000a) 'Managing traditional Chinese family firms across borders: four generations of entrepreneurship in Eu Yan Sang', in L. Douw, C. Huang and D. Ip (eds), *Chinese Traditional Enterprise in Prosperity and Adversity*, London: Kegan Paul, pp. 168–98.

——. (2000b) 'Limits to the growth of family-owned business? The case of Chinese transnational corporations from Hong Kong', *Family Business Review*, 13: 55–70.

Yong, C.F. (1977) 'Leadership and power in the Chinese community of Singapore during the 1930s', *Journal of South East Asian Studies*, 3(2): 195–209.

——. (1991) *Chinese Leadership and Power in Colonial Singapore*, Singapore: Times Academic Press.

Yu, T.F.L. (1997) *Entrepreneurship and Economic Development in Hong Kong*, London and New York: Routledge.

Zeitlin, M. and Ratcliff, R.E. (1975) 'Research methods for the analysis of the internal structure of dominant classes: the case of landlords and capitalists in Chile', *Latin American Research Review*, 10(3): 5–61.

Zheng, W.T.V. and Wong, S.L. (1999) 'Chinese entrepreneurship, business networks and trust', in S.K. Lau, M.K. Lee, P.S Wan and S.L. Wong (eds), *Indicators of Social Development: Hong Kong 1997*, Hong Kong: Chinese University of Hong Kong Press, pp. 201–32.

In Chinese

Apple Daily [蘋果日報] (1999a) 'Children of two wealthy Chinese families marry' [菲兩華人大富對親家], 20 May.

——. (1999) 'The second generation of well-known families' [名人第二代], 3 September.

——. (1999) 'Lam (Pak-yan) buys his adopted son Kin-hong, a wife; Kin-ngao and Kin-ming don't attend the wedding: a silent protest' [林伯為養子娶妻, 親兒唔俾面, 建岳建名缺席, 無聲抗議], 11 September.

——. (2000) 'Nobody can help me' [無人可以我手], 23 October.

Bao, E.D. [包爾冬] (1997) 'Jiang Jie-shi and his sworn brothers' [蔣介石和拜把兄弟], *E-er Duo-si: Journal of Academic and Art Bi-Monthly* [鄂爾多斯文藝雙月刊], 84: 14–20.

Capital. [資本雜誌] (1988a) 'The emergence of the Chau Tsun-nin and Chau Sik-nin families' [周俊年, 周錫年家族發跡史], December: 142–64.

——. (1988b) 'The emergence of the Wing On Kwok family' [永安郭家發跡史], September: 138–50.

——. (1988c) 'The end of the Ronald Li era and the Li family' [李福兆時代的結束與香港豪門李氏家族], January: 74–9.

——. (1988d) 'Business and politics: the twins' [政治與商業: 一對孖生子], March: 144–7.

——. (1989a) 'Hysan Development Holdings: the Lee family' [希慎興業: 利氏家族], January: 104–29.

——. (1989b) 'The emergence of the Hui Oi-chow family' [許愛周家族發跡史], December: 84–99.

——. (1990a) 'The emergence of the Tang Shiu-kin family' [鄧肇堅家族史], April: 130–7.

——. (1990b) 'Tang Wing-cheung: New Star in the Business World [商界新彗星 – 鄧永鏘], May: 110–14.

——. (1991) 'Soya milk and fast food: the emergence of the Lo Kwai-cheung family' [豆奶快餐的故事: 羅桂祥家族史], July: 74–89.

——. (1995) 'Premium issue: DHL/SCMP Hong Kong Business Awards [香港商業管理大], December: 1–130.

Chan, H.W. [陳克華] (1964) 'Chaozhou in brief' [潮州概說], in C&E Association (ed.), *Yearbook of Cultural and Educational Association of Chaozhou Residents in Hong Kong* [香港潮汕文教聯宜會會刊第一期], pp. 86–9.

Chan, K.W. [陳荊淮] (1994) 'A description of the economic development of Chaozhou merchants in Hong Kong' [香港潮商經濟發展述略], in the Editorial Board of the Cultural and History (ed.), *The Chaozhou Merchants* [潮商俊彥], Guangdong: Guangdong People's Press, pp. 89–125.

Chan, P.L. (1983) *Essays in Commemoration of the Golden Jubilee of the Fung Ping Shan Library, 1932–1982* [馮平山圖書館金禧紀念論文集: 一九三二 – 一九八二], Hong Kong: University of Hong Kong Press, pp. 3–12.

Chan, P.M. [陳沛敏] (1993) 'A sauce and condiments empire – Lee Kam Kee' [醬油王國: 李錦記], *Capital*, April: 74–80.

Chan, S.K. [陳述經] (1974) 'The southwest movement of Chaozhou people and the evolution of Chaozhou culture' [潮人東南遷徒與文化的演變], in *The 60th Anniversary [1921–1981] of Hong Kong Chaozhou Chamber of Commerce*, Hong Kong: Chaozhou Chamber of Commerce, pp. 144–6.

Chan, S.M. [陳信明] (2000) 'The Ying Kee Tea Shop: earning a reputation for 50 years in Hong Kong' [英記茶莊: 飲譽香江五十年], *Three File Magazine*, 12: 3–5.

Chan, T.L. [陳進利] (1992) 'Brothers' battles invite others' preying eyes' [兄弟相爭, 魚翁虎視], *Forbes*, October: 74–80.

Chan, T.L. and Ho, W.F. [陳進利, 何華方] (1992) 'The past, present and future of Yeo Hiap Seng' [楊協成今昔與未來], *Forbes*, October: 68–75.

Chau, Y.F. [周日輝] (1926) *Lineage Record of the Si-Long Chau Family* [石龍周氏家譜], Hong Kong: Commercial Press.

Chen, Q.N. [陳其南] (1985a) 'Branch and kin group: the traditional Chinese family system' [房與傳統家族制度], *The Study of Sinology* [漢學研究], 3(1): 127–48.

——. (1985b) *Marriage, Family and Society* [婚姻, 家族與社會], vol. 2, Taipei: Wansun Books Store.:

——. (1988) 'The problems of Chinese family ethics and business management: a comparison with Japan' [家族倫理與中國企業經營的問題: 兼與日本作比較], *Hong Kong Economic Journal Monthly*, 136: 42–6.

Chen, Q.N. and Qiu S.R. [陳其南, 邱淑如] (1984) 'The traditional family system and business organization: a comparison between Chinese, Japanese and Western family systems' [傳統家族制度與企業組織: 中國, 日本和西方社會比較], in Industrial and Commercial Times (ed.), *A Study of Chinese Management* [中國式管理研究會實錄], Taipei: Industrial and Commercial Times Press, pp. 17–26.

Cheng, C.Y. [鄭赤炎] (1996) 'Examining the evolution of the Chaozhou Chamber of Commerce and its political adaptation' [從潮州會館的變演看潮州人的政治适應力], in C.Y. Jao [饒頤慶] (ed.) *Essays on Chaozhou Studies* [潮州學論文集], Hong Kong: Chinese University of Hong Kong Press, pp. 145–66.

Cheng, M.P. [鄭文蓓] (1997) 'Wang Lo Kat: the end of bitter days' [王老吉良茶苦盡甘來], *Investment and Finance* [投資與金融], 20 October: 24–5.

Chiu, Y.N. [招艷顏] (1996) 'Nine decades, three generations' [九十年, 三代人], *Forbes*, February: 53–5.

Choi, C.C. [蔡志祥] (2001) 'Networks and family business: the case of Kin Tye Lung']關係網絡與家族企業: 以香港乾泰隆及其聯號為例], in C.Y.H. Chu *et al.* (eds) *Economy and Society: A Social-Cultural Analysis of Hong Kong, Taiwan and the Chinese Mainland*, Taipei: Sheng Zhi Cultural Publishing Limited, pp. 193–205.

Choi, P.K. [蔡寶瓊》(1990) *Starting New Business: 50th Anniversary of Vitasoy*

(1940–1990) [厚生與創業: 維他奶五十年 (1940–1990)], Hong Kong: Vitasoy Products Company Limited.

Chow, K.F. [鄒家鳳] (1998) 'A century-long recipe: treasures for the stomach' [古方風行一世紀: 肚皮之寶], *East Magazine*, 271: 102–3.

Chuang, F. [莊輝] (1990) 'Wing On concentrates on the department store business' [永安集團著重發展百貨業], *Wealth Monthly*, November: 68–71.

Chuk, C.T. [祝春亭] (1996) *The War in Hong Kong's Business Circles* [香港商戰風雲錄], Guangdong: Guangzhou Press.

Chung, C.W. [宗菁華] (1999) 'The Bank of East Asia gets new blood' [新血進駐東亞], *Next Magazine*, 463: 128.

——. (2000) 'Professor Fung doesn't want to go' [馮教授未去馬], *Next Magazine*, 558: 143.

Fung, B.Y. [馮邦彥] (1997) *Hong Kong Chinese Business Groups: 1841–1997* [香港華資集團: 1841–1997], Hong Kong: Joint Publishing Limited.

Guangdong Sheng Dituce (ed.) (1994) *Atlas of Guangdong Province* [廣東省地圖集], Guangdong: Guangdong People's Press.

Han, T. [行者] (1980) 'Evolution and change in Hong Kong's wealthy families' [香港大富之家的變遷與嬗遞], in Y.C. Qi *et al.* (eds) [齊以正等], *The Rise and Fall of the Wealthy Families in Hong Kong* [香港豪門的興衰], Hong Kong: North and South Poles Monthly Press, pp. 11–17.

Ho, M.C. [何文翔] (1991a) *Biographies of Wealthy Businessmen in Hong Kong* [香港富豪列傳], Hong Kong: Ming Pao Press.

——. (1991b) *Biographies of Wealthy Businessmen in Hong Kong: Part Two* [香港富豪列傳之二], Hong Kong: Ming Pao Press.

Hung, S. and Bun, K. [鴻碩, 賓加] (1988) *Large Super-rich Families* [巨富與世家], Hong Kong: Ming Cheong Publisher.

Kwan, W.L. and Leung, K.K. [關慧玲, 梁家權] (1999) 'Uncle Lam (Pak-yan): dethrones the prince, sacks senior management' [林伯大開殺戒, 廢太子, 斬高層], *Next Magazine*, 466: 36–42.

Kwan, W.L., Chan, Y.Y. and Leung, K.K. [關慧玲, 陳旭英, 梁家權] (1998) 'Uncle Lam (Pak-yan): I will come back to count the debt' [林伯: 我要返來算賬], *Next Magazine*, 453: 46–54.

Kwok, F. [郭峰] (1980) 'Kings of the department store: the Wing-on Kwok family' [百貨業大王: 永安郭家], *North and South Poles Monthly*, 120: 4–8.

Lai, C.H. [黎肖嫻》 (1990) 'From Chaozhou people to Hong Kong people: the emergence of the Chaozhou merchants' [從潮州人到香港人: 香港潮籍富豪的崛興], *Capital*, November: 138–53.

Lam, M.Y. [林萬任] (1992) *The 70th Anniversary of Chaozhou Chamber of Commerce Association Report* [香港潮州商會七十週年紀念聯歡大會刊], Hong Kong: Chaozhou Chamber of Commerce.

Lam, Y. [林原] (1993) 'The wealthy families of Europe' [歐洲巨富], *Hong Kong Economic Journal Monthly*, 191: 17–27.

Law, Y.W. and Chan, K.M. [羅綺萍, 陳健文] (2000) 'Wealth and dreams: Gordon Wu' [富貴浮雲: 胡應湘], *Apple Daily*, 19 November, B1.

Lee, F.Y. [李科儀] (1998) 'Café De Coral: Lo Tang-cheung' [大家樂: 羅騰祥], *Next Magazine*, 449: 118–22.

——. (1999) 'Lo Hong-shui, earns big money in time of market slump' [羅康瑞: 逆市賺大錢], *Next Magazine*, 461: 102–4.

Li, Y.Y. [李亦園] (1982) 'Changes in the contemporary Chinese family: an anthropological inquiry' [近代中國家庭的變遷: 一個人類學的探討], *Bulletin of the Institute of Ethnology, Academica Sinica* [中央研究院民族學研究所集刊], 54: 7–23.

Liu, N.F. [廖雅芳] (2000) 'Didier Li: son of large family and godfather of the rave party' [世家子李國緯成: 教父], *Capital*, November: 70–2.

Lo, S.W. and Wong, H.Y. [盧少華, 黃曉燕] (2000) 'Explaining his absence at Lam Kin-hong's wedding' [缺席弟弟林建康婚禮], *The Sun*, 12 September: A2.

Lui, C.W. [呂志華] (2000a) 'Victor Fung's wealth expands rapidly' [馮國經財技過人身家暴漲], *Sing Tao Daily*, 19 July: A7.

——. (2000b) 'Wealth can last beyond three generations: Li and Fung' [利豐富不止三代], *Sing Tao Daily*, 18 July: A9.

——. (2000c) 'Henry Cheng: acts too slowly and lets opportunities slip by' [鄭家純以慢打快錯失先機], *Sing Tao Daily*, 2 November, B15.

Ma Pak Leung Company. [馬百良 (有限公司)] (2000) *Ma Pak Leung: Since 1822* [馬百良成立於 1822], 13 November, Hong Kong: Ma Pak Leung Company.

Mak, F. [麥輝] (1992) 'Scion of a famous family: Chow Cham-wang' [名門之後: 周湛煌], *Forbes*, December: 19–24.

Ming Pao Daily News. [明報] (1 January 1997–31 December 2000) Court news column.

Ng-Lun, N.H. and Ho, P.Y. [吳倫霓霞, 何佩然] (1996) 'The function and evolution of the Hong Kong Chamber of Commerce, 1921–1980' [香港潮州商會功能的演變], in C.Y. Yao (ed.), *Essays on Chaozhou Studies* [潮州學論文集], Hong Kong: Chinese University of Hong Kong Press, pp. 145–78.

Oriental Daily. [東方日報] (2000) 'Ex-wife's brother marries, Julian Hui (Chun-hang) hosts wedding, it's as if nothing has changed' [前親家娶媳, 許世勳夫婦到賀, 許晉亨穿梭打點, 似身份未變], 17 November: C4.

——. (1996) 'A review on the business ability of second generations' [二世祖守業功夫大檢閱], 28 January.

Pan, G.D. [潘光旦] (1947) *Prominent Jiaxing Families in the Ming-Qing Dynasty* [明清兩代嘉興的望族], Shanghai: Commercial Press (reprinted in 1991).

Pan, G.D. and Fei, H.T. [潘光旦, 費孝通] (1947) 'The civil examination in the Ming and Qing period' [明清朝代的科舉], *Journal of Social Sciences*, 4 (1): 1–21.

Pick, T. [碧滔] (1980) 'Why can't wealth last beyond two generations?' [君子之澤, 兩世而斬: 為甚麼巨大財富大都過不了兩代就散掉了？], in Y.C. Qi [齊以正] (ed.), *The Stories of the Super Rich in Hong Kong* [香港兆萬新富列傳], Hong Kong: Arts Book Store, pp. 34–49.

Poon, S.K. [潘少權] (1995) 'The Li brothers: the scions of prominent Hong Kong families' [香港貴族之後: 李家國字輩兄弟], in Hui Pak-kin, Leung Wai-ling and Poon Siu-kuen (eds), *The Second Generation of Wealthy Families in Hong Kong* [香港富豪第二代], Hong Kong: Commercial Press, pp. 28–36.

Qi, Y.Z. [齊以正》 (1980) 'The founders of the Wing On Group: Gocklock and Gockchin' [永安集團的創始人: 郭樂與郭泉], *North and South Poles Monthly*, 120: 8–10.

——. (1981) 'The second generation of the nouveau rich' [香港暴發戶和他們的第二代], in Y.C Qi. and L. Tam [齊以正, 譚隆等] (eds), *A Record of the Upper Classes* [上流社會搜奇錄], Hong Kong: Arts Books Store, pp. 163–71.

——. (1984) 'The super rich, inheritance and wealth' [超級巨富, 繼承人, 財富去向], in Y.C. Qi *et al.* [齊以正] (eds), *The Super Rich, Inheritance and Wealth* [超級巨富, 繼承人與財富去向], Hong Kong: Arts Books Store, pp. 45–9.

——. (1985) 'You and me: who's right?' [此胡來, 彼胡去, 孰是孰非], in Y.C. Qi (ed.), *The 'Glory' Board of Hong Kong's Business Circles* [香港商場「光榮」榜], Hong Kong: Arts Books Store, pp. 93–101.

Sima, S.C. [司馬嘯青] (2000) *Taiwan's Five Great Families: Old Money* [台灣五大家族], Taipei: Jade Mountain Press.

Sing Tao Daily [星島日報] (2000) 'Son gets married, father (Stanley Ho) is pleased' [乖仔成家立室, 娶維他奶千金, 何鴻燊老懷安慰], 17 November.

——. (2001) 'Adrian Li and Katie Lo: marriage between two great families' [李民橋羅寶盈兩大富豪家族結姻親], 25 February.

——. (2008) 'Conflict among three brothers of Sun Hung Kai Property' [新地三兄弟內], 19 February.

So, S.M. [蘇瑞雯] (1998) 'Lo Kai-fook: a leopard doesn't want to hunt anymore' [羅開福: 不再獵食的豹], *Capital*, December: 14–20.

Sze, W.M. and Fu, S.H. [施慧鳴, 傳斯翰] (1999) 'Uncle Lam wants a fight with Fung Siu-ping' [林伯要砌封小平], *East Magazine*, 329: 20–8.

To, F. [杜輝] (1996) 'Recapturing the market: the fourth generation of Lee Kam Kee' [李錦記第四代掌舵人復興江山], *Capital*, June: 66–72.

Tsui, Y.W. [徐意偉] (1986) 'Another chapter in Hong Kong history: the story of the Fung Ping-fun family' [香港歲月又添一集: 由馮秉芬家族被告說起], in Y.C. Qi *et al.* [齊以正] (eds), *The Rise and Fall of Wealthy Families in Hong Kong* [香港豪門的興衰], Hong Kong: North and South Poles Monthly Press, pp. 35–44.

Wang, K.Y. [王健儀] (1986) *Creating and Inheriting a Family Enterprise* [創業垂統], Hong Kong: Wang Lo Kat Tea Shop.

Wang, L. [王齡] (1949) *A Compendium on Chaozhou Sojourners in Hong Kong* [香港潮僑通覽], Hong Kong: no publisher.

Wang, S.H. [王崧興] (1985) 'Sino-Japanese family system: a comparison' [中日家族制度的比較研究], in Tam Yue-him (ed.), *Sino-Japanese Cultural Interchange: Aspects of Archaeology and Art History*, papers of the International Symposium of Sino-Japanese Cultural Interchange, 1: 51–61.

Wong, B.N. and Wang, C.L. [黃貝旎, 王者馨] (1999) 'The successors of Li Ka-shing and Li Siu-kay' [第二代接班人: 李嘉誠叻過李兆基]. *Next Magazine*, 464: 124–32.

Wong, J. [黃霑] (1981) *Distinguished People* [數風流人物], Hong Kong: Publications (Holding) Limited.

Wong, L.S. [黃麗裳] (1999) 'The day Lam Kin-ming changed his destiny' [林建名扭轉命運的一天], *Next Magazine*, 462: 92–6.

Yu, P.K. [余炳強] (1999) 'Hui Chun-hang: I don't know where my Wife goes' [許晉亨: 我不知道太太去了那兒], *Next Magazine*, 465: 34–40.

Yue, Q.P. [岳慶平] (1989) *Family, Nation, and The Chinese* [家國結構與中國人], Hong Kong: Zhong Hua Press.

Yuet, M. [月明] (1992) 'Three generations of the Si-long Chau family' [石龍周族三代談], *Wealth Monthly* [財富月刊], 63: 12–15.

Zheng, V. and Wong, S.L. [鄭宏泰, 黃紹倫] (2007) *Ho Tung: Grand Old Man of Hong Kong* [香港大老: 何東], Hong Kong: Joint Publishing (Hong Kong) Limited.

——. (2008) *Hong Kong General: Ho Shai-lai* [香港將軍: 何世禮], Hong Kong: Joint Publishing (Hong Kong) Limited.

Index

eBooks

eBooks – at www.eBookstore.tandf.co.uk

A library at your fingertips!

eBooks are electronic versions of printed books. You can store them on your PC/laptop or browse them online.

They have advantages for anyone needing rapid access to a wide variety of published, copyright information.

eBooks can help your research by enabling you to bookmark chapters, annotate text and use instant searches to find specific words or phrases. Several eBook files would fit on even a small laptop or PDA.

NEW: Save money by eSubscribing: cheap, online access to any eBook for as long as you need it.

Annual subscription packages

We now offer special low-cost bulk subscriptions to packages of eBooks in certain subject areas. These are available to libraries or to individuals.

For more information please contact webmaster.ebooks@tandf.co.uk

We're continually developing the eBook concept, so keep up to date by visiting the website.

www.eBookstore.tandf.co.uk